THE INDIANS

THE INDIANS

By the Editors of

TIME-LIFE BOOKS

with text by

Benjamin Capps

TIME-LIFE BOOKS, NEW YORK

THE OLD WEST

Series Editor: George Constable
EDITORIAL STAFF FOR "THE INDIANS"
Editor: Ezra Bowen
Picture Editor: Carole Kismaric
Text Editors: Jay Brennan, William Frankel
Designer: Herbert H. Quarmby
Staff Writers: Erik Amfitheatrof,
Michael Drons, Sam Halper, John von Hartz,
Timberlake Wertenbaker, Peter Wood
Chief Researcher: Joan Mebane
Researchers: Robin Busch,
Elizabeth D. Meyer, Frances Gardner,
Mary Kay Moran, Wendy Rieder, Kathryn Ritchell,
Jane Sugden
Design Assistant: Anne B. Landry

EDITORIAL PRODUCTION
Production Editor: Douglas B. Graham
Assistant: Gennaro C. Esposito
Quality Director: Robert L. Young
Assistant: James J. Cox
Copy Staff: Rosalind Stubenberg (chief),
Roberta Frost, Florence Keith
Picture Department: Dolores A. Littles,
Barbara S. Simon

THE AUTHOR: Benjamin Capps grew up on a ranch in West Texas, the ancient hunting ground of the belligerent Comanches. Since childhood he has been fascinated by the Old West and especially by the culture of the Plains Indians, whose tribal lands he has carefully explored. His sixth novel, *The White Man's Road,* won the Western Heritage Award as the best Western novel in 1969; he completed a seventh, *The True Memoirs of Charley Blankenship,* just before commencing work on *The Indians.*

THE COVER: During the first half of the 19th Century the mystique and panache of the fighting tribes drew many painters onto the Great Plains, where they recorded the lives of these nomadic people. On a year-long, 3,000-mile expedition a 27-year-old Swiss artist, Karl Bodmer, made the cover portrait of a Mandan chief, whose tomahawk, war paint and proud carriage capture the spirit of the Western warriors. The frontispiece, a photograph of a Dakota Sioux named Many Horns, was taken in 1872 by Alexander Gardner, another sensitive chronicler of the Indians.

Valuable assistance was provided by the following departments and individuals of Time Inc.: Editorial Production, Norman Airey; Library, Benjamin Lightman; Picture Collection, Doris O'Neil; Photographic Laboratory, George Karas; TIME-LIFE News Service, Murray J. Gart.

CONTENTS

1 | The faces of a proud people

Who were the Indians of the Old West? Everyone knows them—the hawk-faced men with braided hair and war feathers, their copper skin stretched over high cheekbones, their expressions penetrating and fearless. The tribal names are familiar too: Comanche, Cheyenne, Sioux, Kiowa, and others—all resonant of fierce valor, calling up images of painted horsemen with lances and bows. These tribes and their warriors, like the Comanche at right, dwelt on the Great Plains. To most whites they represented the model of all Western Indians—the men trained from birth to hunt and fight, measuring manhood by their boldness in battle; the women raised to sustain the warriors, sharing in celebrations of victory or slashing their bodies in moments of grief.

For some tribes these images were true, but only partly true. For the Western Indians as a whole they were only the most visible and spectacular manifestations of a broader, more complex story. From the Mississippi to the Great Basin on the far side of the Rockies lived more than 30 distinct tribes, each with its own language and way of life. Some were nomadic hunters who followed the buffalo. Some were primarily farmers who tended peach orchards or raised corn and melons in the fertile river valleys.

Some were pirates of the plains, who raided other tribes for horses, corn and tobacco. The Indians' realm was culturally diverse, but the far-flung villages were connected by a network of trails over which flowed such goods as Pacific seashells in exchange for deerskins.

All of these Indians, whether they were warriors or farmers, shared a common destiny—to be forced aside by the white man. By the middle of the 19th Century they were being pushed from their lands by white farmers, miners, cattlemen and the U.S. Cavalry.

The outcome of the confrontation with the whites was never really in doubt. Although they won some key battles, including one as late as 1876, the Indians were too few, too fragmented and too poorly armed to fend off the waves of intruders. In 1840, before the onslaught had fairly begun, no more than 300,000 Indians roamed the West. But although their battle was hopeless, pride and defiance shone in their faces and rang in their words. As Kiowa Chief White Bear said in 1867, "I do not want to settle down in houses you would build for us. I love to roam over the wild prairie. There I am free and happy." Nine years later White Bear committed suicide in a prison hospital.

Otter Belt, Comanche

A Navaho boy, name unknown

Two Hatchet, Kiowa

Particular Time of Day, Pawnee

Nalin, Apache girl

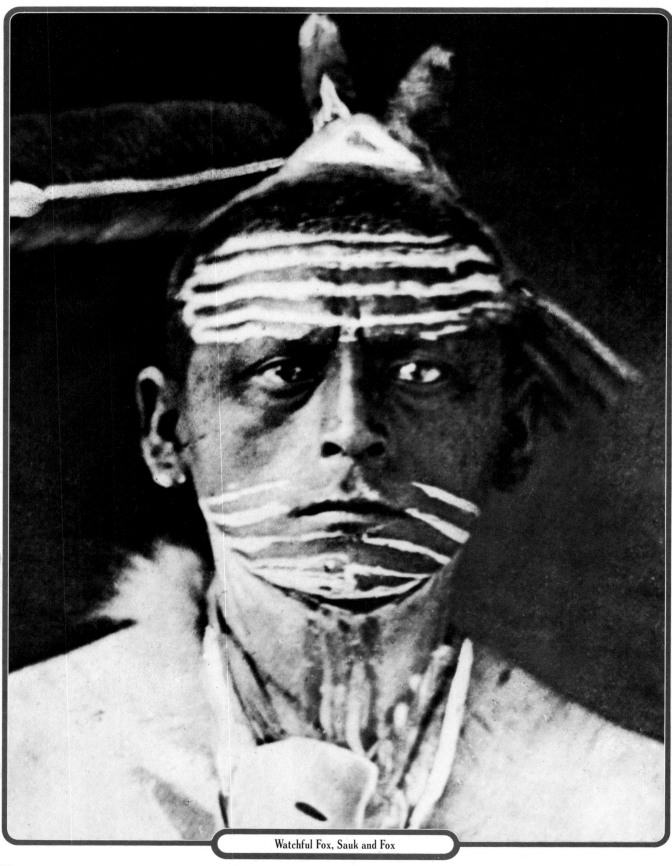

Watchful Fox, Sauk and Fox

Spotted Eagle, Sioux

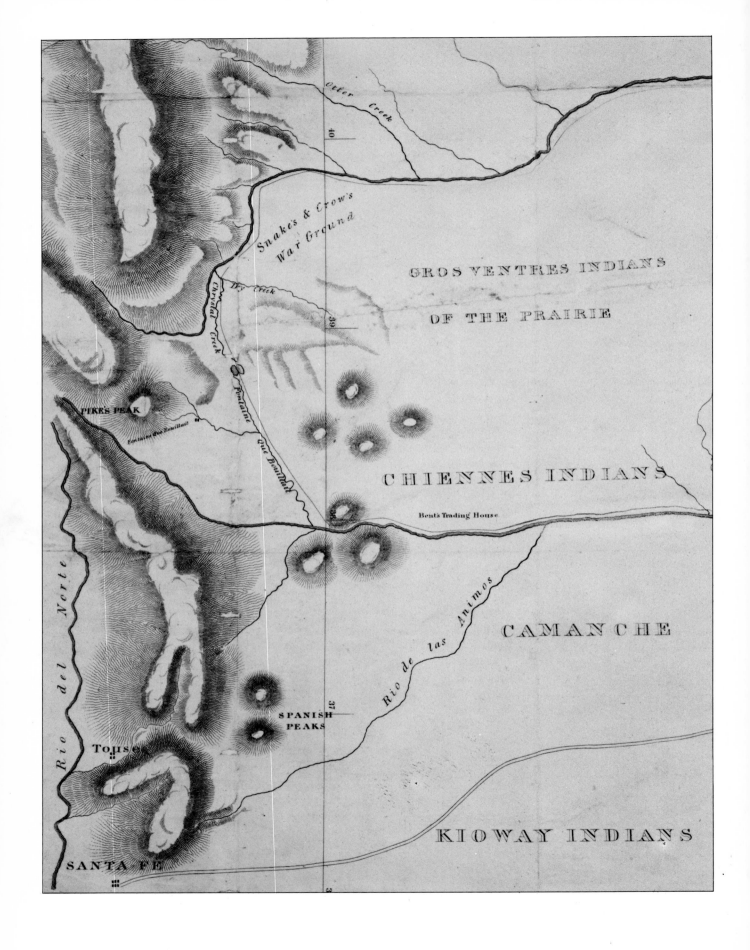

A grand alliance among the tribes

It was the time of year when the buffalo have shed most of their long hair and the brown calves follow at the cows' flanks, when prairie plums are hard and green and the sun bears down hot upon the rolling high plains. A great Indian peace council was gathering, and the time selected for it had not been conceived in the context of white man's thinking. White men would have said the year was 1840. But by the Indian way of counting years it was seven winters since the great shower of meteors, which they called the Winter the Stars Fell. It was nine summers since the Comanches had lanced to death a hairy paleface, said by Mexicans to be the famous explorer named Jed Smith. It was only two summers since the people who were now considering peace had fought a bloody battle against each other on Wolf Creek.

Now they traveled from north and south over hundreds of miles of treeless grasslands toward their selected meeting ground on a river that had been a kind of boundary between the enemy tribes. They called the river the Flint Arrowpoint, or Arrowpoint; white traders called it the Arkansas. Altogether, some 5,000 Indians were gathering here. From north of the Arrowpoint came Southern Cheyennes together with some of their Arapaho allies; from the south traveled the Kiowas, along with some of their Comanche allies. And the parties at the council would also represent Northern Cheyennes and Arapahos, living as much as 600 miles to the north, and Comanches, living 600 miles to the south.

The Cheyenne leaders had chosen a council ground at a point two hours' walk downstream from Bent's Fort, a high-walled adobe structure built by white trad-

ers, one of whom had married into the Cheyenne tribe. They had rejected the vicinity of the fort itself as a meeting place. For one thing, the firewood was all gone there, part of it cut down for the construction of the buildings, the rest taken by the Indians and whites who had subsequently camped at the fort. For another, the grass had been grazed to the ground. But six miles downstream from the fort the valley widened into a broad flood plain on either side of the river, with ample groves of cottonwoods and willow clumps—an ideal campsite, with space and shade and water and wood. Grass was plentiful both north and south of the east-flowing stream, and would provide grazing for the many horses the Cheyennes hoped to receive as gifts from their erstwhile enemies.

The Cheyennes and Arapahos arrived first, on the north bank of the river. They must have entered the valley with conflicting emotions. It was always good to come to a river, and this river was an oasis in a semi-desert. The land from which they came was forbidding in its distances, its monotony. There a cloud and its shadow on the ground were a relief to the eyes; a single hawk wheeling in the air was a thing to watch. In that land the soil was gray, and even now, in early summer, the sparse vegetation did not cover its surface. Away from the watercourses the largest plants were scattered sagebrush, Spanish dagger, prickly-pear cactus. The cottonwood trees that grew along the river bottom seemed like giants; their whitish-gray furrowed trunks were larger than a man could reach around, and some towered four times as high as a tipi. Their leaves rustled continually, gently, whispering of shade and bathing and the pleasures of camp.

But this flood plain by the bank of the Arrowpoint was no ordinary campsite. No sooner did the Cheyennes and Arapahos enter the valley than they began to look south with anticipation—and perhaps with some

The great Indian peace council of 1840 was held near Bent's Trading House on the Arkansas River, shown flowing from west to east in the center of this map.

15

A Kiowa encampment nestles among cottonwood trees near the Canadian River. A grove like this one, with the trees towering over the highest tipis, provided an especially welcome campsite on the flat, semiarid land of the plains.

apprehension. One does not meet with once-deadly enemies without wondering, even at a peace council. Yet these former enemies were bringing the promise of plentiful horses. The Cheyennes and Arapahos owned some, but never enough. The Kiowas and Comanches were rich in horses.

The Cheyennes made their camp in a circle straddling a small creek, with a break in the circle toward the east, where the sun rises. Every band of the tribe had its precise appointed location, and as always each tipi faced the rising sun. The Cheyennes, observing all their traditional formalities, pitched a large-scale camp. A circle was not necessarily the most convenient arrangement, but it was impressive. Let those people from the south who had sued for peace see how a proper and disciplined tribe camps. And another thought may well have occurred to the Cheyennes: if the southern leaders would willingly enter the heart of the Cheyennes circle, it would surely help to prove the southerners' sincerity and trust.

High Backed Wolf, principal chief of the Cheyennes, ordered a special lodge built in the center of the camp circle, a framework of poles shaded on one side with lodge coverings and open on the other. It was large enough to entertain a dozen or more visiting chiefs.

As yet, however, there were no signs of the Indians from the south. Hunting parties rode downstream to try for some fresh deer meat. Women explored the small creek and the river's banks for driftwood, which they carried to their lodges or dragged back by horses. Frequently they glanced south. Many of the women carried scars on their arms and legs where they had slashed themselves in grief over loss of a father or husband or son in fights against the very Indians who were approaching from the south.

Three days after the Cheyennes and Arapahos had made camp they began to see lone riders — scouts — far out across the river on the ridges along the southern skyline. Then they saw gray dust clouds rising in half a dozen places. The land out there was hilly, and from the banks of the river it was hard to see what was coming. But some of the cottonwoods had trunks that divided near the ground, and their giant limbs sloped enough so that they could be climbed. Up these, half-grown boys and girls scrambled, by the aid of rawhide ropes or by sheer agility, to gain a better vantage point.

They called back and forth to those on the ground, and one can imagine their shrill cries.

"I see them coming! Yes! Straight out there! A village of people! Pack horses! People riding! Loads on travois poles!"

"How many loose horses?"

"It looks like a hundred — more than a hundred!"

And from another tree: "Look to the left! Under the dust! Many horses!"

"Loose horses? Count them!"

"It must be five hundred!"

And from still another tree watcher — "Eeee! A thousand coming over the ridge! They keep coming! More than a thousand! And I see dust away back!"

Finally they could hear them coming, a trembling thunder of hoofbeats on the earth. The newcomers were bringing at least 8,000 horses, more than most of the encamped Cheyennes had ever seen or dreamed of. They converged toward the peace-council site from the gray-green grassland, all six divisions of the Kiowas in some dozen bands — men, women and children as well as some Mexican captives who were their slaves. With them came two proud bands of Comanches.

The men and boys herded the loose horses to water at convenient spots along the stream, then drove them back away from the river. The women brought the hardworking pack and travois horses onto the sandy flats south of the stream and began to spread up and down the valley. The band chiefs selected general locations for their followers; the women, significantly, chose lodge sites. Nominally unimportant in the hierarchy of the tribe, the women actually held considerable influence simply by virtue of doing most of the work around a camp. They looked for shade, for firewood, for nearness to water, for grass on which to picket a special horse or two, for closeness to friends or to the prestigious people of the band. They thought of picking a place with good drainage in the event of a shower. The best spot was northeast of a giant cottonwood, where the midday sun would be blocked off, but not directly under the branches, for the large leaves would drip for hours after a rain.

As the women on the south bank raised their lodges they were aware that curious and critical eyes across the stream were appraising their skill. The Kiowa women bound their three main tipi poles with rawhide toward the tips and raised the tripod, added extra poles

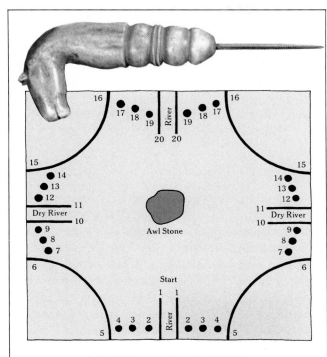

A FAVORITE GAME FOR WOMEN

A pastime popular with Plains Indian women, the awl game, was played on a blanket around which players, or teams, moved in opposite directions. Each position (numbers on diagram) was pegged through the blanket with an awl (top), an Indian woman's tool ordinarily used for perforating hides. In the Kiowa version of the game a player threw four sticks at the awl stone (center); each stick was flat on one side and curved on the other, and one of the sticks had a special mark. Each flat side up counted for one point, and when the special mark came up the player was entitled to an additional throw. A player who "fell into a river" or landed on an opponent's position had to start over. Dry rivers were safe. The first player to complete the circle was the winner.

to the circular framework, tied the poles again at the tips, hoisted the heavy fitted cover of buffalo hide with a final pole and unfolded it around the framework to a beautiful cone. They would show those Cheyennes how to make a proper camp. Why did those superstitious people insist on camping in a circle? Some of them were a long carry from water. The Kiowa women, with great cooperation and good nature, set up a camp that filled the flood plain south of the river.

Some of the tipis on both the south and north banks of the river were decorated with geometrical designs, re-

ligious symbols or simple pictures commemorating a warrior's deeds. A few were painted solid red; the owner of one of them was appropriately named Red Tipi. But most of the hide-covered cones were the plain tan color of the buffalo hides from which they were made, blackened at the top from smoke.

A few of the Kiowa women soon set out to scour the south banks of the river for driftwood. Others began to build brush arbors — cut poles set in the ground, bound across with light limbs and piled with leafy branches on top. Open at the sides, they provided cool, shady places for outdoor cooking, sitting, visiting. This industrious activity began to create a curiously domestic atmosphere that flowed back and forth across the Arrowpoint. Within the memory of many now present the Kiowas, Comanches and Cheyennes had been at peace. They had ways of life in common. There could be no treacherous intent here, with women and old ones and children setting up living arrangements just over a stream that a boy could throw a stone across.

When the newcomers had settled Cheyenne Chief High Backed Wolf mounted his horse and rode across the river (the stream, no longer swollen by spring rains and melting snow, ran only knee deep). He invited the southern chiefs to come over to feast in the special lodge the Cheyennes had built. Kiowa Principal Chief Little Mountain, War Chief Sitting Bear and all the band chiefs accepted. They gathered together to cross the river, dressed, like the Cheyenne leader, in their finest, but with no war paint or weapons or shields.

They wore soft buckskin shirts, leggings, moccasins, all of them fringed and beaded here and there or hung with shells or bits of tinkling metal. They wore silver pendants on leather thongs or necklaces of shells, beads, bears' claws or elks' teeth; on their braided hair were wrappings of fur or tanned skin. As leaders of their people they had a marvelous capacity for ignoring the mundane and superficial. They might have mosquito bites on their arms and necks, even fleas or ticks beneath their fancy clothes requiring sometimes a judicious bit of scratching; yet their look was proud, that of men who knew their worth. Their copper-skinned faces, some wrinkled from long years beneath the sun, were serious, thoughtful, deliberate.

Among these Indians peacemaking was largely a matter of feasting, ceremony and gift giving, all designed to demonstrate goodwill and good intent. After High Backed Wolf went unprotected among the Kiowas and Comanches, and the southern chiefs had gone to feast in the lodge at the center of the Cheyenne circle, any remaining tension in the camps relaxed completely. The day became a gala occasion. The bands of a tribe, numbering only a few hundred persons at most, did not come together often or stay together long, for their horses would soon eat all the grass around a camp. Here was a rare opportunity to meet old friends and kin, to exchange news and gossip, to feast, to joke, to play games, to gamble, to trade, to race horses.

Naked children ran squealing among the tipis, riding stick horses, chasing each other, pausing sometimes to stare wide-eyed at all the strangers passing. Boys a little older set out on exploring and hunting expeditions through the willow brakes, carrying half-sized spears and bows and arrows; if they did not locate any birds or prairie dogs or rabbits they stood ready to attack grasshoppers and dragonflies. The larger boys played war or brought their personal ponies to a clearing to demonstrate riding skills, hanging on the side of a galloping mount, then swinging deftly down to scoop up an object from the ground.

The girls helped their mothers as long as help was needed. Some of them played house using dolls of stuffed deerskin, or pressed into service their own little brothers and sisters. Others visited cousins they had not seen in a year, to chatter and to show off beadwork they had done back in the winter.

The women visited and gossiped and helped one another. Those who had fresh meat invited their friends from other bands to eat with them. Some women and girls went along the river bottom and gathered a supply of green wood along with their firewood. They chopped off lower cottonwood branches or cut down large bunches of the head-high willows so that their cook fires would be smoky enough to discourage the mosquitoes, gnats and the green flies that came from nowhere to plague every camp.

Hundreds of dogs milled among the lodges, searching for discarded meat and bones and investigating one another. Here and there two dogs would circle stiff-legged and then spring upon each other in a snarling, rolling fight. The woman nearest to the battle would seize a handy weapon—a riding whip, a stick of wood—and

The winters' tales of the Dakotas

The painted buffalo robe at right is at once a calendar, a work of art and a chronicle of the Dakota Sioux. Following Dakota custom, a warrior named Lone Dog recorded upon this hide a spiral of years, reading from the center outward, with a significant picture or symbol for each year. The span of time runs from 1800 to 1871, the major period of white invasion. Yet the white man plays almost no direct part in this pictorial history. Lone Dog's winters include seven references to trade with the white man and four references to epidemics of such white man's diseases as measles and smallpox. Surprisingly, there is no indication of battles with the white invaders, yet there are 24 symbols referring to intertribal conflicts. Below are enlargements of five typical symbols; the numeral accompanying each is keyed to the corresponding numeral on the robe.

1. A gruesomely appropriate symbol is a man's body blotched by smallpox, which swept through the Dakota nation in 1801 and 1802.

2. A shower of meteors that fell on November 12, 1833, recalls the Winter the Stars Fell. There are several other references to physical phenomena, including an eclipse 36 years later.

3. The symbol of a tipi pierced by arrows represents the slaughter of all the inhabitants of one Shoshoni village by the Dakotas in the winter of 1839-1840.

4. In 1840-1841, a peace with the Northern Cheyennes was symbolized by a handshake—a custom adopted from the white world.

5. A pony represents a successful raid during which the Dakotas stole 30 horses in the winter of 1841-1842.

enter the fray, whereupon the two combatants would both surrender to her and scamper away, yelping.

A rich mixture of smells soon permeated the valley, that of wood smoke, of rotting meat thrown away, of human wastes behind the thick willows, of steaming cooking pots, of broiling meat dripping fat onto coals. The smell seemed neither good nor bad to them: it was simply the smell of life.

The men had few tasks. Some went hunting, for buffalo, deer and antelope watered in this stream from miles away. But most of them simply enjoyed themselves. They talked of hunting exploits, of raiding forays, of the places their bands had been in past months. They swapped arrows, buffalo robes and horses. The more energetic got up wheel games in which the players threw arrows or sticks at a rolling hoop laced with rawhide; they shouted and bragged with good-humored gusto at the game and gambled on their skill with every kind of property from a dozen small glass beads to a fine robe with two weeks of woman's labor in it. Inevitably they raised questions about the relative speed of favorite horses. They laid out courses, both north and south of the river, and began to run races. Urged on by yells of partisan sportsmen, the mounts kicked up streams of the tan-gray bottom sand; the men gambled recklessly on the results.

As evening came on, the women threw new wood on their fires to make light for games or dancing. The favorite game of the women was the awl game *(page 19),* played around a blanket and accompanied by shrieks of consternation and merriment. Another pastime, for either men or women, was the button game. The only equipment for it was a small decorated piece of wood (the button) that could be hidden in the hand and a pile of tally sticks to keep score. Two teams sat across a fire from each other. A player on one of the teams switched the button from one hand to the other and passed it, or pretended to pass it, to a teammate —and all this to the accompaniment of a chant or song of nearly meaningless sounds that jumped and halted and rose in time with the movements of the team that held the button. The other team intently watched the movements—even the facial expressions—of their opponents. The moment of truth came when one of the watchers shouted, "That one!" Then the man he pointed at had to open his hand, and the teams gained or lost

tally sticks according to the accuracy of the guesser. As always, the players put a little extra spice into the game by gambling on their skill.

They danced social dances in a dozen places. The drummers brought out their painted drums and set them up, several men around one instrument. The beat rose: *TUM! Tum, tum, tum. TUM! Tum, tum, tum.* Men and women danced side by side, forming a circle that contracted and expanded, sometimes following each other in a snakelike parade. Men sang in deep voices. Women sang in shriller tones. Occasionally an old man chanted in a plaintive minor key. Hand rattles made of gourds or stiffened hides or dried buffalo scrotums swished to the measure of the drums.

An observer listening to the sounds carried on the night air might have thought that he stood in the middle of a giant carnival. The fires scattered in the valley cast their glow on the trees and the moving people. The tribes did not visit across the river this night, but each side knew that the same celebrations were taking place on either shore of the Arrowpoint.

The camp dogs howled through the hours of darkness. They responded to one another across the stream as if their masters had never been enemies. Out on the prairie knolls wolves listened and faintly answered.

Across the short stretch of land between the Cheyennes' camp and the river ran the tracks of the white man's iron wagon tires. These marked the Santa Fe Trail. The Indians who camped here in that summer of 1840 probably saw no threat in the trade that moved over this road. They knew it began in some uncertain place in the East, where people had mastered the secrets of making glass beads and gunpowder and iron tools, and led past Bent's Fort and away southwest. Over the trail the previous year whites had brought Eastern goods worth about $250,000, an appreciable amount of money for the period; yet the whole commerce had been carried in only 130 wagonloads, and the wagons seemed small against the immensity of the plains. If a caravan came along now, it would judiciously detour around the Indians.

Perhaps more significantly, the encampment also lay astride another line, less understood by the natives and surely given no validity by them: an international boundary. In that year of 1840 the Cheyenne-Arapaho alliance was camped within the United States; the Kiowa-Comanche alliance was camped in either Mexico or the Republic of Texas, depending upon whether the rebellious Texans could keep their recently won independence and the land they claimed.

In 1840 about half of what is now the Western United States lay south and west of this border. The boundary had been an old Spanish-French line (map, page 33). It came out of the Gulf of Mexico north along the Sabine River (now the western border of Louisiana), went west along the Red River to the 100th meridian, then north to the Arkansas (this same Arrowpoint) River about where Dodge City would be built, upstream through the Indian council ground all the way to the Continental Divide, north along the highest peaks of the Rockies to the 42nd parallel of latitude, then due west to the Pacific. And the lands on both sides of the border were about to be intensively developed by English-speaking white men.

The fact that the Plains Indians knew nothing of such lines and their portent is part of the irony of their historical situation. The year 1840 proved to be something of a turning point for Western Indians. But the story of these people had been one of change for many decades, and change would continue to disrupt their lives during the decades to come.

For centuries the Spanish had exerted influence on some of the native Americans, chiefly in the country running up through the mountains on a line from El Paso to Santa Fe and in California. Spaniards brought the Indians Christianity, slavery in Spanish mines and various trade goods, but they held back guns as a matter of policy. They had failed to control certain tribes, notably the Comanches and Apaches, and had also failed to keep Spanish horses from being stolen and spread all over the West.

French fur traders had been dealing with Western Indians for over a hundred years. The French had explored most of the Mississippi Valley and had sent their priests and traders west up every tributary river into the Great Plains. They had got along well with the native people —many a voyageur took an Indian wife—and even exerted an influence on the English language. Witness such lasting French words for tribes as Nez Percés (Pierced Noses) and Gros Ventres (Big Bellies). For the drag made of two poles lashed together and pulled by dog or horse we have the French word *travois,* and for buried and hidden supplies or valuables, *cache.*

In 1840 one big-time trader, Pierre Chouteau, in St. Louis, bought 67,000 buffalo robes, all of them taken and skinned and tanned by Indians. In the same year Chouteau ordered an array of products for trade with Indians: blankets, bolts of bright cloth, cheap smoothbore guns, 300 dozen butcher knives, 500 pounds of pigeon-egg beads and, according to one report, 9,000 pounds of blue and white chalk beads. The amount of whiskey he used to oil the wheels of commerce was not made a matter of record.

In the fur trade, too, change was in the wind in 1840. The great beaver-trapping days were at an end; the Green River Valley in Wyoming would see no more wild rendezvous where Indians and mountain men and traders came together. Trapper Kit Carson, who had been in the West about 15 years, would trap one more winter at Brown's Hole on the Green River, then conclude, as he put it later: "Beaver was getting very scarce." Whereupon he would go to Bent's Fort and hire on at a dollar a day as hunter to provide fresh meat for Bent's employees. The era of plains and mountain crossing had begun. The trade between Missouri and Santa Fe along the Arkansas River was shifting into high gear, and in 1842 the first sizable train of white immigrants would leave Missouri for Oregon. The time of gold discoveries lay ahead.

By 1840 the Plains Indian culture, based upon exploitation of the buffalo by means of horses and iron tools, had reached the peak of its development. These fighting horse-mounted Indians were raiding and trading and hunting over vast distances. They already had got most of the benefits they were to receive from encroaching Europeans. What the whites would bring later would be mostly unwelcome—and resisted. The Indians vaguely felt it already and had begun to muster what power they had against the oncoming settlers, cattlemen, miners and railroaders.

The tribesmen undoubtedly considered themselves numerous, but the size of a population is a comparative matter. In fact the Western Indians were pitifully few. It is a reasonable guess that in 1840 some 300,000 Indians dwelt in what is now the Western United States, about the same as the number of people who then lived on Manhattan Island. The West was not man's country, but a semiarid wasteland given over mainly to antelope, rabbits, bighorn sheep, prairie dogs, coyotes, buffalo, elk, wolves, deer and bear.

The Indians scattered over this land were in no sense one people. In some ways their differences were greater than those between the Swedes and the Arabs or the French and the Chinese, for they spoke many languages and hundreds of dialects, had a diversity of values and religions and lived at different levels of achievement in commanding their environments and destinies.

Mark Twain, traveling in the West in 1861, described the Indians he saw in the Utah-Nevada country as "the wretchedest type of mankind I have ever seen." These people of the Great Basin region, among them the Paiutes and the Gosiutes, gathered the few seeds, berries and roots that grew in their sagebrush flats and badlands, and they hunted insects, rabbits, reptiles and mice. By contrast, in the eastern half of what would become Oklahoma lived Indians known to whites as the Five Civilized Tribes, recent arrivals from the East. Of these, the Cherokee tribe, numbering about 19,000, was in the process of unifying its factions. During 1839 they drafted a new constitution for the Cherokee Nation. In midsummer 1840, as the warrior Indians of the south and central plains were making peace on the river near Bent's Fort, the Cherokees put their constitution into effect at a meeting in Tahlequah, off the same river but some 500 miles downstream. They would set up a public school system the following year and in three years would have 18 schools in operation. In four years they would begin publishing and printing the *Cherokee Advocate,* Oklahoma's first newspaper, in English and Cherokee. In 11 years they would open two seminaries for higher learning.

The Cherokees considered all men to be brothers, but in worldly matters they may well have thought of themselves as older and wiser brothers. Yet their less civilized neighbors on the Great Plains would still be free, proudly fighting—and pitifully dying—three decades after the Cherokees had successfully mastered the ways of reservation life. The stronghold of these Plains Indians was the buffalo country stretching from the valley of the Saskatchewan in Canada south to central Texas. Here lived the tribes that would establish the image of the American Indian—the flamboyant horseback warrior in a feathered headdress. The Blackfeet,

on both sides of the Canadian border, and the Crows, along the Yellowstone and its tributaries, were original inhabitants. In recent decades they had come into contact with a powerful tribe from the east, the Teton Lakota, or Western Sioux. Sometime between 1840 and 1845 a certain baby boy was born to a woman of these Lakotas. When he was still a boy he gained the name of Crazy Horse. His life was to be violent and dramatic; many white men later wrote of his deeds, though no photograph of him was ever taken. In the wars ahead against the U.S. Cavalry there were to be two important engagements that left no white survivors. The baby boy was fated to be a leader for the Indians on both occasions.

Farther south ranged the northern and southern divisions of the Arapahos and Cheyennes, and beyond them the Kiowas. In the southernmost plains the Comanches, numbering perhaps 10,000, dominated the land through their mobility and fighting spirit. These were the four tribes that met by the river in the summer of 1840 to make peace among themselves.

The gathering on the Arkansas was a result of careful consideration by tribal leaders. They knew that both the geopolitical situation and the Plains Indian way of life were in a state of flux. It was a dynamic time, a time of movement, new homelands, advantages gained or lost, new enemies or new friends made, new and better trading situations. Relationships were changing not only between Indian and white but between Indian and Indian as well. It was clearly a time for discussion and cooperation, and the first necessity was intertribal peace.

The Arapahos might have favored peace solely on account of their temperament. They had fought many a battle alongside their Cheyenne allies, but with some reluctance. Observers have described them as friendly, accommodating, religious, generous. Certain of the neighboring tribes called the Arapahos the Cloud People, or the Blue Cloud People, a name perhaps referring to their easy dispositions.

The other three tribes had more definite motives for peace, reasons related both to their histories and to recent events. The Cheyennes still remembered that their grandfathers had once farmed in the area of Minnesota and western Wisconsin. They had failed to get trade

"They must necessarily yield"

While the tribes at the ceremonious council on the Arkansas River looked toward peaceful coexistence on the High Plains, the highest councils of the United States government in Washington had very different plans for them — in fact for all Indians. The government — and most voters — regarded them as a lesser race that must be expelled from settled regions, driven onto reservations or exterminated. President Andrew Jackson, a former soldier who had fought against the Creeks and Seminoles in the South, was brutally forthright in 1833 when he told Congress in the speech excerpted below what the nation's Indian policy should be.

My convictions upon this subject have been confirmed. That those tribes cannot exist surrounded by our settlements and in continual contact with our citizens is certain. They have neither the intelligence, the industry, the moral habits, nor the desire of improvement which are essential to any favorable change in their condition. Established in the midst of another and a superior race, and without appreciating the causes of their inferiority or seeking to control them, they must necessarily yield to the force of circumstances and ere long disappear. Such has been their fate heretofore, and if it is to be averted it can only be done by a general removal beyond our boundary and by the reorganization of their political system upon principles adapted to the new relations in which they will be placed.

guns as early as some of the adjacent Indians and had faced the choice of being submissive or moving west; they chose the latter. Somewhere in the course of their migration they had, as they put it, "lost the corn," meaning that they had almost entirely ceased farming. Perhaps they literally had lost their seed in a year of drought along the Missouri River; more likely, they had given up farming deliberately for a more active life of buffalo hunting, of fur trapping and trading.

In the region of the Black Hills, in what would become South Dakota, the Cheyennes became typically nomadic Plains Indians. In time they wandered south into the rich buffalo country. Some went no farther than Wyoming, others pressed clear down to the Arkansas River. Known as men of pride and strong will, they seemed to prefer war to peace. And not long after reaching the Arkansas in their migrations, they came into conflict with the Kiowas.

The Kiowas had traveled over part of the same migration path as the Cheyennes 50 years earlier. Coming out of the mountains in the upper Missouri River region, they had moved to the Black Hills, had learned the ways of Plains Indian life from the Crows and had turned south. In the late 18th Century they had met the Comanches on the southern plains, fought them and made peace with them.

The Cheyennes lived at peace with the Kiowas, at first, in a tentative, skeptical sort of way. Enmity developed slowly. The Cheyennes stole a few horses. They killed a few Kiowas here and there. It seemed only natural to put on a little pressure. They had come down to the Arkansas River, why not push on farther? In 1837 a Cheyenne war party had made a clear test of Kiowa mettle. A group of 48 elite Cheyenne warriors of the Bow String Society rode boldly south, looking for horses, scalps — and trouble.

Among the Kiowas was a brilliant war chief named Sitting Bear, born about 1801 and now in his prime. He had the complete trust of his tribe and wore a long thin black mustache in the style of the ancient Kiowas. Angered by the brash Cheyenne invasion, Sitting Bear led a band of Kiowa braves to intercept the Bow String warriors. He swooped down on the invading war party south of the Antelope Hills like an eagle curving down on a ground squirrel, trapped them and wiped them out to a man. Sitting Bear and his men scalped and stripped them, then laid them out in a row on the prairie as if to make them easy to count.

Since none escaped, the Cheyenne people did not know what had happened to the Bow String war party. But a few Arapahos, those inveterate friends of everyone, visited the Kiowas, who were holding a big war dance, and recognized some of the hair of their slain friends; whereupon they remembered their oldest loyalty and went north to tell the Cheyennes. For the Cheyennes the occasion called not for a mere revenge raid, but for carrying their sacred striped arrows against the hated Kiowas — in other words, for all-out war.

Pipes of prayer and friendship

No rite was more widely practiced by Indians than smoking. When an Indian lit a mixture of tobacco and various aromatic herbs — called kinnikinnick — in the stone bowl of his pipe his intent was often deeply serious. The smoke that he exhaled was seen as a breath of prayer, and the pipe itself was regarded as an intimate channel of communication to the spirit world. Pipes were also used to sanctify communication between men. An early fur trapper named Alexander Ross noted that pipe smoking was "the introductory step to all important affairs, and no business can be entered upon with these people before the ceremony of smoking is over."

Ceremonial pipes, like the Crow pipe below, were the personal property of a chief, medicine man or warrior. They were smoked according to a grave and precise ritual to pledge an oath or ratify a treaty, which inspired the white man's phrase "peace pipe."

The pipes were also used as passports when traveling and for conciliation in even the most private disputes. If a brave ran off with someone else's wife, etiquette decreed that he send an old man to the husband bearing a pipe. If the husband smoked the offering, it meant that he would not take revenge on the lovers. Many men owned an unadorned everyday pipe, because smoking was also a casual habit. But the older men sometimes felt obliged to warn the young warriors against excessive smoking; it could cut their wind and thus reduce their stamina in a battle.

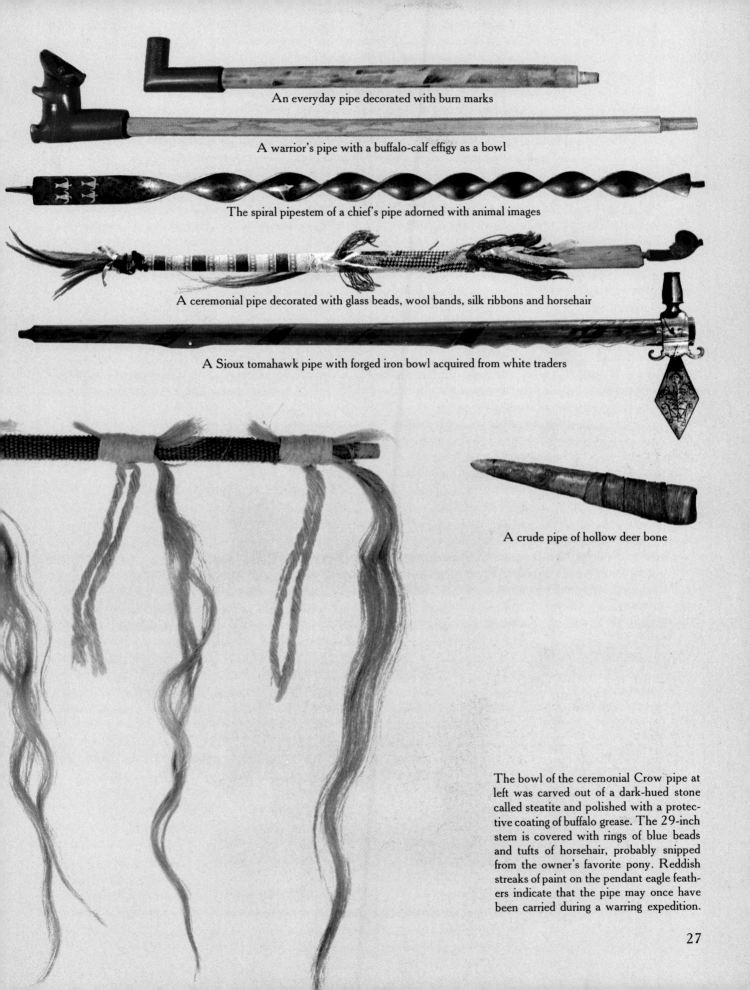

An everyday pipe decorated with burn marks

A warrior's pipe with a buffalo-calf effigy as a bowl

The spiral pipestem of a chief's pipe adorned with animal images

A ceremonial pipe decorated with glass beads, wool bands, silk ribbons and horsehair

A Sioux tomahawk pipe with forged iron bowl acquired from white traders

A crude pipe of hollow deer bone

The bowl of the ceremonial Crow pipe at left was carved out of a dark-hued stone called steatite and polished with a protective coating of buffalo grease. The 29-inch stem is covered with rings of blue beads and tufts of horsehair, probably snipped from the owner's favorite pony. Reddish streaks of paint on the pendant eagle feathers indicate that the pipe may once have been carried during a warring expedition.

27

Careful, patient labor went into the making of a ceremonial pipe, and a good one might be worth the price of a horse or several buffalo robes. Pipe bowls were shaped from soft stone of varying colors, with red considered the most beautiful. (The red stone was later called catlinite, after the painter George Catlin who visited the sacred site in Minnesota where it was quarried.)

The carving of pipe bowls was usually done by specialists. Using metal tools introduced by the Europeans, these skilled craftsmen could fashion the stone into bold images such as a horse in full gallop (*below*), or they could execute fine details of bas relief like the wavy pattern of buffalo fur on the bowl at bottom. After they had carved a bowl they would smooth and polish its surfaces by rubbing them with an abrasive variety of water grass.

The pipestems were made of gray ash, willow or cottonwood. All of these woods have soft, pithy centers that the pipemaker either hollowed out after having split the stem in half or burned out by using a hardwood stick or, later, a piece of heated wire. Although some of the tobacco smoked by the Indians grew wild, various tribes cultivated it in order to have a predictable supply available and to be able to trade it to other tribes. Both the planting of seeds and the harvesting of tobacco leaves were occasions for ritualistic prayers and dances. The Blackfeet even made tiny moccasins that were left out in the fields as gifts to the tobacco spirits, whom they visualized as gnomes one foot tall. Since the raw tobacco tasted strong, the Indians adulterated it with sumac leaves, bearberries and willow bark. This mixture might be carried inside a pouch like the one at right.

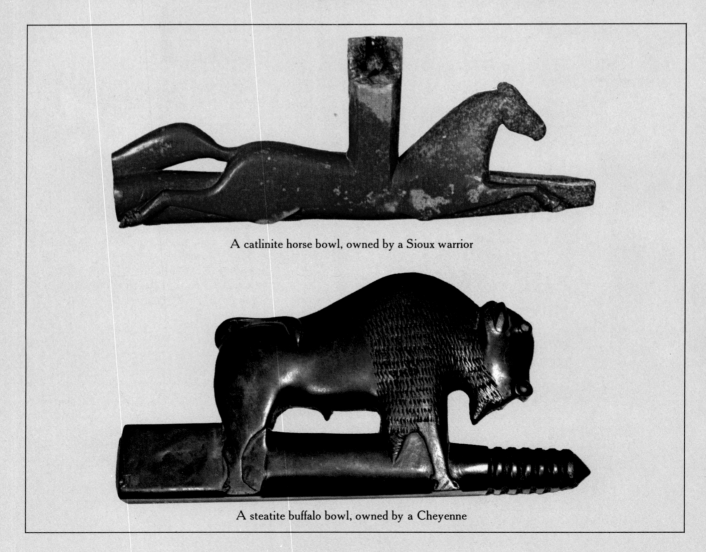

A catlinite horse bowl, owned by a Sioux warrior

A steatite buffalo bowl, owned by a Cheyenne

A Sioux carried this beaded buckskin tobacco pouch and quilled tamping stick.

Tomahawk bowl

Double bowl

Inlaid bowl

A popular Indian pipe bowl, the tomahawk, was actually introduced by the white man as a trading item. Indian craftsmen copied the motif, as in the catlinite bowl at top inlaid with ornamental strips of lead. Some bowls commemorated heroic deeds. The bowl at center is called a double horseback bowl, because it was smoked by a warrior who had ridden through enemy fire to sling a wounded companion over the back of his pony and rescue him. Others, like the bowl inlaid with catlinite at bottom, were prized as status symbols.

A full year passed before the two tribes clashed. At Bent's Fort the Cheyennes traded for all the muzzle-loading flintlocks they could afford (the price was five good buffalo robes per gun). Then, taking along as many Arapaho allies as they could muster, they headed south to hunt Kiowas and found them in the sand-hill country on Wolf Creek, some 140 miles northwest of modern Oklahoma City. They had decided to take no prisoners. One of the scouts who located the enemy that day, in the spring of 1838, was a warrior in his 30s, Black Kettle, a handsome, thoughtful man who would become an important civil chief of the Cheyennes in the turbulent decades ahead.

The Cheyennes struck viciously and, at first, successfully. Some of them ambushed and killed a party of 30 men and women out buffalo hunting; then a few hours later the main force caught a scattered group of women digging for roots south of the creek and killed a dozen of them. But now the camp was aroused, and the Kiowa braves mounted their horses to defend themselves. The battle was joined, and it surged back and forth for hours. Two Cheyenne chiefs, Gray Thunder and Gray Hair, fell, as did a number of important warriors. Parties of the attackers tried to break into the camp, but the Kiowa women threw up defensive breastworks in the sandy soil and cut down small trees to form barricades against the oncoming horses.

The Cheyenne and Arapaho women and children watched the battle from a nearby hill. Many an individual did deeds of valor to be bragged about later, but the northern attackers could not take the camp. As the sun touched the horizon in the west they pulled away, gathered their people and headed back north. Later the Cheyennes would claim that it had been a victory, but they would also say they had not observed the proper ceremonies in moving their sacred arrows against an enemy and that was the reason for the limited success.

The battle of Wolf Creek taught a lesson to thoughtful Indians on both sides. People as fierce and stubborn as Cheyennes and Kiowas cannot live at war with only the shallow Arkansas River separating them. The Cheyennes were, in the face of necessity, realists. It was one thing to make occasional raids against the Pawnees to the east, or the Shoshonis or Utes out in the mountains, or the Crows still farther out in the rugged country to the north, even though such adventures might bring on reciprocal raids. It was something else again to live at war with an enemy who occupied your backyard and had no intention of retreating. The Kiowas found the situation equally uncomfortable.

Both sides also had other motives for wanting peace. The Cheyennes wanted more horses, and their southern neighbors had an abundance of them; the Kiowas wanted to do business at the trading post of the Bents, those white friends of their enemies. The Kiowas may have believed that they could not lose a protracted war as long as the powerful Comanches were their allies, but they knew that they would suffer greatly while such a war proceeded. Furthermore, both the Kiowas and their Comanche allies had been decimated by an epidemic of smallpox during the previous winter.

The Comanches were the key to everything. Of the four tribes moving toward peace they were the most numerous, the most widespread, apparently the most secure in domination of their region. For more than a hundred years they had been lords of the southern plains, an area bigger than all New England. They had defeated or driven out many other tribes, including the tough Apaches. Moreover, they had waged effective war against the Spanish and French. Recently they had discovered a new threat on their southeastern frontier —a warlike group of white men called Texans.

Earlier in 1840 a delegation of important Comanches had gone to San Antonio to meet with those whites and discuss the possibility of accommodation with them. The Texans had requested that the Indians surrender a reported total of some 200 whites captured from the Texan settlements. The Comanches brought with them only two of their captives: a young girl whom they had wantonly tortured and a Mexican boy. Seeing only this pitiful pair, and revolted by the girl's mutilation, the Texans had become incensed and attempted to seize the peace delegation and hold them hostage until all the captives were returned. One does not seize Comanche dignitaries. They fought back hard, but the whites, having the advantage, killed a dozen chiefs and 20 warriors.

The Comanches immediately tortured to death some of the whites they held in their camps, but that was not enough. It seemed clear that these Texans were as aggressive as themselves—and treacherous in the bargain. They must be taught a stern lesson and given to un-

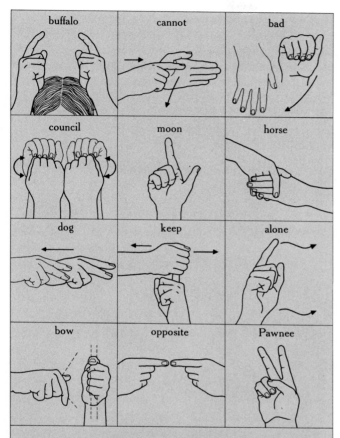

buffalo	cannot	bad
council	moon	horse
dog	keep	alone
bow	opposite	Pawnee

THE SILENT LANGUAGE OF THE PLAINS

A Sioux chief, Iron Hawk, pointed out that while the Great Spirit gave whites the power to read and write, "he gave Indians the power to talk with hands and arms." By means of signs like those shown above a Plains Indian could communicate with a speaker whose language was unknown to him. Though communication by gesture is probably older than speech itself, no system has ever proved more versatile and expressive than that developed by the Plains Indians.

derstand who it was that really controlled this country.

One problem bothered the Comanche Nation as it planned a major strike through Texas in the fall—the Cheyennes. The Comanches did not want to wage a two-front war. It had not taken the lords of the south plains long to make a decision; they told their friends the Kiowas to attempt a peace feeler toward the leaders of the Cheyenne-Arapaho alliance. The Comanches would let the Kiowas handle most of the ceremonies; they themselves would send only enough emissaries and

gifts to make clear their agreement to the proceedings.

In the Kiowa Nation one division, called the Kiowa-Apache, was noted for being friendly and peaceable. They sent up a delegation to an Arapaho camp headed by Chief Bull and told Bull that the southern tribes were prepared to consider peace. In the course of the meeting a raiding party of Cheyennes also stopped at the camp. They would not smoke with the Kiowas; as simple warriors they had not the authority to make this formal symbol of peaceful commitment. But they quit their raid and immediately turned back to carry the word to the Cheyenne chiefs. Within a matter of days the Cheyenne people had agreed and arranged a preliminary conference on the Arkansas River some 70 miles east of Bent's Fort.

To this site came the Cheyenne and Arapaho chiefs, led by High Backed Wolf, that old Cheyenne fighter and diplomat, who had consulted the most important warriors of his tribe and had been given authority to conclude peace. Two days later representatives of the southern alliance arrived: Kiowa Chiefs Little Mountain, Sitting Bear, Eagle Feather and others. All the leaders from both sides sat down in a line, and Eagle Feather, acting for the southern tribes, passed a lighted pipe. Each man solemnly took a puff. The ceremony meant that their hearts and minds were at one, and that their intentions were not in conflict.

The next item of business concerned a mysterious bundle wrapped in a Navaho blanket. It had been brought to the conference by the Kiowas and, as tactfully as possible, Chief Eagle Feather revealed that it contained the scalps of the Bow String warriors. He offered to give them back to the Cheyennes. High Backed Wolf considered the matter, then said: "Friend, these things if shown and talked about will only make bad feeling. Do not let us see them or hear of them."

The leaders from the south had also brought with them a youngster, a chief's son. Now, in gratitude for the initiative of the other side, the Cheyennes offered blankets as presents and threw them on the ground around the boy until all that could be seen of him was his head sticking up in the middle of the pile of gifts. Afterward they all feasted and planned a larger council for the final peacemaking.

Kiowa Little Mountain asked the other side to choose a site for the big meeting, specifying that it must be a wide place for large camps and many horses. The Cheyennes chose a place upstream on this river, about six miles below Bent's Fort, where they frequently traded. The leaders of both sides left the preliminary conference with confidence that a good peace could be made. During the next two weeks messengers rode over the south and central plains informing the various bands of the time and place for the big council.

The four major tribes involved spoke five distinct languages. Communication would be difficult, but not at all impossible. In the first place many of the tribesmen were multilingual. Nearly every leader spoke more than one language. From captives and from intermarriage in more peaceful times they had developed an abundance of competent interpreters. They had, in addition, the sign language *(page 31)* in which all the plains tribes were proficient. With a few hundred signs, many varying in meaning according to context, and through ingenious combinations of these signs, an Indian could express thousands of thoughts from the simple device of pointing to himself for "I" or "me" to the complicated expression of the verb "to be." The latter idea was shown by the right hand clenched upright in front of the chest, then moved down a few inches, almost as if one were stamping a document, the motion firm and steady; it meant "to be" or "to remain" or "to sit." Undoubtedly those who spoke in signs learned to be especially attentive and sensitive to the intent and meaning of the persons before them.

The main council gathered at the wide bottomland of the river; and any remaining tensions in the great encampment disappeared after the southern chiefs feasted in the special lodge. The chiefs smoked together, made speeches praising one another's worthiness and bravery, and feasted. The Cheyennes observed protocol in providing meat—no bear for the Kiowas, for it was taboo to them; no dog for the Comanches, for to them eating a dog was like eating one's own grandmother.

The climax of the chiefs' meeting came when Kiowa Little Mountain rose to issue a long-awaited invitation: "Now, my friends, tomorrow morning I want you all, even the women and children, to cross over to our camp and sit in a long row. Let all come on foot; they will all return on horseback."

The following day the northern Indians splashed across the stream and sat in long rows, expectant, with

The tribes and their territories

Formidable both as fighters and as hunters, 13 nomadic warrior tribes *(red italics on map)* dominated the heart of the grasslands during the early and middle decades of the 19th Century. But the world they lived in was in swift and violent transition; the tribal locations for the year 1840 shown on this map were very different from what they would have been only 50 years earlier—or later. Some of the fiercest of the warrior tribes, among them the Cheyenne and Sioux, had moved to the wild plains from the wooded territory around the upper Mississippi and Great Lakes. Other, less powerful Indians, such as the Iowa and Missouri, had been forced by white pressure out of the regions that carried their names.

The horse-borne nomads who roamed the Great Plains subsisted mainly by hunting buffalo. They fought hard among themselves and sometimes found the grasslands contested by tribes like the Pawnee and Mandan, who for the most part lived and farmed in permanent villages but hunted buffalo during the summer and sometimes raided the nomads for horses.

To the southwest were the Pueblo Indians, sophisticated farmers who lived in huge apartment houses of adobe or stone and shrewdly traded horses and corn to the southern nomads for buffalo robes and other products. Nearby were the deadly Apaches, once dwellers of the southern plains but by now mostly driven to the region that would become New Mexico, where they were periodically harassed by their powerful enemies, the Comanches.

Through the central and northern Rocky Mountains, the Utes, Shoshonis, Nez Percés and others occasionally sallied out into the buffalo country. Every summer, for example, the Nez Percés rode eastward over the high passes to hunt buffalo and to trade with, or raid against, the plains tribes.

By the 1840s tribe-against-tribe fighting had less effect on the Indians' settlement patterns than the growing incursions of white men. As white pressure upon the West increased, only the largest and most powerful plains tribes—among them the Sioux, Cheyenne, Blackfoot and Comanche—could hold out for any length of time; smaller tribes, such as the Arikara and the Crow, often became allies of the whites against warrior nations that had been their traditional enemies.

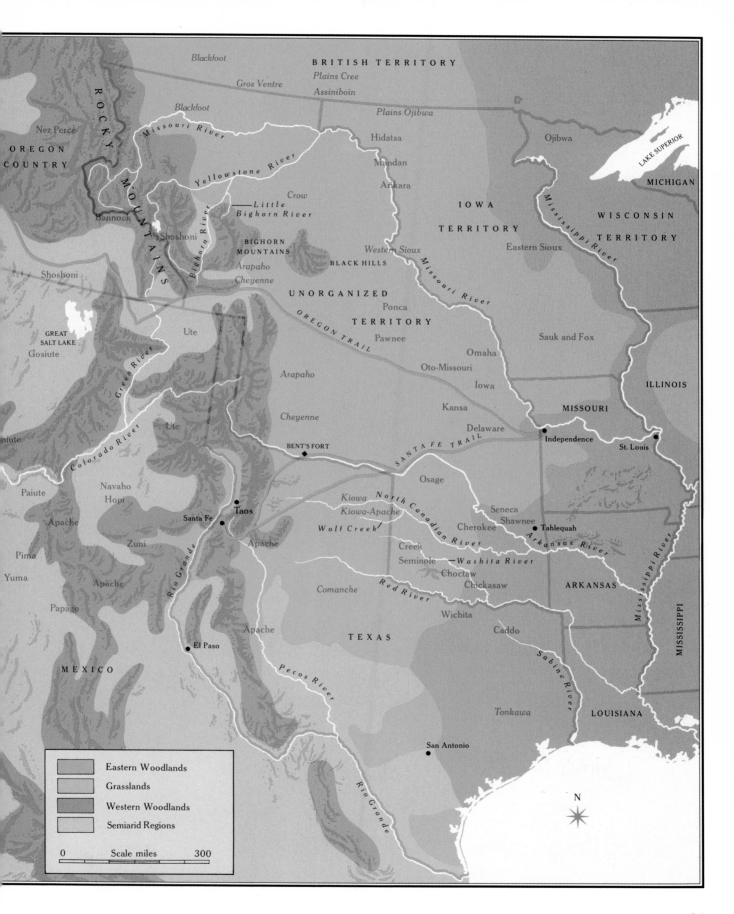

BRITISH TERRITORY

Blackfoot

Gros Ventre

Plains Cree

Assiniboin

Plains Ojibwa

Blackfoot

ROCKY

Nez Percé

OREGON
COUNTRY

Missouri River

M
O
U
N
T
A
I
N
S

Bannock

Shoshoni

Yellowstone River

Crow

*Little
Bighorn River*

Hidatsa

Mandan

Arikara

Ojibwa

LAKE SUPERIOR

MICHIGAN

IOWA

TERRITORY

WISCONSIN

TERRITORY

Mississippi River

Shoshoni

Bighorn River

BIGHORN
MOUNTAINS

Arapaho

Cheyenne

BLACK HILLS

Western Sioux

Eastern Sioux

GREAT
SALT LAKE

Gosiute

Ute

Green River

Colorado River

UNORGANIZED

TERRITORY

Ponca

Pawnee

OREGON TRAIL

Omaha

Oto-Missouri

Iowa

Missouri River

Sauk and Fox

ILLINOIS

MISSOURI

Arapaho

Ute

Cheyenne

BENT'S FORT ◆

Kansa

Delaware

● Independence

SANTA FE TRAIL

● St. Louis

Paiute

Navaho
Hopi

Santa Fe

Apache

● **Taos**

Kiowa

Kiowa-Apache

Wolf Creek

North Canadian River

Osage

Seneca

Shawnee

Cherokee

● Tahlequah

Arkansas River

Mississippi River

Paiute

Zuni

Apache

Creek

Seminole

Washita River

MISSISSIPPI

Pima

Yuma

Apache

Choctaw

Chickasaw

ARKANSAS

Rio Grande

Papago

Comanche

Red River

Apache

● El Paso

Wichita

Caddo

TEXAS

Pecos River

Sabine River

MEXICO

Tonkawa

LOUISIANA

Rio Grande

● San Antonio

N

	Eastern Woodlands
	Grasslands
	Western Woodlands
	Semiarid Regions

0   Scale miles   300

Proud and impassive, Sitting Bear glares at
the camera in 1870. Some 30 years had
passed since the council on the Arkansas;
in 1871 he would perish by deliberately
provoking the bullets of the U.S. Cavalry.

the men in front, then the women, then the children. The giveaway was an important institution. It was a form of conspicuous consumption showing the wealth of the giver and his careless disdain for property. But it also flowed out of real generosity and the desire to show goodwill. Most important, it showed insight into human psychology. People sometimes have differences that cannot be settled by rational dialogue or argument, but if one side presents a valuable and needed gift the differences may be wiped out as if by magic.

To make the giving a solemn and orderly ceremony the southerners presented small sticks as counters to those who sat in the long rows. The first to pass along was the slender Kiowa War Chief Sitting Bear, his left arm holding a great bundle of sticks, his black hair and long drooping mustache sparkling with grease. Four times in early manhood he had danced the exhausting sun dance for the good fortune of the tribe. Since then he had remained in the eyes of his people a man of grace and dignity, and now he had also become their most trusted war leader. He passed out his armload of sticks, then went to the bushes and broke off more to pass out; in all he gave 250 horses out of his own herd.

During the distribution of the sticks the Kiowas and Comanches sent their boys and their Mexican slaves out into the hills to drive the horses into the flats where the camps stood. They drove in horses of every description and color, some flighty, some docile, and the beasts made a crowded melee among the tipis and cottonwood, the herders shouting to control them. The northern Indians flocked toward the donors who had given them sticks and had their particular gifts pointed out to them. Everyone old enough to ride got at least one mount; some got six or more.

High Backed Wolf then invited all the southern people to come to his side of the river the following day. Over there, inside the big camp circle, the Cheyennes brought out exotic foods traded at the fort for the occasion: steaming kettles of rice and pots of dried cooked apples, hot stews of meat and bone marrow, the gravy thickened with ground corn meal — and to sweeten the food, New Orleans molasses.

When they had eaten, High Backed Wolf cried out to his people to bring presents. They brought brass kettles, beads, blankets, calico, guns. High Backed Wolf cautioned his guests that his warriors liked to fire a gun into the air before giving it away. For a time the camp was in an uproar as the Cheyenne men fired the noisy muzzle-loaders; then they presented the guns, still warm and smoking, to the visitors.

Thus they made peace. Some of the bands remained at the site several days to wade the river back and forth, to make new friends, to gamble and to continue with the round of other sports and games. The old griefs and hatreds were wiped out. Parties rode upstream to trade at the adobe fort. The Bents were pleased at the new customers, but refused to provide whiskey while so many former enemies were present.

The four tribes never broke the peace made at the Arrowpoint, but their agreement amounted more to a nonaggression pact than to any organized coalition against the forces that threatened them all. The following October, having settled their problem of a two-front war, the Comanches staged the biggest raid they ever made into Texas. They pressed their attack through the white settlements all the way to Linnville on the Gulf Coast, and some frightened whites even put out to sea in boats to escape them. The raid was significant as a symbol of what lay in store; it seemed to be successful, and many horses and much plunder were gathered. But as the marauders retreated west the whites gathered their forces in pursuit, and the Texas militia struck a smashing blow at the invaders in the Battle of Plum Creek. It would always be a moot point as to who was the victor, but the clear lesson was that the Comanches could not teach the Texans a lesson.

The peace of 1840 between the Indians of the south and central plains was a very humane accommodation to the immediate situation, yet the Indians of each tribe would face more in the future than they faced on this day. The fate of Sitting Bear, a noble savage if ever one existed, epitomized what was happening. In one of the most brave and defiant acts ever done by a man, he would die as a prisoner of the U.S. Cavalry 31 years later, literally forcing his captors to shoot him down. In his death he mutely testified to the inability of the Indians to guide the long sweep of Western history, but here on the Arrowpoint he had already made history of a kind. See him in the summer sun walking on the river sand before the rows of Indians, ceremonious, graceful, a demigod with lice. He had slain them generously, and now he gave them 250 precious horses.

Celebrating victory, Hidatsa women sing and raise enemy scalps on long, thin poles.

The Indian as the white man found him

In 1833 the Indians of the upper Missouri, like the rest of the plains tribes, were still sovereigns of their land, although agents of fur companies had already started the process of cultural destruction. That year two rare visitors voyaged up the Missouri River intent not on profit, but on knowledge. One was a middle-aged German prince, Maximilian of Wied-Neuwied, who preferred the study of natural history to ruling his tiny state. He brought along a young Swiss artist, Karl Bodmer.

Traveling more than 2,500 miles, these benign observers visited the Mandan, Hidatsa, Assiniboin, Blackfoot and other tribes. While Maximilian took notes, Bodmer made more than 400 sketches of the looks and customs of the Indians. His sketches were the basis of a later series of meticulous colored engravings, such as the rendering of the Hidatsa scalp dance (below) in which the women led the celebration after a successful skirmish with the enemy. Their work was fated to be the final record of some of these people. Only a few years later a smallpox epidemic, brought by white men, ravaged several tribes in the upper Missouri.

Playing a game near their village, two Hidatsa youths attempt to spear a ring on the ground while their elders look on.

Mandans gather in a lodge that visitor Maximilian found "spacious, tolerably light, and cleanly," despite the horses.

Near their village of 60 lodges, Mandan women ferry firewood across the Missouri in boats made of buffalo hides stretched over willow rods.

In the buffalo dance, led by the two esteemed warriors wearing whole buffalo heads, Mandans feign the milling movements of their prey.

A lone Mandan worshiper wrapped in a buffalo robe prays to the sun and moon idols made out of animal skin, grass and twigs.

After trading pelts for guns, knives and tobacco, Assiniboins break camp at Fort Union to follow the buffalo.

2 | The wide world of the horse Indians

A Plains Indian spent almost all of his life on a horse. As a child, when the camp was on the move, he shared his mother's saddle. Later he rode to the hunt and into real battle. Much later he might look forward to spending his remaining years as the rich and venerable owner of a large herd.

When explorers first came upon these mounted tribesmen they were so impressed by the Plains Indians' horsemanship that they called them the horse Indians. These formidable riders had first seen horses in the late 17th Century after the Spaniards brought them from Europe into southwestern America. Previously the Indians had lived as farmers and small-time hunters on the fringes of the plains, doing their work and traveling afoot.

The Western Indians got their first mounts by stealing and trading among the Spanish settlements of the Southwest. By the middle of the 18th Century tribes like the Comanches owned large herds of horses, and on them they ventured into the vastness of the Great Plains, which before were rarely crossed — or penetrated — to hunt the buffalo. Now many tribes abandoned their fixed abodes and became nomadic hunters, following the wanderings of the game herds, sleeping in movable lodges and designing a whole new way of life based on mobility.

In many tribes the high time of the horse culture lasted barely a century; a mounted brave was an unpleasant enemy to white men, who, accordingly, proceeded to wipe him out. But during the brief time these Indians dominated the plains, they made thorough use of this one gift of white men to lead venturesome, varied and often glorious lives as hunters, horsemen and warriors.

Mounted Navahos move toward their stronghold, the Canyon de Chelly in Arizona.

A sprawling encampment of Sioux is thronged with horses, some used in hunting or war, others to haul possessions on simple drags or, in later days, on the white man's wagons. So crucial were horses to the Plains Indians' way of life that the U.S. Army made killing them a major objective.

Indians considered their battle horses as extensions of themselves and dressed them accordingly. In artist George Catlin's sketch at top a horse parades in the same trappings as his Sauk and Fox rider. At bottom a Crow chief and his horse both wear elaborate headdresses.

New freedom with the coming of god dog

Sometime in the autumn of 1787 a raiding party of 250 Blackfoot warriors mounted their horses in western Canada, some 300 miles north of the present Montana line, and rode out of camp. They were off, wrote David Thompson, a Hudson's Bay Company man who was living among them, "to war on the Snake Indians." But the Snakes (Shoshonis) were not to be found, and the Blackfoot party "continued further than usual, very unwilling to return without having done something." Finally, after riding some 1,500 miles, they discovered a number of Spaniards leading a long pack train of horses and mules. The raiders sneaked toward the Spaniards and suddenly rushed down on them with terrifying war whoops. The Spaniards fled, "leaving the Horses and Mules to the war party."

The warriors paid no attention to the cargo the train was carrying—"a great weight of white stone." They quickly dumped it, slashing the cinches that held it on the animals, and headed north on the long trek home with their captured animals. It was a fine raid. They trotted into the camp where Thompson was staying, with about 30 horses and a dozen mules together with a number of bridles and tooled-leather saddles.

The Blackfoot men did not know—nor would they have cared—that the white stone they had left strewn on the ground was silver ore. To the warrior tribes of the plains, the horse was worth far more than silver. Confronted with the intimidating distances of the Great Plains, these nomadic people lived by the horse. With their mounts they easily followed the migratory buffalo herds, moved their villages to fresh hunting grounds, raided for all manner of booty and traded with other tribes and whites at places hundreds of miles from their home ranges. So central was the horse to the culture of the people of the plains that a tribe's, or an individual's, wealth was commonly measured in numbers of horses, and the horses, in turn, helped determine the size of

tribal bands because of their need for grazing room.

Yet at the time of the Blackfoot raid the horse was comparatively new to the Great Plains, having been there less than 150 years. There were no horses at all in the West—or anywhere else in the Americas—when the Spanish conquistador Hernando Cortes landed in Mexico with 10 stallions and six mares in 1519. Not many tribes attempted to live in the forbidding heart of the open grasslands. And those that did were poor in goods and often hungry. Limited to foot travel, they could carry little with them. Tribes like the Shoshoni and the Blackfoot in the North tried to eke out a living primarily by stalking buffalo. Some, like the Apache in the South, learned to make crude efforts at subsistence farming. More commonly these hunting Indians traded for food, such as maize, with the Southwestern Pueblos or with Indians on the eastern margins of the plains.

The horse changed all that, and quickly. As the Spaniards arrived in increasing numbers to exploit the region that would be Mexico and the Southwestern United States, they brought with them quantities of horses for mounts and pack work. These were fine beasts, with excellent bloodlines—mixtures of Arabian, Barb and Andalusian—and they multiplied rapidly. In the early 17th Century the Spaniards were still moving northward, mining, ranching and founding missions. Their horses moved with them, and it was at the Spanish centers that the Indians had their first extensive contacts with the new animals. Spanish policy forbade giving or trading either guns or horses to the Indians, for the conquistadors knew how important the exclusive ownership of both items had been in their conquests. But they used some of the Indians as grooms, herdsmen and cattle workers and either deliberately or by example taught these Indians to ride. When other tribes came to the area to trade or to beg food from the prosperous Pueblos in their established farming communities,

49

they too learned something about the new animals.

Although the white man tried to maintain his monopoly, the Spanish system of ranching with large herds on open ranges resulted in much straying. Many of the strays were never recaptured and became the ancestors of the wild mustangs of the West, but inevitably a number of them fell into Indian hands. Moreover, as the Indians gained some horses and came to understand their potential, they began to raid the Spanish herds, growing more daring as they acquired increasing mobility and striking power. One major windfall for the Indians occurred in 1680, when the Pueblos rose in violent revolt against their white masters, killing or driving out every Spaniard in the New Mexico area. Several thousand horses were left ownerless, to be taken by any Indian who had the chance and the ambition.

Indian-controlled horses spread from the Southwest in two principal streams (map, opposite). Only 40 or 50 years after the Pueblo revolt, both the Shoshonis, to the north, and the Comanches, who had begun moving south onto the plains from the Rocky Mountains, had a number of horses, and the Comanches were threatening not only the Spanish settlements but the homelands of the Apaches as well.

As each succeeding tribe first caught sight of the horse, its people reacted with astonishment and wonder, since the only domesticated animals they had ever seen before were their own scruffy dogs. Thompson talked with an old warrior who recalled his band's first sighting of the horse. It had been in his youth during the 1730s, only half a century before that noteworthy Santa Fe raid, when horses were still new to the plains. "We pitched away in large camps with the women and children on the frontier of the Snake Indian country," the old man recalled, "hunting bison and red deer which were numerous, and we were anxious to see a horse of which we had heard so much. At last, as the leaves were falling we heard that one was killed by an arrow shot into his belly, but the Snake Indian that rode him got away. Numbers of us went to see him, and we all admired him. He put us in mind of a stag that had lost his horns; and we did not know what name to give him. But as he was a slave to Man, like the dog, which carried our things, he was named the Big Dog."

Despite such admiration on the part of many Indians, the horse did not appeal equally to every tribe.

For example, the Pueblos, though they were among the first to learn the value of horses, continued their largely horseless life style. Dwelling as they did in permanent communities with adequate supplies of food, they did not really need the horse and tended to use it primarily as a trade item. To the Apaches, the horse meant more. The Apaches stole mounts from other Indians and from the Spaniards, raided with them against more sedentary tribes and battled with them against such tribes as the Comanche pressing down from the north. Yet their devotion to the new animal was never very deep or permanent. In fact, most Apaches were as much inclined to eat a horse as to ride it, and they had reasons. For one thing, by 1750 many of them had been pushed into some of the driest reaches of the Southwest, a wasteland consisting of rocky mountains, eroded breaks and sandy plains, offering little sustenance for horses or for people. Through necessity they quickly learned to live in this harsh country, to travel through it afoot like the coyote or mountain lion, to blend in so that they were nearly invisible. They became, in the words of an admiring commentator, "one of the toughest human organisms the world has ever seen." Under the circumstances, the horse was often more valuable to them as food than as transportation.

There was a parallel reason, subtle but valid, why the Apaches made less than a wholehearted commitment to the horse. Innately, they were not so flamboyant as certain other tribes. It was not their way to daub bright war paint on their faces and show themselves

---

HOW THE HORSE SPREAD ONTO THE PLAINS

The principal sources of horses for Western Indians were Spanish ranches established during the 16th and 17th Centuries in the area that now comprises northern Mexico, New Mexico and Texas. Horses spread north as a result of both intertribal trading and livestock raids, and in the 18th Century the regions around Santa Fe and San Antonio became the major diffusion centers. West of the Rockies the animals moved toward the Shoshoni trading center; from there they traveled either toward the Northwest or swung eastward into Crow territory. Another trunk route ran east of the Rockies from Santa Fe onto the plains, where it merged with the flow of horses from San Antonio and eventually rejoined the western route at the major trading centers on the northern plains. There Indians who had received guns from early French and English white traders bartered the weapons for horses brought in by the other tribes.

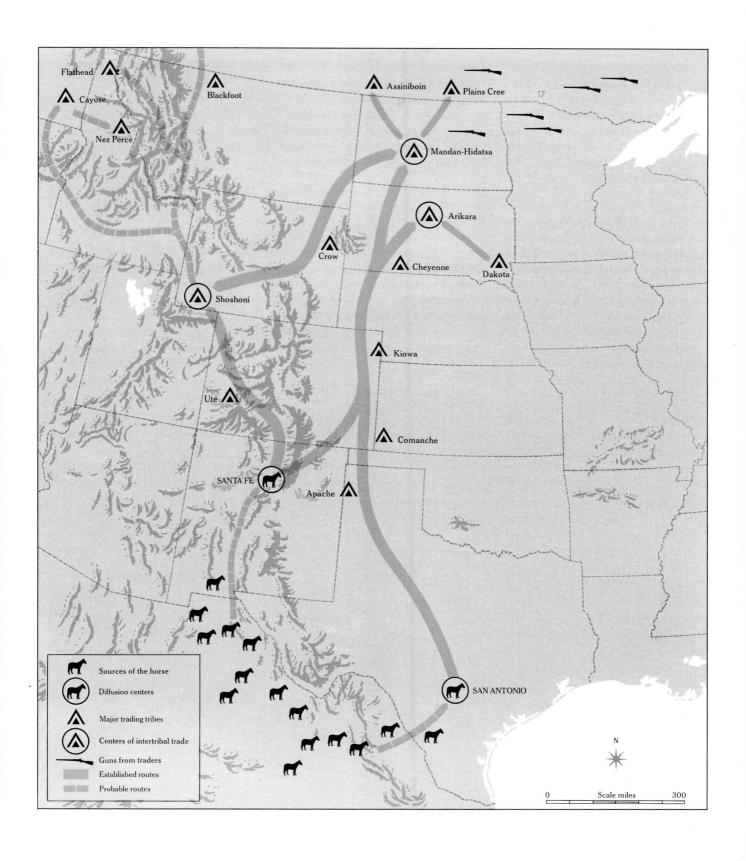

Flathead

Cayuse

Nez Percé

Blackfoot

Assiniboin

Plains Cree

Mandan-Hidatsa

Arikara

Crow

Cheyenne

Dakota

Shoshoni

Kiowa

Ute

Comanche

SANTA FE

Apache

SAN ANTONIO

Sources of the horse

Diffusion centers

Major trading tribes

Centers of intertribal trade

Guns from traders

Established routes

Probable routes

N

0   Scale miles   300

In a lively Catlin painting a Comanche struggles with a wild horse he has roped and hobbled, while his companions continue the chase. Since these mustangs were few and the fastest ones always got away, Indians only went after wild horses when they could not steal from whites or other tribes.

high on horseback to their enemies; instead, in their harsh land they often preferred to use stealth and cunning on foot both in war and in hunting.

By contrast, other tribes—Blackfoot, Sioux, Cheyenne, Arapaho, Kiowa, Comanche—not only took to the horse as if to the saddle born, but seized the opportunity the horse afforded to acquire mastery of the Great Plains. In fact, it may be said that the horse actually created the nomadic Plains Indian as he was encountered by white Americans in the 19th Century —mounted, mobile and fierce, a proud warrior to whom husbandry was anathema and who reveled in both the chase after game and the charge against an enemy. From being marginal hunters or farmers plodding at the edge of hunger, many tribes rode the horse into a new life.

Mounted, the Indians could pursue game so efficiently as to ensure a surplus of meat and hides. They could pack up and move entire villages *(pages 56-57)*. They could trade conveniently with other Indians and white men hundreds of miles away. They could plunder and raid rivals all over the plains. In very definable ways the horse also changed social structures within the tribes, making some people rich and powerful while others remained weak and poor. With the horizon no longer limited by the distance an Indian could travel on foot, it could even be said that the horse altered the psyche of the plains people. For the feel of a beast obeying a man's will gives him a sense of power. It makes him an Arab, a Mongol, a conqueror. It makes him a Plains Indian. In all, the changes wrought in many tribes by the horse were as great, relatively, as those that steam and electricity would one day bring to the white man.

Not surprisingly, some of the Western tribes came to look upon the horse with an almost religious awe. To the Sioux the animal was a medicine dog; the Comanches called it a god dog. Similarly, other tribes used words implying that the horse was mysterious or sacred. But one of the most meaningful of the Indians' descriptions was the mundane Blackfoot term big dog, for it was an indicator of the real, pragmatic value of the horse. Until its arrival in the New World, the dog had been the Indians' only beast of burden—other than Indian women, who carried whatever loads the dog did not. And the horse, of course, was a far larger and stronger beast of burden than the dog (or woman). The Sarsis were even more specific in their nomenclature.

53

They called the animal seven dogs, implying a comparison in working ability between the horse and the dog. The name was apt. The Indian work dog, which was similar in size and appearance to a large gray wolf, could carry approximately 50 pounds on its back and pull about 75 pounds with a travois, or pole drag. So loaded, a train of dogs could move five or six miles a day. A horse could be packed with 200 pounds or pull a 300-pound burden with the travois and make 10 or 12 miles in a day. Thus the work ratio in favor of the horse over the dog did in fact approximate 7 to 1.

One surprising improvement the bigger draft animal brought almost immediately was in the size of people's dwellings. In the past the limit on loads had made it impossible to transport a large, heavy tipi cover or a set of sizable poles. In consequence, the tipis had been small and cramped, no more than five or six feet tall. Now, with the bigger beasts of burden, the Indians could afford to build lodges 12 to 15 feet high, with more room inside for family, visitors and for storing possessions. The horse was an immediate blessing, too, for the very old or infirm members of the tribes. Formerly, there had been no solution but to abandon those who could not walk. Now incapacitated people could be moved on the horse-pulled travois.

Though such effects on household matters were fundamental to plains life, other changes were more dramatic. One was the role of the horse as an instrument —and an objective—in raids. To steal the god dog in a raid not only meant immediate new wealth to the raider, but horse stealing also came to be much admired as a proof of manhood. The Comanches were particularly adroit as horse stealers, carrying out most of their raids with small parties. The horses of the Apaches and Spaniards were prime targets. An observer on the plains wrote that a Comanche could crawl into a "bivouac where a dozen men were sleeping, each with a horse tied to his wrist by the lariat, cut a rope within six feet of the sleeper, and get away with the horse without waking a soul."

The Comanches also gloried in large-scale raids, where the warriors would ride out in sufficient strength to dominate the target area. On such forays they would set up a raid camp, then spread out to collect horses and any property they could pack away. This was of-ten done in the sparsely settled country on the northern frontier of Mexico. A traveler who had gone from Mexico City to Santa Fe in 1846 reported the effects of Comanche raids: "For days together I traversed a country completely deserted on this account, passing through ruined villages untrodden for years by the foot of man." Within the span of a single year "upwards of ten thousand head of horses and mules have already been carried off, and scarcely has a hacienda or rancho on the frontier been unvisited and everywhere the people have been killed or captured."

On one memorable plundering expedition the Comanches traveled so deep into Mexico with their Kiowa allies that they saw bright-plumed birds and "tiny men with tails" climbing around in trees — an indication that the raiders may have reached the Yucatán Peninsula.

As the horse spread and intertribal raiding grew more intense, the plains became like an ocean with a hundred pirate strongholds from which bold men sallied forth to prey on the unsuspecting. No single law held sway, for there were many peoples, each with its own laws. Cheyennes preyed on Kiowas; Kiowas harried Pawnees; Sioux raided Crows. Even after they had been driven from the plains, the prowling Apaches, in certain circumstances, used the horse for their forays. The later Apache leader Geronimo tells in his autobiography of a raid from his base in Arizona in 1865: "Heretofore we had gone on foot; we were accustomed to fight on foot; besides, we could more easily conceal ourselves when dismounted. But this time we wanted more cattle, and it was hard to drive them when we were on foot." Mounted, they rode into Sonora from somewhere southwest of Tombstone, Arizona, and continued as far south as the mouth of the Yaqui River on the Gulf of California. Then they turned north, "attacked several settlements, and secured plenty of supplies."

Of all these warring tribes, no people made more efficient, consistent and steady use of the horse than the Comanches. Perhaps more than any other nation, they lived by the god dog, doing with it all that other tribes did, but in most cases just a little better. From the 1750s until well into the 19th Century mounted Comanches dominated the southern plains, driving out weaker tribes, as did the Cheyenne, Sioux and other tribes to the north. Spain could build her missions and presidios in the woodlands to the east or through the

So attached were Indians to their war horses that they sang to their steeds and carved effigies to those killed in battle. In the figure below, made by a Sioux, the holes painted red represent the horse's wounds.

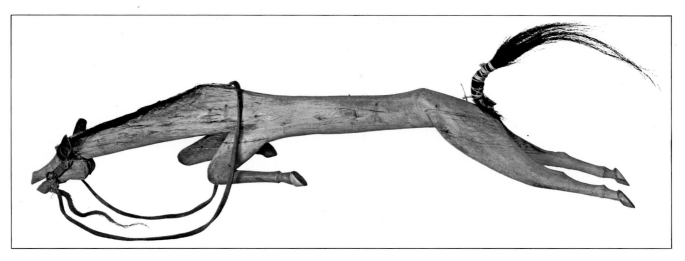

dry Southwest all the way to the Pacific, but she could establish herself only in isolated spots south of the Great Plains and only as far north as San Antonio. From there on the Comanches had become lords of the southern plains; the overextended Spanish forces, conquerors of the Aztecs and Incas, finally were to be blocked by the Comanches and their allies.

The artist and Western explorer George Catlin, who observed a demonstration of the Comanches' horsemanship in 1834, paid them this tribute: "I am ready without hesitation to pronounce the Comanches the most extraordinary horsemen that I have seen yet in all my travels, and I doubt very much whether any people in the world can surpass them. A Comanche on his feet is out of his element, and comparatively almost as awkward as a monkey on the ground, without a limb or branch to cling to; but the moment he lays his hands upon his horse his *face* even becomes handsome, and he gracefully flies away like a different being."

Comanches and other Plains Indians found that the horse vastly increased their efficiency on the hunt. It presented them with the means to exploit the buffalo *(page 66)* as never before.

The new mobility gained from the horse also increased trading over long distances. Commerce between tribes had been carried on for ages, long before the coming of the white man or the horse. Sea shells, salmon oil and dried fish from the Northwest coast, for instance,

My horse be swift in flight
Even like a bird;
My horse be swift in flight.
Bear me now in safety
Far from the enemy's arrows,
And you shall be rewarded
With streamers and ribbons red.
Sioux warrior's song to his horse.

passed through many hands and eventually found their way over the Rockies in exchange for such articles as eagle feathers and fine war bonnets made from them.

One practical item southern and eastern Plains Indians needed was the lodgepole for the frames of their tipis. The poles had to be some 20 to 25 feet long, light enough to be carried on a horse and strong enough to bear the weight of the buffalo-hide tipi cover. The Comanches' own territory, for example, was almost barren of suitable trees, but fine, straight poles grew almost ready-made in what came to be called the lodgepole pines of the northern Rockies.

In the past this process of exchanging back and forth across the regions of the plains frequently had taken months or years. After the use of the horse became general, trading accelerated tenfold or more, and the horse itself became a basic standard of exchange *(page 62)*. One of the main intertribal trading centers in the Southwest was located at Taos, where Pueblo Indians had long held trade fairs that were later broadened in scope by the Spaniards with European goods. Comanches first attended a Taos fair early in the 18th Century. Like other plains tribes, they brought dried meat, animal skins, tallow and salt, which they exchanged for maize, squash, melons, blankets, pottery and decorative turquoises. Meanwhile, far to the northeast, the villages of the Mandans, the Hidatsas and the Arikaras became trading centers *(map, page 51)* of equal importance.

An Indian family moves out from camp near Fort Keogh, Montana. The bentwood cage at left kept children from falling off the platform.

Horse power for moving a family and its goods

A village of nomadic Plains Indians following a large buffalo herd or escaping an enemy often had to pack and move in a great hurry. Clothes, weapons, household utensils and even the tipis had to go onto the backs of horses or onto the platforms of the A-shaped drags called travois. This called for some adroit packing, as indicated by the diagram at far right.

Before the horse came to the plains a camp could not expect to move more than six miles a day. And the weight of goods was restricted to what women and dogs could carry (men had to carry arms in case the camp was attacked).

The horse changed all this. A horse-borne camp could travel 30 miles in an emergency. A lodge, which was once no more than five to six feet high, could now reach 15 feet and still be transportable — though it required three horses: two for the dozen or so poles and one for the heavy buffalo-hide covering. A wealthy chief, whose towering lodge might be held by 30 poles, each over 30 feet long, used 15 horses for the poles alone.

In time both the number and quality of an Indian's possessions came to de-pend on the number of horses he owned. And these differences in wealth were never more obvious than when the camp was on the move. In a rich man's entourage a favorite wife, mounted on a horse carrying elaborately decorated saddlebags and parfleches (*right, above*), led a long procession of other horses bearing the family goods. Middle-class families followed, with fewer horses and perhaps some dogs to help the transport. And finally the poor man's wife trailed along in the slums of the moving camp, walking in the dust behind the one overloaded family horse.

A parfleche *(left)*, strapped to the horse's side, was stuffed with dried foods; clothes and small utensils went into a saddlebag *(right)*.

The main part of a travois consisted of two long shafts tied crosswise in front of the horse's head with a thick buffalo tendon. To secure the travois in place, strips of buffalo rawhide were wound around the shafts and lashed to the crosspieces that comprised the platform. Travois were made and owned by the women, who took great pride in their craftsmanship. Any woman who failed to remove all of the buffalo hair from the rawhide line, or who allowed its width to be uneven, was considered an incompetent housewife.

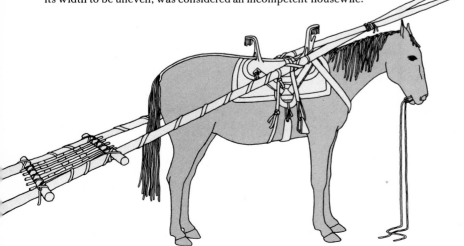

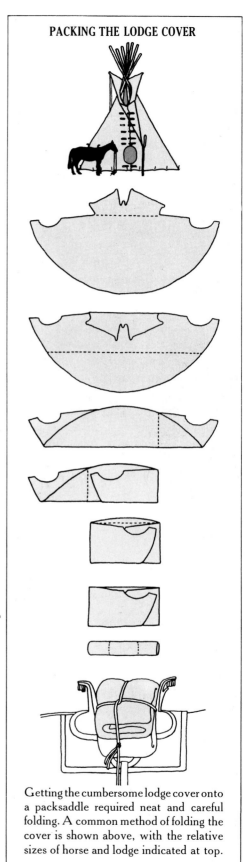

PACKING THE LODGE COVER

Getting the cumbersome lodge cover onto a packsaddle required neat and careful folding. A common method of folding the cover is shown above, with the relative sizes of horse and lodge indicated at top.

Virtually all of the Plains Indians used quirts when mounted. The Crow quirt shown here had long rawhide tails for whipping the horse and a heavy wooden handle for clouting an enemy in close combat.

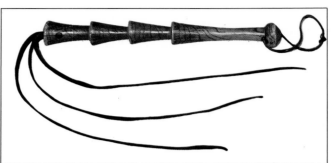

In the 19th Century, Indians also came to trade at the posts established by whites who had pushed west from the Mississippi to deal in furs and in other native commodities. During the 17th, 18th and early 19th Centuries, for example, the principal fur-trade item offered by the Indians was the beaver pelt, much sought after for the European fashion market. In the 1830s, when the supply of beavers declined and the fashion changed, white traders at posts like Bent's Fort on the Arkansas bought enormous quantities of buffalo robes, readily available as a result of the increased efficiency of mounted Cheyenne and Arapaho hunters. There was also a brisk trade in stolen horses and mules, many of them carrying Spanish, Mexican and Texas brands. Some of this livestock was even marked with the brands of ranches as far away as California. The Indians occasionally brought in wild horses, too, but the traders at Bent's Fort bought more than one herd that had cost the lives of a family in the stealing.

In return, the Indians received an array of white man's goods, some of which had an impact on plains life comparable to that of the horse itself. At trading centers on the northeastern plains, and at Taos and other pueblos, Indians were able to obtain wonderfully useful, durable items, such as steel hatchets, metal arrowheads, saber points for lances and well-tempered knives. Formerly the Indians had used stone tools to remove and cut the tough hide of the buffalo and to slice its meat into strips to make jerky for rations. Good stone knives were quickly made and efficient, but they were brittle and less useful for fine cutting of animal hides and flesh than were metal ones obtained from traders.

Another white man's product that had an even more pronounced effect was the gun, obtained from French and English traders. The early caplock, matchlock and flintlock guns were clumsy to load and fire from horseback; the fact was that a bowman had all the advantage in rate of fire, being able to get off 20 arrows to the musketman's one ball. A frontiersman testified that he had "as leave be shot at with a musket at the distance of one hundred yards, as by one of these Indians with his bow and arrow." Nevertheless, the new weapon, even in its early days, did possess a critical advantage: a tribe with guns could win against one without them because of the noise, smoke, surprise and effectiveness of the new weapon when it found its target. It was, for example, the gun in conjunction with the horse that enabled the Comanches to prevail over the Apaches. And later when breechloaders and repeating firearms came in, the first tribe to get them could dominate in almost any confrontation.

One wholly unfortunate result of the trading with whites was the acquisition of liquor, which many Indians became inordinately fond of. In fact, some refused to trade without it. In later years nearly all English-speaking traders used liquor as a tool to soften up customers even though there were regulations against selling or giving it to them. Frontier merchants justified the practice with an age-old argument: everybody else was doing it. As one warrior after another foundered under the impact of whiskey or rum, many whites shrugged off the consequences. It is doubtful, however, that many white men could have imbibed much of the stuff tendered by some traders in the late 19th Century. One recipe called for 1 quart pure alcohol, 1 pound black chewing tobacco, 1 bottle Jamaica ginger, 1 handful red pepper, 1 quart black molasses and Missouri water as required. The trader's hope was that his Indian customer would become generous and easy to trade with and then, instead of growing bellicose, would become drowsy or sick. Often the prescription worked.

Unhappily, too, the horse-induced escalation of trade, particularly in the Southwest, brought increased sales of another item: human beings. The slave trade had originally been started in the New World by the Spaniards to ensure themselves a supply of labor for the gold and silver mines of Mexico. Later, halted on their northward advance by the ferocity of the mounted plains tribes, they encouraged the trade in slaves as a method of keeping the tribes from uniting against them, buying Apaches or Comanches or any other hostile Indians that were brought to them as captives. The tribes,

The most common Indian bridle, known as the war bridle, was made of a length of rope with a so-called lark's-head knot in the middle. The knot, tightened around the horse's lower jaw, formed the bit; the rope ends served as reins.

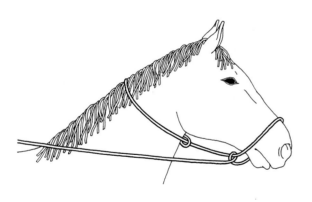

To break a horse for riding, the Indians occasionally used a halterlike bridle. The nose loop and single rein gave the rider a strong contact with the horse's head, and a hard pull on the rein cut the animal's wind, bringing it to a halt.

regrettably, were all too eager to supply prisoners.

One summer, for example, in late July an estimated 1,000 Comanches invaded the Chama district of New Mexico, killed seven people, wounded others and kidnapped three boys. The Spanish governor sent soldiers to chase the raiders, with no success. On August 15, 100 Comanches attacked the pueblo of Pecos, killed nine people and captured seven. Pursuit was more successful this time; Spaniards surprised the Indian camp some 200 miles from Santa Fe and killed 40 Comanches. On August 18 the Indians struck the village of Albuquerque, killed five people, kidnapped four sheepherders, slaughtered 400 sheep and ran off all the horses. Pursuit was impossible; the local militia was off fighting Navahos. But on August 27 Comanches came to trade at Taos as if all were peaceful, and they were permitted to sell captives, as well as livestock with Spanish brands.

In an earlier even less-admirable incident, a band of raiders, probably Apaches, brought some Caddoan children to one of the pueblo trade fairs. For one reason or another Spanish customers refused to buy the children, whereupon the raiders cut the throats of all the small prisoners in full view of the horrified spectators. To prevent such massacres, the King of Spain authorized the payment of ransom for prisoners even when no need for slaves existed, thereby ensuring the continuance and expansion of the trade. Even after the departure of the Spaniards the slave trade flourished among the tribes themselves until well into the 19th Century, creating hostilities that endured for years.

Within the intimate social structure of each tribe the horse was also responsible for certain fundamental changes. The status of women improved—initially because they were relieved of some of the burdens they had borne on their own backs. In consequence they gained more leisure for handicrafts and for social life. Ironically, however, among the nomadic tribes the relief women gained from traditional labors was only brief. Any surplus time now available was given over to dressing, tanning and working the buffalo hides the hunters brought in. Partly because of the hunters' need for this kind of assistance, polygyny, which had previously been practiced in a modest way in various tribes, became increasingly popular among affluent males. With his extra horses, a well-to-do hunter could acquire several wives to work on the hides. One Blackfoot chief noted that his "eight wives could dress 150 skins in the year whereas a single wife could only dress ten."

In addition, the horse brought with it class divisions for many tribes. In early times, the foot-bound people had spent almost all their energies gaining the bare necessities, and there had been little or no surplus left over to divide after the survival of the band was assured. But after the horse created a more abundant society, three loose classes grew up: a privileged class that was expected to be generous and responsible for the general welfare of the band, a middle class sharing most of the benefits of the upper class but with fewer possessions and sufficiently independent so that a family could leave one band and join another at will, and a lower, underprivileged class consisting of people poor in horses and other possessions and dependent on the generosity of the powerful upper class. Though status was based to some degree on heredity, the wealth in horses brought by prowess as a warrior and hunter was a critical measure of social status. Therefore any man of competence could change his class standing and that of his family by raiding against a rival tribe.

Although Indians preferred the domesticated animals obtained by stealing, another way a man might increase his wealth was by catching wild horses. This was particularly true of the Comanches, for their domain included the best early ranges of the wild mustangs. The Indians used many methods of taking wild horses. They built corrals of posts and brush, with wings extending from both sides so that horses could be driven toward them and then chased into the enclosure. On their own mounts they ran down and caught with the lariat animals that had grown thin and weak in the winter or those that had become fat and sluggish in the summer — or sometimes horses that simply had drunk their fill of water and for the moment could not run well. Good wild horses were difficult to catch; in fact, the fast, long-winded ones nearly always got away. In an effort to capture such prizes the Comanches would pursue them in relays, taking advantage of the fact that each herd tended to remain within its own grazing grounds and when pursued would normally run in a large circle. Riders with fresh mounts would take over the chase at regular intervals. By this relay chasing technique the coveted mustangs could sometimes be run to exhaustion and finally lassoed, even though the process might take two or three days without stopping.

To tame a newly caught horse the Comanches first would choke the animal with ropes and throw it to the ground. The new owner then would blow his breath into the horse's nostrils, perhaps as a symbol of mastery. Next he would halter the animal with a length of rawhide looped around the lower jaw and tied fast around its neck, and secure the other end to a gentle old mare for a few days. While the green horse was tied to the mare, the owner would handle it enough to make it accustomed to human beings, and when it was set free the animal would stay near the mare. In breaking a horse to ride, a man would take it onto a boggy or sandy place or into the deeper water of a river or stream. There the animal would find bucking more difficult; for the man the inevitable spills would be less painful.

The Comanches and some other tribes were in one way wiser than the Spaniards with horses. Spaniards rode only stallions, which are especially skittish in stressful circumstances like charging an enemy line. Indians gelded most of their male horses. First, a gelding is more tractable and thus more easily trained than a stallion. Second, by gelding most males and keeping only those with superior characteristics to use at stud, the Indians continually improved the breed.

The greatest breeders of horses among American Indians were the Nez Percés. The explorer Meriwether Lewis wrote in his journal in 1805 of the Nez Percé horses: "They appear to be of excellent race, lofty, elegantly formed, active, and durable; many of them appear like fine English coursers; some of them are pied with large spots of white irregularly mixed with a dark-brown bay." The pied horses Lewis observed were first-class Appaloosas.

Although the Comanches were not quite so meticulous in horse breeding as the Nez Percés, they were every bit as shrewd in discovering the characteristics of a good animal. They would watch a growing colt, observing its form and color and spirit. When it was a year or two old they would begin to test it for speed, stamina, fearlessness and trainability. If it showed little promise, ample employment could nevertheless be found for it. A warrior would ride an ordinary animal for simple traveling and lead his war or buffalo horse, saving it for more exacting work. For hunting and fighting he avoided riding a mare, if possible. Mares were generally used by women and younger children. Any old swayback would be made to carry a pack or pull a travois.

If, however, an animal was superior, the warrior who owned it would make a war or buffalo horse of it, sometimes using the same animal for both the battle and the hunt. In war such a horse had to be able to stand not only the whooping and screaming of the fight, but to respond alertly to commands transmitted by pressure from

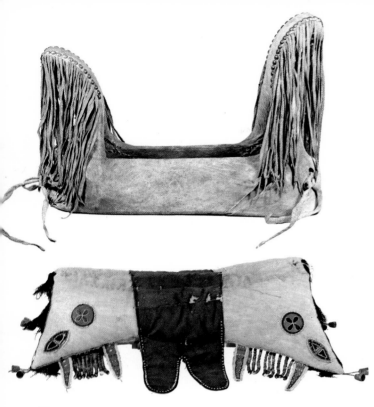

Though many Indians preferred the convenience of bareback riding, they also used saddles, especially for long trips and ceremonies. Women rode astride an adaptation of the high-bowed Spanish war saddle *(top)*. Men preferred the soft pad saddle, like the Apache one shown directly above stuffed with buffalo hair and grass. The Cheyenne blanket *(below)*, decorated with beads, went under a saddle for dress occasions.

its rider's knees or a shift of his weight while the warrior's hands were engaged in striking at the enemy.

Some superior horses learned to gallop in a straight line, parallel to the enemy, while the rider hung over one side with only one of his heels showing over his mount's back. This enabled the warrior to unloose arrows from underneath the horse's neck while being shielded by its body. The galloping rider was supported by a loop of horse or buffalo hair woven into the animal's mane and slung around one shoulder. He then locked a leg over the horse's back and the other under its belly. This spectacular technique was, however, only rarely employed in battle. It left the entire side of the war horse vulnerable and made accuracy exceedingly difficult.

Hunting buffalo, a horse had to have many of the same characteristics as those displayed in battle — sufficient speed and fearlessness to enter the fringes of a nervous, fleeing herd without guidance by reins; enough quickness to avoid the charge of a wounded bull; and the deep wind to stay with a racing herd for miles.

A Comanche had great esteem for his favorite horse. He combed it and petted it and for safety's sake usually picketed it at night near his lodge. One Comanche, Post Oak Jim, once told an anthropologist: "Some men loved their horses more than they loved their wives." To kill a man's favorite horse was tantamount to committing murder.

The Plains Indians generally made their own riding gear, largely modifying Spanish designs but also following their own ideas. They made equipment of twisted or woven horsehair or buffalo hair, rawhide, and tanned leather. Sometimes a steel bit might be attached to the bridle. But the Indians preferred to guide their mounts only by a thin rawhide thong or a rope of braided buffalo hair looped over the lower jaw *(page 59)*. When hunting or fighting they did not wish to encumber their horses with much weight and therefore rode bareback or with a simple hide or hide-pad saddle stuffed with buffalo or deer hair. For women's and old men's use, and for the securing of packs, more elaborate saddles were made of a wood or wood-and-horn frame bound about with sinew and wet rawhide. Shrinking as it dried, the rawhide covering held the parts firmly in place. Such saddles *(at left)*, cushioned with a folded buffalo robe or piece of bearskin, were fitted with stirrups made of green wood bent to shape and then dried.

A bustling market for traders

To the Indians of the plains, the horse meant more than an increase in the mobility of warriors and buffalo hunters or relief for women from some of the backbreaking labor of moving camp. Horses came to represent wealth. For both the individual owner and the tribes they became a major medium of exchange. Moreover, the horse enabled the Indian to travel increasing distances to trade horses and other prized goods like buffalo robes and beaver pelts at the posts established by white merchants.

By 1840 there were an estimated 150 trading posts like the one at right. Since the mounted Indians could pick and choose among traders, competition between the entrepreneurs grew intense, and the trade goods they offered became increasingly varied and exotic. Beside such essentials as cloth, tools and firearms, there were bells and mirrors from Leipzig, clay pipes from Cologne, beads from Venice and shell ornaments from the Bahamas.

While the Indians wanted such gewgaws and traded eagerly for them, they could be quite hardheaded in bartering for the goods they really needed to sustain or improve their way of life. They were, of course, canny judges of horseflesh, and when dealing with whites or fellow Indians they would demand upwards of half a dozen animals for a well-trained, long-winded horse that could overtake a buffalo.

Furthermore, they knew how to parlay one good trade into another. As early as the latter half of the 18th Century, the Arikaras would trade one mount for a rifle, a hundred rounds of ammunition and a knife. Then they would use the weapons to raid whites or other tribes for still more horses.

As with any other commodity, the value of horses as a medium of exchange varied with supply and demand. In the early 1800s, on the upper Missouri where horses were relatively scarce and buffalo abundant, a fine horse might be worth 10 buffalo robes. Later the price dropped to as low as three robes. The exchange rate also varied according to the wealth of the Indian trader. A rich man was expected to pay more for goods than did his poorer neighbors (for example, nine horses versus two for a dress shirt and leggings). Below are some other comparative prices in the trading markets of the High Plains.

A SAMPLING OF TRADE VALUES

1 ordinary riding horse
- = 8 buffalo robes
- = 1 gun and 100 loads of ammunition
- = 1 carrot of tobacco weighing 3 pounds
- = 15 eagle feathers
- = 10 weasel skins
- = 5 tipi poles
- = 1 buffalo-hide tipi cover
- = 1 skin shirt and leggings, decorated with human hair and quills

1 fine racing horse = 10 guns

1 fine buffalo horse = several pack animals

1 buffalo robe
- = 3 metal knives
- = 25 loads of ammunition
- = 1-gallon metal kettle
- = 3 dozen iron arrowpoints
- = 1½ yards of calico

3 buffalo robes = 1 white blanket

4 buffalo robes = 1 scarlet Hudson's Bay blanket

5 buffalo robes = 1 bear-claw necklace

30 beaver pelts = 1 keg of rum

10 ermine pelts = 100 elk teeth

Indian traders gather in the great inner court of Fort William (later Fort Laramie). This painting was done by artist A. J. Miller in 1837, a year in which more than half a dozen plains tribes traded at the post.

One fascinating side benefit for the Indians from their preoccupation with the horse was a profound knowledge of the geography of the Western land. On their prolonged raiding and trading forays they acquired an intimate familiarity with regions so distant from the home ground that their forefathers might have heard of them only in rumors, if at all. The American trader Josiah Gregg, who was about to set forth across the plains, discussed the lay of the terrain with a Comanche chief, Big Eagle. Gregg found Big Eagle apparently "well acquainted with the whole Mexican frontier from Santa Fé to Chihuahua and even to the Gulf, as well as with all the prairies." For proof, Gregg asked for a map, which Big Eagle was able to sit down and draw "with a far more accurate delineation of all the principal rivers of the plains — the road from Missouri to Santa Fé, and the different Mexican settlements than is to be found in many of the engraved maps of those regions."

Another dividend from the horse was just plain fun. Sioux boys, like those of many tribes, played rough, competitive games with their horses, hugely enjoying themselves. The name of one Sioux game was throwing-them-off-their-horses. The boys would strip naked and choose up sides, then mount and charge each other with war whoops, their horses rearing and plunging. They used no weapons but tried to wrestle their opponents off their mounts. A boy on the ground was "dead," out of the game. This sport inevitably produced many lumps and bruises — and many skilled horsemen and toughened warriors. In fact, it was the conviction of General George Crook (considered by many of his contemporaries to be the U.S. Army's most competent Indian fighter) that, the Comanches notwithstanding, the Sioux were the greatest light cavalry the world has ever known.

One of the most popular of all plains sports was horse racing. Virtually every big intertribal meeting had its round of races. And at any time one warrior might bet literally everything he owned that his favorite animal could beat that of another brave. The attachment of these rough sportsmen to their favorite racers was illustrated on one Kiowa calendar. Each drawing on the calendar symbolized a notable event for a particular year. In the winter of 1852-1853 a Pawnee stole a Kiowa race horse named Red Pet, the fastest in the tribe. This was such a major tragedy that it was chosen as the pictograph for that winter.

For the Comanches, too, horse racing and gambling on the outcome of races were as much a part of life as raiding or capturing wild animals. One of the most memorable races in the history of the tribe occurred in the mid-19th Century when a Comanche band camped near Fort Chadbourne in West Texas. Some of the Army officers at the fort taunted the apparently reluctant Indians into a horse race, and the garrison assembled to watch. The Comanches bet buffalo robes and some $60 worth of plunder for an equal value of flour, sugar and other goods. They then brought out their racer, which Colonel Richard Dodge later described as "a miserable sheep of a pony, with legs like churns, a three-inch coat of rough hair stuck out all over the body, and a general expression of neglect, helplessness, and patient suffering that struck pity into the hearts of all beholders." The Indian jockey, a large man, who looked "big enough to carry the poor beast," belabored his mount with a large club from start to finish. To the officers' surprise, the mangy beast was a neck ahead at the end of the 400-yard course.

The officers then brought out their next best horse. The bets were doubled on both sides, and a second race was run. The outcome, amazingly, was exactly the same. The sorry, shaggy Indian pony won by a neck.

But the officers had — or thought they had — an ace in the hole: a blooded Kentucky mare that was a tried winner. As soon as this splendid animal appeared, the Indians doubled their bets again.

At the shout "Go!" the Indian jockey threw away his club and gave a whoop. His ugly mount kicked dirt on the Kentucky mare all the way. Fifty yards from the end of the course the Indian turned around backward on his horse, made faces and motioned for the white rider to come on. Afterward the Comanches confided that they had just come from visiting the Kickapoos up in Oklahoma and had won 600 ponies from them with this one shaggy race horse.

The Comanches might well have shared with the officers another secret that by 1850 these proud warriors and master equestrians had come to believe: that it was *they* who had introduced the horse to the white man and that the Great Spirit had created the horse for the particular benefit of Comanches. And perhaps he had.

An Indian Horse Dance

Galloping right up to a big bull, a mounted
hunter draws his bow for the kill. Before
they got the repeating rifle from white
men, Indians preferred the bow and arrow
for bringing down buffalo from horseback.

The dramatic hunt for the buffalo

In peacetime the primary task of the nomadic Plains Indians was buffalo hunting, shown in these paintings by George Catlin, a Philadelphia artist who spent six years among the Western tribes. The buffalo was more than just meat; it supplied virtually everything an Indian needed to stay alive, from spoons to housing *(pages 74-75)*. Because of this importance—and in tribute to its strength—the buffalo was worshiped as a sacred animal, its spirit praised before every hunt *(below)*.

The essential instrument for a buffalo hunter was his horse, which he often chose and maintained with more care than he gave his wife. It had to be fast enough to overtake a stampeding herd and strong enough to hold a gallop for long distances, since even a mortally wounded bull could run a mile before dropping. A good horse was expected to hold steady during a stalk, despite the buffalo's large size that spooked untrained animals. If the buf-

falo grouped together for protection, the horse had to plunge into the pack, nimbly avoiding the slashing horns.

Small wonder that the animal occupied a favored place in an Indian family. When thieves from other tribes were known to be near, the buffalo horse was brought into the tipi. This forced the women to sleep outside.

For a buffalo hunt a brave stripped down to a breechcloth and moccasins, tucked a sheath knife in his belt and carried a short lance or a three-foot bow with a quiver of about 20 iron-tipped arrows. Around the neck of his horse was a trailing rawhide thong, which a rider would grab if he fell to slow the horse with his dragging body so he could remount. Once he had closed on his quarry, the hunter tried to puncture its diaphragm and collapse its lungs by hitting a spot just behind the last rib. Even if the arrow or lance was accurate, the powerful beast generally took at least three hits before it finally fell.

In a tribal ritual before a hunt Sioux dancers circle the silhouette of a speared buffalo painted in the grass.

An impressive sight on the open plains, a mature bull buffalo such as this one stood about six feet tall at the humped shoulders and weighed up to 2,000 pounds. The Indians regarded the hump's back fat and the tongue of the buffalo as the choice cuts.

To cool off in summer a buffalo would gouge a hole in a damp spot with its horns, then squirm around until it created a moist, cool wallow. The round areas of grass that filled in these wallows were mistaken by white settlers for Indian dance circles.

Before they acquired horses, the Indians who tried to live off the buffalo on the fringes of the plains led a risky and arduous existence. Although the beasts on occasion congregated in immense herds numbering in the hundreds of thousands and stretching beyond the visible horizon, more commonly the buffalo traveled in small bands of five to 50 that appeared and disappeared overnight. With dim eyesight and wits to match, a buffalo might seem easy prey for the cunning Indian hunters. Yet, through its sheer size and ferocity when attacked, the buffalo created many widows in the tribal camps.

When they hunted the buffalo without horses the Indians were forced to devise many different hunting methods, some subtle, some cruel and none of them consistently effective. Hunters disguised as white wolves crept up on grazing herds (below). Others donned buffalo skins and tried through bleats and motions to lure the beasts over an escarpment, risking death if the herd suddenly stampeded. More commonly, entire tribes were organized to form shouting, robe-waving columns that would try to stampede a herd over a cliff while men waited below to finish off the survivors with lances. In winter the Indians drove the animals into deep snow (overleaf) or onto frozen lakes, where the animals lost their footing and were much easier to approach and kill.

Because healthy buffalo in herds did not fear wolves, Indian hunters draped themselves in the skins of white wolves to stalk their quarry.

Indian hunters on snowshoes made of buffalo rawhide move in on a band of animals trapped in the deep snow. Sinking from their own weight, the helpless buffalo are speared by Indian lances or finished off with muzzle-loading muskets that the Indians have plenty of time to load and reload.

Mounted hunters surround a herd of buffalo, then attack with lances and arrows. The boldest hunters would drive their horses into the mass of animals, while others waited to kill those that tried to escape.

Wounded buffalo that eluded the hunters were dispatched by wolves, but not without a fight. One buffalo was seen battling after the wolves had torn out its eyes, tongue and nose, and had shredded its legs.

The climactic method of killing buffalo by mounted Indians was a noisy, lethal battle called a surround. Within 15 minutes an entire band of the animals could be destroyed this way, but seldom without loss or injury to hunters and horses. The surround started as two columns of mounted hunters gradually closed in on a herd. When the buffalo found themselves attacked from two sides they began to run. The hunters' two columns came in and converged at a gallop, shrieking and waving arms to turn the leading buffalo back into the herd. With the confused and terrified buffalo swirling in circles, the Indians rode around them, firing arrows and charging with lances. Trapped and wounded, the buffalo lashed out with their horns, sometimes goring a horse and throwing the rider who might be trampled as he tried to escape. In the chaos the buffalo even attacked one another, while clouds of dust rose high into the air above the battleground.

After the last buffalo had been killed, the women came in to help the hunters, each wife identifying her animals by the special painted markings on her warrior's arrows. Two Indians could dress an entire animal in an hour. A good hunter might have as many as half a dozen wives to do his skinning and butchering for him, since the better hunter a man was the more people he could afford to support in his lodge. The buffalo hides and most of the meat were taken back to camp on pack horses — never on the prized hunting horses. But because some parts of the buffalo, such as the brains and small intestines, could not be preserved, they were often immediately devoured on the field in a victory celebration. When the last pack horse had carted off its heavy load the plain was often littered with buffalo hearts purposely left behind by the Indian tribes. They believed that the mystical power of these hearts would help to regenerate the depleted herd.

The all-purpose beast of the plains

Every part of the buffalo not used for food was put to some other purpose. Horns, bones, hoofs, hides and innards became household items, such as those listed here. Even the dung of the buffalo was saved to use as fuel. The most versatile portion of the animal was its hide. The thickness — and uses — of the skin varied according to the age and sex of the animal. The thickest skin came from old bulls and went into shields and the soles of winter moccasins. The thinnest was that of unborn calves for berry bags. Between these extremes was cowskin, whose intermediate thickness allowed it to be fashioned into any number of items from rafts to ball coverings for a game called shinny.

In addition to these natural variations, the Indians treated the skins to give them different properties. An untreated skin, called rawhide, was tough and stiff in texture, but after tanning *(pages 112-113)* it became soft and pliable. For winter garments and blankets the hair was left on the hides; for other uses the hides were scraped clean. Sometimes a hide would age in such a way that it ultimately would serve two very different purposes. The upper part of a cowhide tipi cover, made rainproof by the grease and smoke of many cooking fires, was eventually salvaged by the industrious Indian women who would cut it up and stitch it into clothing to be worn during the wet season.

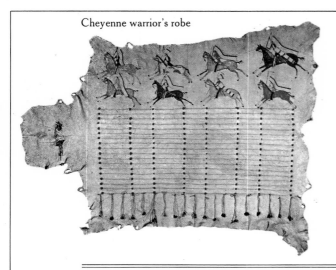
Cheyenne warrior's robe

CLOTHING

Robes *(hide with hair)*
Caps with ear flaps *(hide with hair)*
Moccasins *(hide)*
Moccasin soles *(bull rawhide)*
Leggings *(hide)*
Mittens *(hide with hair)*
Shirts *(hide)*
Coats and capes *(hide with hair)*
Dresses *(hide)*
Belts *(bull rawhide)*
Underclothes *(calfhide)*
Breechcloths *(hide)*
Headdress ornaments *(hair, horns)*

TIPI AND FURNISHINGS

Tipi covers *(cowhide)*
Tipi door flaps *(cowhide)*
Tipi linings *(cowhide)*
Bedcovers *(hide with hair)*
Cache-pit covers *(rawhide)*
Tipi ornaments *(hair, tail)*
Medicine cases *(rawhide)*
Trunks *(rawhide)*

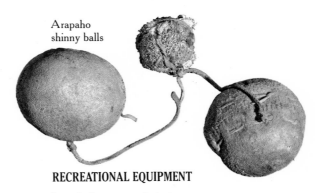
Arapaho shinny balls

CEREMONIAL OBJECTS

Sun-dance altars *(skull)*
Rattles *(hoofs, rawhide)*
Horse masks *(hide, horn)*
Winding sheets for dead *(hide)*

RECREATIONAL EQUIPMENT

Ice-sled runners *(ribs)*
Dice *(bone)*
Ball stuffing *(hair)*
Ball coverings *(calfskin)*
Netting for lacrosse hoops *(rawhide)*

Oto burden strap

RIDING AND TRANSPORTATION GEAR

Burden straps *(hide)*
Frame-saddle coverings *(rawhide)*
Pad-saddle coverings *(hide)*
Saddle-rigging straps *(rawhide)*
Stirrup coverings *(rawhide)*
Cruppers *(rawhide)*
Parfleches *(rawhide)*
Saddlebags *(rawhide)*
Double saddlebags *(rawhide)*
Tobacco pouches *(calfhide)*
Berry bags *(hide of an unborn calf)*
Bridles *(rawhide, hair)*
Honda rings *(horn)*

Hackamores *(rawhide)*
Lariats *(rawhide)*
Picket ropes *(rawhide)*
Hobbles *(rawhide)*
Saddle blankets *(hide)*
Travois hitches *(rawhide)*
Pole hitches *(rawhide)*
Miscellaneous tie strings *(rawhide)*
Horse blankets *(hide)*
Horse-watering troughs *(rawhide)*
Horseshoes *(rawhide)*
Rafts *(cowhide)*
Snowshoes *(rawhide)*

Cheyenne shield

Sioux hide scraper

TOOLS AND UTENSILS

Arrow straighteners *(hump)*
Fleshing tools *(tibia and femur)*
Meat and berry pounders' hafting *(rawhide)*
Hoes *(shoulder blade)*
Mauls' hafting *(rawhide)*
Cooking vessels *(paunch)*
Water buckets *(paunch)*
Spoons *(horn)*
Cups *(horn)*
Ladles *(horn)*
Knives *(bone)*
Hairbrushes *(rough side of tongue)*
Fuel *(dung)*
Fly brushes *(tail)*
Glue *(hoofs, hide)*
Tanning agents *(brains, fat, liver)*
Soaps *(fat)*
Thread *(sinew)*
Sewing awls *(bone)*
Hide scrapers *(bone)*
Paint brushes *(hip bone, shoulder blade)*
Quill flatteners *(horn)*
Tool for dehairing rope *(skull)*

WEAPONS

Shields *(rawhide from bull's neck)*
Bow backings *(bull sinew)*
Bowstrings *(bull sinew)*
Arrowheads *(bone)*
Arrowhead and feather wrappings *(sinew)*
Powder flasks *(horn)*
Cover and hafting of war clubs *(rawhide)*
Ornaments for clubs *(hair, beard)*
Knife sheaths *(rawhide)*

3 | An ingenious way to live

The Plains Indians' solutions to such fundamental human needs as food, shelter and social order reveal them as a people of resourcefulness and ingenuity —qualities most visibly proclaimed by their dwellings. The tipi *(page 92)* was perfectly fitted to the housing requirements of the roving buffalo hunters. This buffalo-skin tent was portable, easily erected, waterproof and, owing to a clever wind-deflecting device of smoke flaps, well ventilated even with a fire burning inside.

Although the tipi has come to be a symbol of Plains Indian life, many tribes spent a great deal of the year, when they were not on the move, in permanent structures of earth or grass. But none of the Plains Indians' dwellings could match those of the Pueblos, their southwestern neighbors, who resided in terraced apartment buildings where one man's roof was another man's balcony.

An Arapaho brave stands in front of his tipi at a temporary encampment in southwestern Oklahoma.

Using their earth lodges as grandstands, Pawnees watch a tribal ceremony. The multifamily dwellings had a permanent framework of posts and beams covered over with layers of willow branches, sod and mud. More than 40 feet in diameter, these lodges even provided shelter for prized horses.

Resembling a huge beehive on the Oklahoma prairie, a Wichita dwelling has a framework of heavy poles similar to that in an earth lodge but is sheathed only with grass thatching, suited to the warmer climate of the southern plains. The thatching was tied down by slender wooden rods.

At the trading center of Taos, New Mexico — a market for horses and foodstuffs among southern plains tribes — Pueblo Indians lived in a sprawling apartment complex constructed of adobe bricks. The individual rooms were small and were added haphazardly whenever more living space was needed.

The well-ordered world of the warrior tribes

When a Cheyenne baby uttered the first cry of its life and opened its small dark eyes upon the world, it faced an ordered pattern of human relationships, institutions and values—a Cheyenne world, shaped to ensure the preservation of the tribe and to foster, though not to guarantee, a satisfying life from babyhood to old age.

During the months before a birth, the mother observed appropriate taboos; she did not, for example, stare long at any unusual person, animal or other object for fear that her unborn child would be marked at birth. And she followed a practice with which a modern obstetrician might agree: she got up each morning before sunrise and took a walk. But she did this for an unscientific reason: she believed that babies grew in the early dawn and that walking helped them grow.

The birth, which took place either in a small special tipi or, more usually, in the home lodge, was attended by older women—the female relatives of the mother and a wise old midwife or two. The mother knelt on a hay-covered robe for delivery, firmly grasping a sturdy upright pole planted in front of her. A medicine man was sometimes employed to sit nearby, singing prayers and shaking a rattle.

After the delivery a midwife tickled the mother's throat with a finger or a feather to make her expel the placenta, or afterbirth, which was then tied in a bag and taken out of camp to hang in a tree. To bury it, the

A case for the umbilical cord

Heavy with child, Winona, a young Sioux, stands among the tipis of an encampment located near Fort Snelling, Minnesota, at the northeastern rim of the Great Plains.

Cheyennes believed, might cause the death of the child. The women greased the newborn baby's skin and powdered it with finely ground dried buffalo manure, decayed cottonwood pulp or ripe, dry spores of the star puffball fungus. The puffball was especially favored for the umbilical cord. Later, when the cord had dried and dropped loose from the navel, the mother would sew it into a small buckskin bag shaped like a turtle or a lizard (left), to be worn around the child's neck or tied to its clothing as a charm to ensure long life.

During the days before the birth the father-to-be acted in a manner that at any other time would have been unmanly for a Cheyenne. He went about carrying firewood and water for his woman, and he spent much of his time worrying over the prospects for a successful birth. Babies were cherished in the tribe, especially boys, for they represented potential warrior strength. Because of the dangers of such masculine pursuits as war and hunting, the women of a tribe generally outnumbered the men. But all children were welcome. Frequently a father, when notified of his new offspring, would fire his gun.

An older relative of the father—a grandparent, uncle or aunt—usually gave the newborn baby a name. A boy was often named after an animal or a physical attribute, with an added descriptive word or phrase: Tall Bull, Spotted Wolf, Little Hawk or Gray Tangle Hair. A girl's name almost always included the word "woman" in it: Owl Woman, Buffalo Calf Road Woman, Little Creek Woman. But nicknames for both sexes were commonly used until the age of 5 or 6. A little boy might be called Moksois as a term of endearment and a girl Moksiis. Both words meant potbelly.

Two Kiowa girls hold up an infant strapped into a cradleboard. Boards like this and the ones shown opposite were usually made by a female relative of the father, often in return for a horse.

Within a few weeks the mother began to lace the baby into a cradleboard, a wooden frame with a soft-skin pouch, which could be carried on the woman's back. The cradleboard was a versatile device. It could be hooked onto a saddle or strapped to a travois; it could be hung up inside a tipi or, if the mother was working outdoors, leaned against the lodge covering. In any of these positions it had one advantage over the white man's crib or baby carriage: long before it could sit up, an Indian baby was able to view the world about it and the comings and goings of other people in an upright posture. Even when the baby was not on the board it was often upright, for its mother might carry it on her back in a blanket sling, with its head raised a little higher than her own.

The mother gave her baby much affection and cuddling and allowed it to nurse at will. Cheyenne children might nurse at their mothers' breasts for four or five years. But the baby suffered one kind of traumatic experience: crying was not tolerated by the Cheyennes. They considered it antisocial at any time; also, a crying baby might give away a camp position to enemy raiders. If a baby persisted in crying after its needs were taken care of, the mother took it out alone in its cradleboard and hung it on a bush, there to cry itself out. When the howling stopped, the mother brought it back to human company. After a few such experiences the baby learned that crying was useless. Thus it took its first step toward the strict self-control of Indian life.

Young children soon became a part of the rigorous life of the tribe, and it was, of course, a life led largely on horseback. By the age of 2 or 3 they were riding with their mothers or were tied in a saddle on a gentle horse. By the age of 5 or 6 a boy might have his own horse—given to him by his father, an indulgent uncle or a grandfather—and be a good rider, able to help herd the horses. Girls the same age began to help their mothers dig roots and carry water and wood.

Cheyenne children became tough, inured to the extremes of a life lived close to nature, traveling under the harsh sun in midsummer, working and playing out of doors in winter. A frontiersman named Jacob Fowler noted Indian children at play on the ice of the upper Arkansas River in the winter of 1821. The children probably included Comanches, Kiowas, Cheyennes and Arapahos, for at that time all four tribes were living in relative peace with one another. Fowler had at best a shaky command of written English—the spelling and grammar of the following quotation have been improved—but he was a keen observer: "The weather is now cold, the river frozen up, the ice a great thickness, and the Indian children that are able to walk and up to tall boys are out on the ice by daylight and all as naked as they came into the world. Here they are at all kinds of sport which their situation will admit and although the frost is very severe they appear quite warm and as lively as I have ever seen children in midsummer. I am sure that we have seen more than one thousand of these children on the ice at one time, and some that were too young to walk were taken by the larger ones and set on a piece of skin on the ice, and in this situation the small one kicks its legs and hollers and laughs at those round it at play. I doubt that one of our white children, put in such weather in that situation, could live half an hour."

Fowler did not distinguish between the children of the various tribes. It is unlikely that he saw Cheyenne children more than a few years old going completely naked, for the Cheyenne were strict in matters of dress and sex. Parents and older advisers rarely chastised their children, but they continuously exhorted them not only to be chaste and virtuous, but to be honest, grave, friendly, modest, industrious and generous so that they would amount to something and would not be shamed and gossiped about in the tribe. Once again early training led directly to the ways of later life. As an adult a Cheyenne would measure his status by the approbation of his tribesmen and literally dread the thought of falling under their criticism or contempt.

Most childhood play, in fact, mimicked adult life. Little girls played with toy tipis and deerskin dolls in miniature cradleboards, and little boys carried small bows and arrows. When slightly older, girls and boys played camp with miniature lodge villages and make-believe families. The boys pretended to go on hunts and raids, taking make-believe captives and counting coups like grown men. They would sally forth on stick horses to hunt buffalo, which were represented by other boys carrying leaves of prickly pear on sticks. An arrow shot into a spot marked on the prickly pear constituted a kill, and the boy playing the buffalo would fall to the earth and "die" — but if the arrow missed, the enraged "buffalo" would charge, and the hunter might find himself swatted on the rear with the cactus. Sometimes the boys caught fish or killed birds or rabbits and brought them in for the girls to cook. Boys and girls also enjoyed the comradeship of their elders. Grandfathers spent many hours telling stories to their grandchildren, passing on the tribal myths and lore.

But as children approached their teens, boys and girls were no longer allowed to play together. The time had come for the family and the tribe to prepare the members of each sex to function as adults. At 12 or 14 a boy went on his first real hunt. When he killed a buffalo — the first was usually a calf — his family praised him highly. His father cried out the news to the whole camp and if the father could afford it, he announced the gift of a good horse to a deserving poor person, or even invited an entire group of needy tribesmen to a feast. In his early teens a boy might go on a raid with a war party that included his father or an uncle. He could be of service to the warriors by taking on such chores as

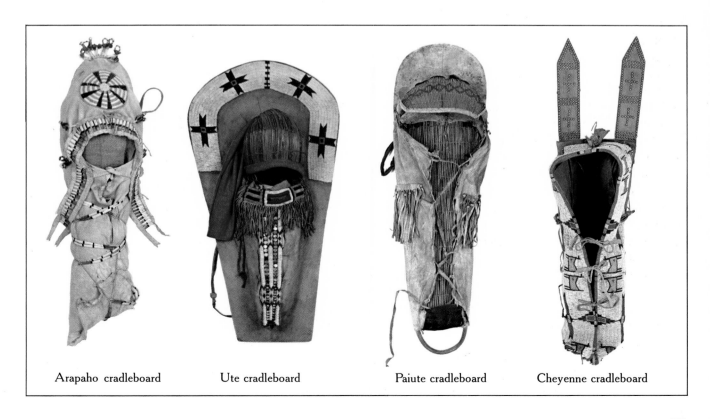

Arapaho cradleboard   Ute cradleboard   Paiute cradleboard   Cheyenne cradleboard

gathering wood and holding horses, and he would be treated with respect by the men — more like a mascot than a servant. In the course of the expedition, the boy tasted danger, watched the men in action and was praised for every manly act.

Cheyennes had no puberty rites for a boy, but every boy saw his older friends honored and looked forward to accomplishments that seemed important; when a boy had killed a buffalo and experienced the hardships and excitement of a war party, he took on the dignity of a man, even though he still might have much to learn. Meanwhile around the age of puberty he entered into rough sports with comrades his own age.

Sioux boys had games typical of the Plains Indians in developing physical endurance and toughness. In the swing-kicking game two rows of boys lined up against each other, each player holding a robe wound over his left arm as a shield. To begin the game one of the boys would shout the question: "Shall we grab them by the hair and knee them in the face until they bleed?" Then the two sides rushed each other, trying to kick a participant down. Few rules existed. Two boys could gang up on one. The object was to protect oneself with the robe and kick an opponent down. Once down on the ground a boy, if not protected by members of his team, was grabbed by the hair and kneed in the face till he bled; then he would be permitted to rise and fight on. The game continued until one of the teams retreated or all the players were exhausted. As an elderly Sioux, Iron Shell, remembered it: "Some boys got badly hurt, but afterwards we would talk and laugh about it. Very seldom did any fellows get angry."

Another hardy Sioux sport was the fire-throwing game. Two teams made brush piles about 50 yards apart and set them afire. Each boy took out several flaming brands as weapons, and the two sides advanced against each other, throwing brands or using them as clubs. The object of the game, amid the smoke and flying sparks, was to cause the opponents to flee and to surround their blazing brush pile. An old Sioux said of the fire-throwing game, "In close fighting, after you have hit an enemy two or three times, your torch goes out. Then you get your share until his stick dies out."

Girls the same age had their own games, exciting but less rough. Cheyenne girls played kickball, trying to see how many times a girl could kick a ball of leather stuffed with antelope hair up into the air without ever letting it touch the ground. Sioux girls played a simple form of field hockey in which they used curved sticks to knock a ball toward the opponent's goal. For the most part, though, Plains Indian girls were trained not to run about the camp; as they grew older they would stay near their home lodges, venturing out only in company. Meanwhile they began to learn how to fashion and decorate moccasins, how to sew and create beadwork, how to cook, and — the last craft a girl would master before she was old enough to marry — how to dress and tan the hides of buffalo and other game.

Cheyenne girls went through a formal puberty rite. At her first menstruation a girl's father called out to the camp that she had become a woman (Indians did not use the word "squaw," which was a white corruption of a term used by East Coast tribes). If he was well-to-do, he might give away a horse. The girl unbraided her hair and bathed herself; the older women painted her body red. She then wrapped herself in a robe and sat near a fire. A coal from the fire was sprinkled with sweet grass, juniper needles and white sage, and the girl bent over the coal, surrounding it with her robe so that the smoke passed over all her body. Then she went to a special lodge where women spent their menstrual periods. Here her grandmother cared for her and gave her instructions on womanly conduct. Finally the girl once again passed through the smoke in order to purify her body and returned home.

Cheyenne women were noted for their chastity. A young unmarried woman customarily wore a leather or rope chastity belt that was tied around her waist, knotted in front and wound down between the thighs. One Cheyenne woman has left a detailed account of her young womanhood, courtship and marriage. Soon after her first suitor began to pay attention to her, her aunt gave her this advice: "It is silly to exchange too many glances and smiles with this young man, especially in the presence of people. He will think you are too easy and immoral. When he comes to see you at night you must never run away from him. If you do so, this indicates that you are silly and not sufficiently taught and educated to respect the attentions of a suitor. You must never consent to marry your suitor the first time he asks you to marry him, no matter how good looking he may be. Tell him you would like to associate with him for some time yet to come. And if he really thinks anything of you he will not be discouraged, but will continue his visits and come to see you. When he comes at night do not let him stay too long, but ask him please to go. If you let him stay till he is ready to go he will think you are in love with him and will surely think less of you. You must always be sure to take great care to tie the hide [the chastity belt]. You must remember that when a man touches your breasts . . . he considers that you belong to him. And in the event that he does not care to marry you he will not hide what he has done to you, and you will be considered immoral. And you will not have a chance to marry into a good family. In short, you will not be purchased, which is surely the ambition of all young women."

The Cheyenne girl heeded the advice but had little time to put it into practice. Soon after hearing the lecture from her aunt some old men from another camp came and proposed to her father that she marry a young male of their family. She did not know her would-be husband, but after consideration her father consented. Next day five good saddle horses and other goods were sent to her lodge. Her male relatives encouraged her to accept the proposal, saying, among other things, that her father was getting on in years. "His eyesight is not very good. This young man will look after the necessary work for your father.

"However," they added, "we do not wish to do anything against your will." The girl remembered that she felt uncertain but said, "I love my father and whatever he deems best for me, that I will do."

Her relatives took the five horses and gave the prospective in-laws five in return. She mounted one of them and rode with a delegation to the nearby camp of her future husband. The young man's women relatives met her and, placing her on a blanket, carried her to his tipi. She went in and sat beside him. The women brought dresses, shawls, rings, bracelets, leggings and moccasins. They dressed her splendidly, braided her hair and painted red dots on her cheeks. Then she returned to her own camp, where her mother and aunt had prepared a marriage feast and where a new tipi was erected for the couple. The in-laws told jokes and funny stories, and recounted exploits of war. Then they went away and left the couple in their new home. After

How an Indian got his name

Indian names were a language unto themselves, laden with descriptive, allusive or even magical meaning. An Indian baby was named soon after birth—usually by a medicine man or a paternal relation—and the entire village participated in the occasion. The infant might be named for an animal, for a physical phenomenon such as thunder that occurred on the day of birth or even for a brave deed that once had been performed by the giver of the name. A woman generally kept the name she received at birth, but a man often replaced his original name with a new one that celebrated a personal act of valor, recalled an encounter with an unusual animal or perhaps was inspired by a dream. However, a man who had a handicap or some other distinguishing characteristic was forever known by an apposite nickname, such as Hump or Big Hand. Because Indian names almost always were based on something objective, they could easily be rendered as pictographs—frequently with a line connecting visual representations of the name and a human head to signify ownership. Below are some Sioux signatures.

Caught the Enemy

Kills by the Camp

Spotted Face

Eagle Horse

He Dog

Stabber

Ten poles form the skeleton of this southern plains lodge. Standing about 12 feet high — a little less than the average — the tipi, when finally assembled, comfortably held all of the family and their possessions.

a year the woman gave birth. She recalled: "It was at this time that I really began to love my husband. He always treated me with respect and kindness."

It had been a typical Cheyenne marriage, but more an alliance between families than a love match. In this case it was also an especially impersonal marriage; probably the girl, though she belonged to a substantial family, was marrying into one of higher rank. Normally the courtship period for young adults might last four, five or even six years, and the girl usually had more power of choice; the suitor ordinarily had a more difficult job in winning his mate. A young man would wait near a spot where his favored girl might pass, hoping for a few words or a smile. Gaining courage, he would appear before her lodge to talk to her about everything but love. If all went well, they might exchange rings of horn or metal in promise of marriage. But it was unlikely that a girl would make such a promise to a young man who had not been to war; until then he was not considered more than a boy.

Young men alone on the prairie — scouting, traveling, herding horses — sang songs about their girls: "My love, it is I who am singing. Do you hear me?" Or they would implore: "My love, come out of the lodge; I am searching for you." And: "My love, come out into the prairie, so that I may come near you and meet you."

Flute playing was supposed to win a girl's heart, and some enchanted flutes were said to cast a spell of love over even a reluctant maiden. These magical flutes were a specialty of Sioux medicine men. They made them out of two grooved halves of a cedar stick, bound and glued together, with five finger holes and an air vent that could be closed with a movable piece of wood carved into the shape of a horse's head. The medicine men also dreamed up the magical music for their instruments, and they would sell both the flute and the song to an ardent young man with an absolute guarantee that no girl would be able to resist him — if the music was played properly. On warm summer nights the lovesick young men could be heard, each of them out in the brush but within hearing of his girl's lodge, tootling his plaintive and erotic tune.

The Sioux had a clearly prescribed method of courting. A boy might meet a girl in front of her tipi, throw his robe over her and himself and, standing in front of her family and perhaps curious younger brothers and sis-

Tipi etiquette

Proper behavior among Plains Indians — as in most societies — was governed by extensive, strict and often subtle rules. The principles below are a sampling of various points of etiquette that Indians knew and heeded when paying a social call at a friend's tipi.

If the door is open, a friend may enter the tipi directly. But if it is closed, he should announce his presence and wait for the owner to invite him to come in.

When a male visitor enters the tipi he goes to the right and waits for the host to invite him to sit in the guest place to the left of the owner at the rear. A woman enters after the man and goes to the left.

When invited to a feast guests are expected to bring their own bowls and spoons and to eat all they are given. No visitor should ever walk between the fire and another person but instead should pass behind the sitters, who for their part lean forward to make room.

Women should never sit cross-legged like men. They can sit on their heels or with their legs to one side.

In a group of men only the older ones should initiate conversation. The younger men should politely remain silent unless they are invited to speak by an elder.

When the host cleans his pipe everyone should leave.

ters, embrace and whisper with her. On a pleasant evening a popular girl might have several suitors waiting their turn. She could refuse to be embraced under the robe if she did not like the boy, and she could duck out from under the blanket whenever she wanted to. Thus the young Sioux courted despite being chaperoned.

Among all the Plains Indians, and among such neighboring tribes as the Apaches, the offering of horses was the universal method of proposing marriage. As a matter of form a suitor usually sent the horses to the girl's lodge and made his official proposal of marriage through a relative or friend. To reject the suitor the girl had the horses sent back to his lodge or simply ignored them; if she took them to water or let them be mixed with her

How the tipi was constructed

Warm in winter, cool in summer and sturdy enough to withstand gale-force winds, the tipi was a remarkably serviceable dwelling—and yet it was so easy to assemble that two women could erect it within an hour.

Although certain details of design differed from tribe to tribe, the tipi was basically a cover made of dressed buffalo hides that were stitched together with sinew and stretched over a framework of poles. Most tribes used a tripod of especially strong poles for the main support. These primary supports were tied together at the top and raised *(bottom, left);* then all but one of the remaining poles were leaned against them, tied in place and,

in windy weather, anchored to a single peg in the ground within the tipi. The frame was not a true cone, but was tilted slightly. This asymmetry served several functions. It provided more headroom in the rear of the dwelling; it permitted better ventilation with an off-center smoke hole; and, since tipis almost always faced east, the greater slant of the front side helped brace the structure against the prevailing west winds on the back.

When the poles were in place the folded hide cover *(below, center)* was fastened to a stout lifting pole and hoisted into position. It was relatively easy at this point to unfold the cover around the poles, peg the bottom edge

down, close the vertical seam with wooden pins and attach the door flap. (In warm weather the bottom edge could be raised for ventilation.) Finally, two lighter poles outside the tipi were inserted in the pockets of the smoke flaps; by moving these poles the flaps could be adjusted to compensate for changes in wind direction, or the flaps could be closed in case of rain or snow. Now complete *(bottom, right),* the tipi was ready for the furnishings. Usually about 15 feet in diameter at the base, it had ample room for beds, back rests, a stack of firewood and other articles of equipment, sometimes arranged according to the scheme shown below, center.

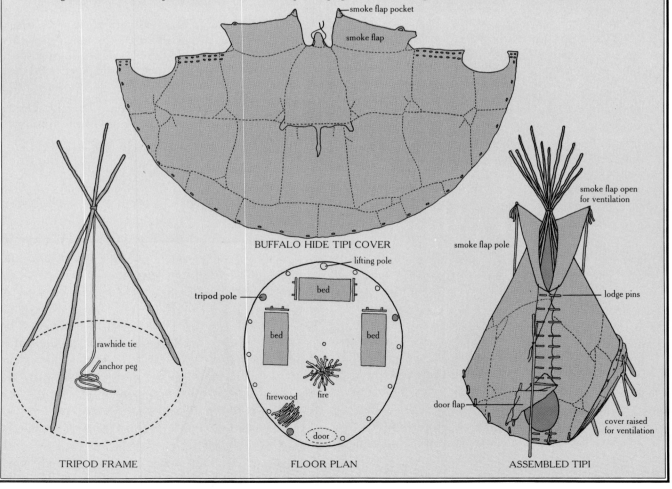

TRIPOD FRAME   FLOOR PLAN   ASSEMBLED TIPI

father's herd, she accepted the proposal. In fact, though, the process was ordinarily no more than a formality. If the choice was really being left to the girl, the young man knew well in advance whether or not she would accept; if it was an arranged marriage, the families had already solemnly discussed and agreed upon it in private. The marriage ceremony itself, which always included a big feast, often took place within the next day or two. At that time the wife made her formal departure from her own family and went to her husband's lodge, bringing with her horses and other gifts equaling his in value.

A Plains Indian man was the head and the boss of his household. He lived in a male-dominated society, and in some cases he treated the women as subjects in a cruel, even inhuman manner. A customary punishment for infidelity was cutting off the wife's nose. Yet despite male dominance most Plains Indian women lived a satisfying, self-respecting life. The relative number of men and women was crucial. Many men were killed in the chase and at war. One result of an excess population of women was plural marriage; and such a society of a few hundred or a few thousand souls, seeing themselves as one tribe, one people, always faced with the possible threat of extinction, adopted the institution of plural wives. Why should a woman of child-bearing age be without a mate simply because women outnumbered men? The fact that these women suckled their children as much as five years and often abstained from conjugal relations during that time made polygyny still more attractive.

Polygyny was widespread, but not universal; in many instances a man and one woman worked out their destinies together without having sexual relations with anyone else. Among the Apaches, who, like the Cheyennes, were noted for the fidelity of their women, the validity of the institution of plural wives was never settled. Some of them believed it proper; some did not. Significantly, these supposedly self-controlled and unemotional people treasured one of the most intimate and personal of all human relationships: the honeymoon. After a pair of Apache newlyweds had completed the marriage ceremony they escaped to be alone a week or more. Before the ceremony the bridegroom-to-be built a shelter several miles from the main camp. In this bower, hidden among trees, festooned with flowers and provisioned for the length of their stay, the couple spent their honeymoon, paying attention to no one but each other until the time came to return to everyday life.

Later on a woman of a Plains Indian tribe might welcome, or even suggest, the bringing of a new wife into the lodge. There was plenty of work for women; if it could be shared with a friendly companion, so much the better. The problem of jealousy was often eased by a man's marrying the sister of his first wife; familiarity and dominance would already be established, and the first wife would remain the female leader of the household. The prize for the largest number of wives among the Cheyennes should have gone, perhaps, to a man named Crooked Neck; he had five, all sisters. Upon being made a chief Crooked Neck gave three wives away, but he spent the rest of his life with the other two.

Divorce was easy. If a Cheyenne man wanted to divorce his wife, he could "throw her away" at a tribal ceremony called the Omaha dance. During this ceremony the irate husband would dance alone holding a stick in his hand; advancing to the drum, he would strike it a mighty blow, throw the stick into the air, or toward a crowd of men, and shout, "There goes my wife; I throw her away! Whoever gets that stick may have her!" The men would dodge to keep from being touched and might tease each other, crying, "I thought I saw you reach for that stick!" Given the Cheyenne concern for public opinion, a woman felt much shamed at being divorced in such a way.

A woman could divorce her husband merely by moving back to her parents' lodge. She usually took the children. If as a young woman she had been given horses by indulgent relatives, she retained property rights in them and in their increase during marriage; upon divorce she took her horses with her.

Among the Crows a distinction was made between the property of husband and wife. Guns, ammunition, bows and other paraphernalia of the hunt and war belonged to the man; the tipi, cooking equipment, hides and such belonged to the woman. Each knew which horses they owned. Thus they were always prepared to go their separate ways. In trading for new possessions the women wanted things that would be hers, the man those that would be his. If considerable affection existed between husband and wife, she often got her way. Later, if she lost her charms for him he might find divorce impractical because she owned most of the property.

The rough-and-tumble of the Indians' lacrosse

In the societies of the Indians who lived in the West, the spirit of competition flourished. Within the daily round of village tasks, time was always found for games, on which players and spectators alike bet with gusto. Favorite sports were horse racing, archery and wrestling, but the most intriguing and dramatic of all Indian games was the mass mayhem of lacrosse, brought from the East by the Choctaws.

The name lacrosse, which came from French traders, referred to the webbed sticks used to carry and throw a wooden or deerskin ball. In the Choctaw version of the game, each of the hundreds of barefoot players wielded two such sticks. Artist George Catlin, in his travels through the western Indian lands, captured the excitement and pageantry of one of these extraordinary contests.

A Choctaw competitor sports a horsehair tail and two sticks.

On the evening before a lacrosse game, as artist Catlin watched from horseback, an elaborate ceremony unfolded on the playing field. Team members assembled around their respective goals, "and at the beat of the drums and chaunts of the women, each party commenced the ball-play dance."

The lacrosse game began with a thunderous rush. As Catlin watched, "an instant struggle ensued between the players, who were some six or seven hundred in numbers, and were mutually endeavouring to catch the ball in their sticks, and throw it home and between their respective stakes."

One source of moral and physical support for a Cheyenne woman was the general practice among married couples of living near the wife's parents. Thus the wife always had more near relatives to aid or defend her than he did. Another source of power was the Cheyenne woman's contribution to the social prestige of her family. A good family had many horses; the man at the head of it was a good hunter and possessed many war honors. But the woman of the lodge had to be a proper woman and a fine housekeeper; she had to keep plenty of parfleches (rawhide bags) filled with dried meat and other provisions; she had to be skillful in the making of clothing and of gear for horses, and in the methods of decorating these items. She had to rear mannerly children, respectful to their elders and well trained in the Cheyenne way of life.

The Sioux were equally concerned with the matter of family rank. A Sioux chief named Red Cloud became one of the best military tacticians and strategists among Western Indians and was at the same time a brilliant diplomat in councils with the whites. Yet he came from a modest family background, and the Sioux never gave him the respect he would have received had he been the son of an important family.

Women ordinarily left warring and raiding expeditions to the men, but they might help defend their own camps, accompany a war party to cook and hold the horses or go to a nearby battleground to strip the enemy dead and carry home the loot. Among the Utes, women who had participated in raids danced their own peculiar war dance in full regalia; the limping, labored step of the dance symbolized the carrying home of captured enemy property.

In some exceptional cases women actually became outstanding warriors. A certain Gros Ventre girl, for example, was taken prisoner by the Crows when about 10 years old. She soon displayed a love of horses and boys' sports, and her captor allowed her to guard his horses and practice with a bow. The girl grew up to be a peerless rider, marksman and hunter. A raiding party of Blackfeet attacked her Crow band one day as they were camped near a trading post. They lost several men but managed to get safely into the post. Five Blackfeet, out of gun range, signaled for a parley. None of the Crow men or white traders would go out to meet them, but the Gros Ventre woman rode out, well armed, to

see what they wanted. The five attacked her in clear view of the fort. She killed one with her gun and wounded two others with arrows; the remaining two fled. She came back into the fort to shouts of praise, and from then on was called Woman Chief.

A year later Woman Chief led a group of male warriors against the Blackfeet, taking 70 horses and two scalps. After this she was permitted to sit in Crow war councils. She led many raids and defended Crow country even against her own people, the Gros Ventres. In the warrior ceremony, in which men would strike a post and publicly recount their brave acts, she would tell of more coups than most of them.

Crow men held her in reverence but would not court such a formidable woman. When her foster father died she took his lodge and family, acting as both mother and father. As a ranking hunter and warrior she demanded the privileges of a man, including the privilege of marriage. Eventually she "married" four women to tan her robes and perform the many domestic duties of her lodge; this was work unsuited to a warrior.

Woman Chief became a living legend among the Crows. Finally the tribe made an uncertain and tentative peace with the Gros Ventres in 1851, and three years later she made a pilgrimage to them. Upon recognizing her, their scourge for many years, they treacherously killed her, never realizing that she was trying to visit her own people.

Other instances of warrior women have been recorded, but all are exceptions to the rule. Normally women gave most of their time to domestic chores, the needs of their families and the social functions of camp life. The gathering of wild plants was one of the more arduous tasks, but the women assumed it proudly. A mature woman was a storehouse of knowledge about a vast array of useful plants, which could be used for dyes, incense or medicine, for smoking alone or mixed with tobacco and, most important, for food.

The most widely used food plant was the prairie turnip, which the French called *pomme blanche* and English speakers called the Indian potato, or Indian turnip. It grew throughout the high plains and was gathered in the spring. Growing to as much as four times the size of a hen's egg, it was eaten raw or in soups and stews, and could be sliced and sun-dried for storage. When Cheyenne women and girls went out to dig prairie tur-

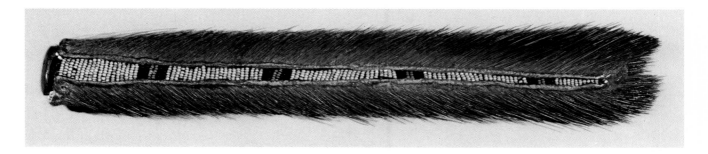

nips they went in small work parties and sometimes treated the expedition as a gay outing. Often as they returned to camp they would engage in ceremonious horseplay, making believe they were a war party and the men of the village their enemies. In sight of their camp they would arrange their roots in a row of piles and line up behind them, having gathered a quantity of sticks and buffalo chips for ammunition. One woman would wave her blanket and give out a challenging war whoop, upon which any men in the camp who were in the mood for fun would rush out and prepare to attack them. Some men would mount scrubby old pack horses. Some would provide themselves with makeshift shields of rawhide bags. Then with much fierce yelling they would charge the women's position, to be met with showers of sticks and buffalo chips. The rules of the game permitted any man who had a proven war record or who had lost his horse in battle to capture some roots for himself if he could make his way through the barrage without being hit. The sport always had many laughing, shouting spectators and provided relaxing gaiety after a day of hard work.

A Cheyenne woman's achievements in decorative craft were valued as highly as a man's deeds in war, and a woman described the objects she had adorned as proudly as a man recited his deeds of battle. Women of special accomplishment formed special associations, most notably the Quillers' Society. This was an exclusive group, half sorority, half sewing circle, that ceremoniously performed the sacred task of decorating leather with porcupine or bird quills.

When a young woman felt concern over an ailing relative, or over a husband's going to war, she might vow that if things went well she would quill a robe for a priest, doctor or warrior. She would go to an elderly member of the Quillers' Society, make her a gift and ask for assistance. To begin with, the old woman would instruct her in the prescribed manner of giving a feast for the society. An elderly male crier would announce the event throughout the camp. When the ladies of the society assembled for the feast each recited a list of robes and other articles they had ornamented in past years. Then the older woman would pray over the young one, instructing her in both needlework and the ceremony of the society. The feast amounted to an initiation, but during the following days the old woman would further instruct the novice and aid her in her quilling project. And when the project was completed the young woman joined one of the most respected institutions of her world. The Quillers' Society served an important function in honoring patient work and beautiful handicraft, preserving designs and sewing methods and earning prestige for a woman throughout her band.

Men also engaged in some of this sort of work, principally the making of drums, ceremonial paraphernalia, smoking pipes, war bonnets, shields, spears, bows and arrows. For the fashioning of some of these items there were craftsmen with special skills, but nearly every man needed to know the art of making bows and arrows. A Sioux arrowmaker, for example, cut sturdy shoots of the gooseberry, cherry, Juneberry or other suitable wood, tied them in a bundle and waited for them to season. A standard Sioux arrow length was the distance from a man's elbow to the tip of his little finger, plus the length of that finger. When the wood was cured the craftsman sanded it smooth by pulling and twisting it through a hole formed by two pieces of grooved sandstone held together in the other hand. He straightened the arrow by sighting down it again and again, taking out the curve by bending it with a bone or horn tool with a hole in it and sometimes applying grease or heating the wood to assist the process. Then, using a special tool of bone or

The art of cooking, plains style

Despite the spartan simplicity of their way of life, the Plains Indians ate a surprisingly varied diet. And in keeping with the need of some tribes to be constantly on the move in pursuit of buffalo, cooking paraphernalia was limited, lightweight and sometimes was made of disposable materials.

The staff of life for the nomadic Indian was, of course, the buffalo. After a successful hunt women would roast chunks of meat on skewers hung over the flame (*drawing, below right*) from a tripod. When food was plentiful the tribes ate three meals a day; but they were seldom wasteful. They threw away none of the animal's edible parts, even breaking the bones and boiling the marrow. Moreover, they cleaned and shaped the entrails into sausage cases, stuffing them with marrow fat and strips of meat that had been seasoned with wild onions and such herbs as sage.

Indian women also made stew with buffalo meat, using the imaginative device shown in the left-hand drawing. They tied the ends of a buffalo's stomach lining or a piece of hide to four poles, then filled it with water and meat and vegetables, such as wild peas and the root vegetable white men called prairie turnips. To make the water boil the women then dropped hot, fist-sized stones into the pouch.

The Indians varied their diet by hunting and trapping elk, deer, antelope, mountain sheep, quail and jack rabbits. Some of the plains tribes would eat fish, which they speared or netted, while certain tribes, such as the Blackfoot, Crow and Comanche, regarded fish as taboo. The desert dwellers caught and roasted snakes and insects. Some plains tribes, like the Mandan and Pawnee, regularly planted crops of corn, beans, squash and pumpkins, which they not only ate but traded to other Indians. In the course of a year women would pick more than a dozen kinds of wild fruits, ranging from persimmons to choke-cherries, and even more varieties of roots and stalks. They peeled fresh sweet thistle stalks that tasted like bananas. They collected milkweed buds and rose hips, and sliced the fruit of the prickly-pear cactus, adding them to buffalo soups and stews.

While the Indians might gorge themselves at the peak of the hunting and harvesting seasons, they knew well that lean months would follow. Accordingly, they preserved buffalo meat by cutting it into thin slices and hanging it to dry. The dried strips, known as jerky, could be pulverized with a stone maul, and the powdered meat mixed with ground and dried berries and fat. The result was a high-protein food called pemmican.

Not only was pemmican nutritious, but it could also be stored away in rawhide cases called parfleches, where it would keep for months. Some tribes stored meat, dried corn and other vegetables and fruit in large jug-shaped caches dug into the ground. Such preserved foods helped to sustain the plains people through the midwinter months, until the grasslands again quickened with wild plants and quivered beneath the hoofs of the buffalo.

TECHNIQUES FOR BOILING AND BROILING

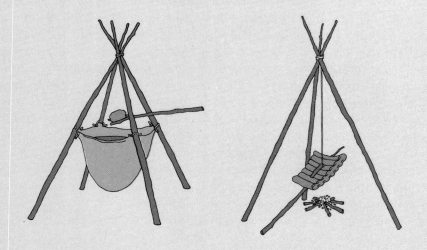

The traditional cooking paunch at left, made from the lining of a buffalo's stomach, lasted for three or four days, when it became soggy and soft from the heat. The Indians then disposed of the paunch by eating it. When broiling meat, plains women hung the skewered chunks on a rawhide strip moistened to keep the leather from burning through.

flint fitted with a sharp tip, he cut fine zigzag "lightning lines" down the shaft. In theory, these lightning marks would help the arrow fly swiftly and true; in practice, they probably also helped to prevent warping. Into a cleft at one end the man bound and glued an arrowpoint —usually iron in the 19th Century—and into the other end three split turkey or buzzard feathers. Excellent glue for finishing the job was made from boiled buffalo hoofs and certain pieces of hide.

Though craftsmanship was honored among Plains Indian men, the greatest prestige obtainable by a man was won through war and raiding—for horses and other plunder, for revenge, or for the extension or defense of tribal territory. War was neither play nor sport, but an extremely serious matter; and one symbol of the pride men took in success in war was the hair of the enemy, worn or displayed as a trophy.

A Crow chief of the early 19th Century named Rotten Belly, a master of raiding and ambush, had his shirt, his leggings and even his buffalo robe fringed with the hair of the foes he had killed. In 1873 Thomas Battey, a Quaker teacher in the employ of the U.S. Indian Bureau, was a breakfast guest in the tipi of an old Kiowa warrior. Battey was seated toward the rear of the lodge and felt something softly brushing his ear; it was a great bundle of human hair hanging from a lodgepole. After breakfast he found an opportunity to study this evidence of his host's prowess, which he later described: "The scalps had been trimmed and stretched, while fresh, upon small hoops, about four inches in diameter, and strung upon sticks, by running a stick like an arrow, only larger and about two feet in length, through them, near one edge. There were three of these sticks, each of which contained a dozen or more of these sickening trophies of his former bravery, the long hair of which hung down." The wife of this Kiowa brave was a Mexican woman who had probably been captured as a young girl, and Battey wondered whether the scalps of her parents were included in the 36 or more scalps he saw.

But the scalping or even killing of an enemy was not the highest war honor among the Plains Indians. Bravery was shown by the scoring of coups—that is, by the touching or striking of an enemy with hand or weapon. Coups struck within an enemy camp ranked highest, and the bravest man was one who entered such a camp armed not with a lance or a bow and arrows, but with a tomahawk or a whip. Better still, he might carry only a stick. But any heroic act in the face of the enemy counted—charging a defensive position alone, rescuing a wounded or unhorsed comrade, having a horse killed under one, being the first to locate an enemy or acting as a decoy in an ambush.

Not so dramatic as war but equally important in the life of a Cheyenne man was hunting. He hunted many animals—deer, elk and bighorn sheep by stalking or by ambush as they came to a water hole; antelope by an organized hunting method of surrounding them or driving them into a camouflaged pit so that they could easily be slain by a ring of bowmen. To catch an eagle, valuable for its feathers, the hunter hid in a pit and waited for the mighty bird to come down to his meat bait; then he reached up, seized the eagle and killed it with his hands. He netted fish and turtles in baskets or with seines of hide, willows or reeds.

His greatest game was the buffalo, which he preferred to kill, even after the advent of the gun, with lance or bow, riding a specially trained fast horse (*page 66*). The buffalo hunt was always dangerous: a buffalo bull—particularly a bad-tempered bull in rut—was hard to bring down and would fight like a cornered grizzly bear even when mortally wounded. Unhorsed, trampled and gored, a few men lost their lives every year when trapped in a stampeding herd or attacked by a maddened buffalo.

In summer and fall, when buffalo were roaming in large herds, an individual or small party was not permitted to hunt alone. Every family had to have its opportunity to get meat and hides before the frightened beasts stampeded and fled. Communal hunts were carefully organized. The civil chiefs decided when a surround was to be made and designated one of the special groups called soldier societies to police each hunt. The society's members enforced their authority strictly so that every hunter had a fair chance at the game. If they found a man hunting buffalo when the no-hunt rule was in effect, they judged him on the spot and usually whipped him with quirts, sometimes beating him until he could hardly walk. They took into consideration the seriousness of the offense, what actual damage had been done to tribal interests and the attitude of the violator. They might cut an ear off his horse or kill it, destroy his weapons, cut up his tipi, even chop up his lodgepoles.

Strong medicine from the flute and drum

As with most aspects of Plains Indian culture, music was closely bound up with their belief in the supernatural workings of the world. Instruments like those at right were played individually and during public dances, and there was Indian music for almost every occasion.

Every young man had a personal song whose melody and words, he believed, were transmitted to him directly by the power of his guardian spirit —a roving wolf, a tree or flower. To find the song he would go alone into the wilderness and fast until the inspiration came to him in a dream. Perhaps it would be a simple avowal of confidence, like the Cree song: "There is only beauty behind me, only beauty before me." He sang this personal song at certain moments of his life so as to renew his contact with the mysterious powers he had seen in his dreams. If his life was conspicuously successful, much of the credit was given to his personal song, and other men might offer him a valuable pipe bowl or some horses in exchange for the rights to the verse.

A young wife might softly croon a lullaby to her baby. And a Cheyenne girl in love would answer a suitor's song with the coy refrain, "Put your arms around me, I am not looking." There were satirical ditties disparaging persons who had annoyed the composer. Warriors had their special songs, like this one sung by a member of the Sioux Kit Fox warrior society:

I am a Fox
I am supposed to die
If there is anything difficult
If there is anything dangerous
That is mine to do.

In public ceremonies singing was combined with dancing and with highly rhythmic music from a variety of instruments. The dancers shook rattles or pounded hand-held drums to underscore their footbeats. Rattles were made of gourds or turtle shells filled with pebbles or seeds. Drums generally were made by soaking a strip of wood in hot water and bending it into a circle; then the drum skin was tightly strapped over the circle with rawhide laces. While some Plains Indian drums had a single drum skin, like a tambourine, there were others, such as the Ute drum on the opposite page, that had skins lashed onto both sides. A few tribes also used rasplike instruments that emphasized the rhythm of a dance. The Utes scraped a piece of elk antler across a notched wooden bar placed on an overturned basket (*bottom, opposite*) to amplify the vibrations.

The whistle and flute were the only Indian wind instruments. Warriors riding into battle would blow on whistles made from the wing bone of an eagle, the bird that symbolized courage. The recorderlike flutes, with finger holes along the top, were carved from a length of soft, straight-grained wood, like willow or box elder, that was split in half and hollowed out; the halves were rejoined with glue made from boiled hide scrapings and bound together with rawhide lace to make them airtight.

Contact with the white man expanded Indian musical concepts by introducing them to written music, and to brass and stringed instruments. The Apaches even made their own version of a violin (*below*) by stretching two lengths of deer sinew over a carved-out wood frame about a foot and a half long. Thus, with a short horsehair bow, they evoked in their ceremonies the unaccustomed fluid tones of the violin.

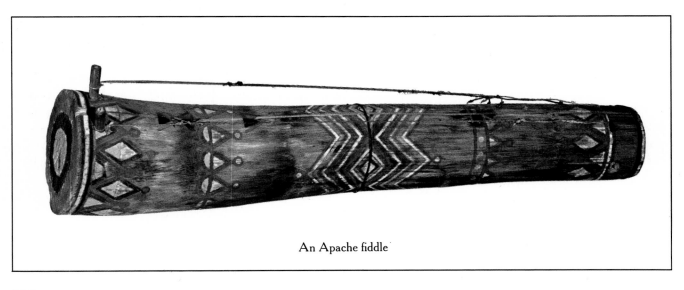

An Apache fiddle

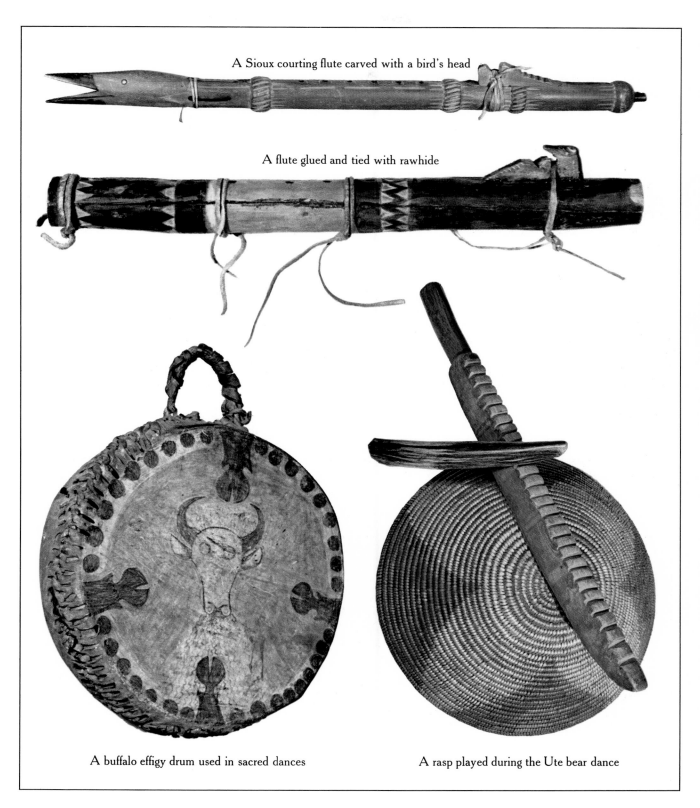

A Sioux courting flute carved with a bird's head

A flute glued and tied with rawhide

A buffalo effigy drum used in sacred dances

A rasp played during the Ute bear dance

These soldier societies were unique to the Plains Indian tribes. Their members were brought together through common battle experiences, and shared their own secrets and ceremonies. They policed not only the hunts, but also the large encampments and the camp moves. They were the epitome of the warrior ethic. The main war chiefs among the Cheyenne bands were chiefs of the soldier societies.

In the Cheyenne tribe there were six such societies: the Fox Soldiers, Elk Soldiers, Red Shields, Dog Soldiers, Bow Strings and Crazy Dogs. Except for the Dog Soldiers, who formed their own distinct band among the Cheyennes, these fraternities were similar in their organization and functions, differing mainly in ceremonial dress, dances and songs. In their ceremonies four of them employed daughters of good families as maids of honor, giving them a role somewhere between mascot and patroness of the society and thereby honoring tribal ideals of womanhood.

Among all the Plains Indians perhaps the most aristocratic and exclusive soldier society was one of the Kiowas'—the Kaitsenko (the Real Dogs, or Society of the Ten Bravest). They were pledged to lead charges and to fight in the van of every battle until they were victorious or perished. Of the 10 members, three wore sashes of red cloth; six wore red elkskin sashes, and the leader wore a broad black elkskin sash that trailed from his neck down to the ground. In a fight to the end it was the leader's duty to pin himself to the ground with a ceremonial arrow through his sash, there to hold fast while the battle swirled around him, until victory — or, with all hope lost, he was unpinned by a fellow member of the society. Chief Sitting Bear, who gave away 250 horses at the great 1840 peace council, wore the black elkskin sash and was still wearing it in 1870. By that time his hair was fading to gray, but he was still erect and proud, and his people considered him the single bravest Kiowa alive.

Government and law varied widely among the Plains Indians. The Utes of southern Colorado, for example, made thievery, adultery, even murder, a private and family matter. If one Ute stole from another, the victim complained to an elder relative of the culprit; the item was returned and the thief was whipped by his relatives. If adultery was discovered, the husband seized his rival's horse; if the husband were the offender the wife might fight the other woman or rob her of her personal possessions. In the case of murder the family and friends of the victim demanded and got reparations, or exacted revenge by killing.

Edwin Denig, a mid-19th Century fur trader on the upper Missouri, observed in some detail the habits of Crow Indians in handling disputes. He wrote: "Smaller pilferings and discord are decided by heartily abusing each other. At this game both men and women are equally adept, and their language affords a fine variety of beautiful epithets, which they bestow upon each other in great profusion. Most of these expressions consist of comparing the visage and person thus abused to the most disgusting objects in nature, even to things not known in the natural world."

Civil discord or criminal acts might set entire bands against each other, and yet they could settle the dispute simply by getting it off their chests. Denig wrote: "The band of the Platte sometimes takes offense at the band along the Yellowstone. Every traveler that comes from one to the other during one or sometimes two years, brings threats, abuse, and defiance. One who did not know them would think that in case the bands met a desperate struggle would take place. Nevertheless, when they meet, after all this parade of threats, they are the most peaceable people in existence. They will remain together for months on good terms. But when they separate, and have a river between them, so that no harm can be done, their war commences and terrible is the abuse shouted across the stream, accompanied by throwing stones that do not reach halfway. Then they go different directions, swearing vengeance."

While all of the Plains Indians had warrior chiefs, not all of them had a very sophisticated civil government. The Crows and the Comanches, among others, had little in the way of overall tribal organization. But such tribes as the Sioux and the Cheyenne did develop a formal, strict system of governing themselves. The Cheyenne Tribal Council had 44 civil chiefs. In fact, a warrior chief who was elected or appointed as a member of the Council was expected to give up his military chieftainship (though he might remain a member of his soldier society). The civil council ruled supreme; in this warlike people military and civil power were kept separate, with the civil government normally in control. War and honors of war were vitally important to the

Cheyennes, but they apparently knew that tribal unity and stability were still more crucial.

To help achieve unity they organized their tribe in a complex way. The Cheyenne tribe was made up of 10 major bands and for good reasons. Their nomadic hunting economy and the need to find adequate grazing grounds for their horses forced them to wander in relatively small groups: the size of a band rarely exceeded more than a few hundred people. Each member of the band knew every other member: band loyalty was important. And a Cheyenne would properly be identified by band as well as tribal allegiance—such as an Omissis Cheyenne, a Hevataniu Cheyenne, and so forth.

The bands rarely came together, except for special ceremonial occasions in the summer months. But when united they worked together politically in a system as equitable and perfectly balanced as that of the white man's federal government in Washington. The equivalent of the white man's Congress was the Cheyenne Tribal Council of 44 civil chiefs. Each band sent four of its members to the Council; the four additional Council members were the principal chiefs of the entire tribe. These tribal chiefs, who were either selected from among the band chiefs or appointed by retiring members of the supreme group of four, were the ones who usually made the ultimate important decisions. All members of the Council generally served for a term of 10 years and chose their own successors. Although the Council might meet only once a year, when the tribal bands came together, and although separate bands might scatter to the farthest corners of the Cheyenne domain during most of the year, the Council held the tribe together in matters of government and high policy. It was thus a vital element of continuity and stability in a world of nomadic wandering and constant change.

A representative to the Council was called a civil chief in his own band. And every civil chief was considered a father and protector of all the Cheyennes in the band. Ideally he was even-tempered, good-natured, energetic, wise, brave, kind, generous. If a member of the band asked a chief for the loan of some object, the chief would usually give it to him. And the four tribal, or supreme, chiefs were expected to be even more magnanimous. Soon after High Backed Wolf became a civil chief he approached a warrior named Pawnee, who had been stripped and beaten by a warrior society for some offense. High Backed Wolf said, "This is the first time since I have become a big chief that I have happened upon such a poor man. Now I am going to help you out." He delivered to Pawnee a stern lecture on Cheyenne behavior, then gave him clothes, a horse, a decorated mountain-lion skin and a six-shooter.

A tribal chief was supposed to show no sexual jealousy. An ordinary man might accept damages if his wife ran off with another, but a chief would refuse damages and try to place himself above any hurt or idea of revenge. In referring to and dismissing the offense he might use the expression "A dog has soiled my tipi."

George Grinnell, the great student of the Cheyenne people, wrote: "A good chief gave his whole heart and his whole mind to the work of helping his people. Such thought for his fellows was not without its influence on the man himself; after a time the spirit of goodwill which animated him became reflected in his countenance. True friends, delightful companions, wise counselors, they were men whose attitude toward their fellows we might all emulate." Since the chiefs of the council were dominant members of their own bands within the tribe, their attitudes set an example for the rest of the tribe.

Not only chiefs, but all elderly people were venerated among the Cheyennes for their wisdom. Essentially a conservative people, these Indians treasured the knowledge and experience of the old, and when one died the loss was deeply grieved. A dead person, regardless of age, was dressed in his or her finest clothing, wrapped in a robe or blanket and placed in a tree, on a scaffold or on the ground and covered with rocks. A man's favorite horses might be killed at his burial place, and his weapons, pipes and other treasured belongings were left with him. A woman was buried with her utensils, her digging stick and sometimes her hide-fleshing tool. Relatives wailed at the grave. Women mourners, especially the mother and wife of the dead person, cut off their hair; if they mourned a man who had died of wounds or in battle they gashed their forehead and legs to make the blood flow and might even cut off a finger.

The Cheyennes believed that there was no burden of guilt to be borne beyond death. According to their faith, the spirit of the departed traveled up a Hanging Road, the Milky Way, to the abode of Heammawihio, the Wise One Above—there to follow the Cheyenne way and to live forever among long-lost loved ones.

The essential role of women

While the men rode off to hunt or make war, the women sustained and perpetuated village life. And their labors won them a similar measure of tribal esteem. Women gathered the fruits and nuts and vegetables for their families; women cultivated the crops if the tribe was semisedentary; women prepared pemmican, sewed hides and made pottery. Women also performed such heavy tasks as raising and lowering tipis, bringing in firewood and digging roots from the sun-baked earth with a sharpened stick. Far from regarding these unceasing chores as drudgery, Indian women carried them out with a sense of satisfaction and even, when they forayed together on berrying or root-gathering expeditions, with a certain joyous camaraderie.

The women took special pride in their role as artisans. The weaving of a basket or the making of a tipi lining was done in a spirit that sanctified the object and dedicated it to the welfare of family or tribe. Productivity and proficiency in crafts established the rank of a woman within her small society. The woman who made the most intricate patterns on clothing or prepared the greatest number of hides gained the same prestige among her peers as a warrior who performed bravely in battle.

In front of an open-pit kiln fueled by chips of dung, Pueblo women inspect clay pots baking in the fire.

A Crow woman brings firewood for her family's encampment near the Yellowstone River.

An Apache woman gathers mescal, a plant whose sweet fleshy base, roasted in pits, was a favorite food for Southwestern Indians.

With a stone mortar and pestle a Cheyenne woman pounds wild cherries, pits and all, into mush that will be used in making pemmican.

Pueblo women wash away the chaff and dirt from their wind-winnowed wheat before putting it out in flat baskets to dry in the sun.

As a first step in the tanning process, Cheyenne women stretched and pegged fresh buffalo hides. In the background, strips of meat hang on a line in the sun to dry.

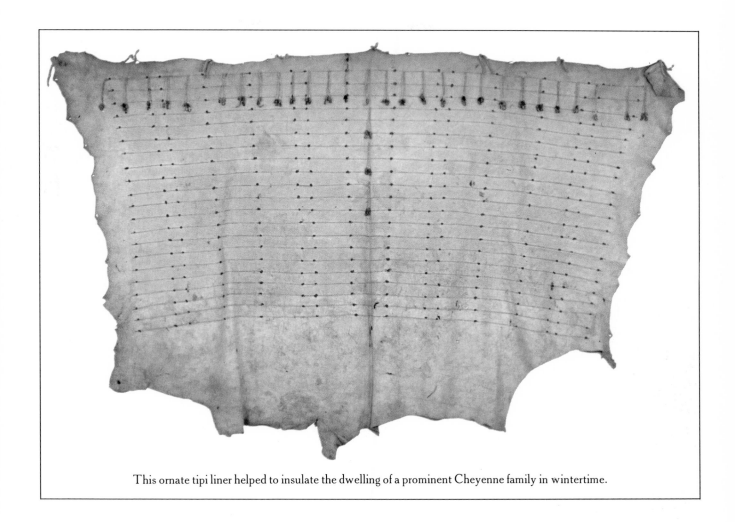

This ornate tipi liner helped to insulate the dwelling of a prominent Cheyenne family in wintertime.

An essential task of a Plains Indian woman was the dressing of hides. The articles made of hide—not only that of buffalo, but of elk, deer, antelope and smaller game—included a majority of a tribe's earthly possessions. An Indian woman started the tanning process immediately after a successful hunt. She first stretched the fresh skin out on the ground, hairy side down, and pegged it in place *(left)*. Working on the exposed side, she removed meat and fat with a flesher, an adzelike blade often lashed to an elkhorn handle. A flesher was a cherished possession, and a good one was often handed down from mother to

daughter through many generations. To finish the cleaning process, a woman used another tool, a stone scraper.

If the hide was intended for winter wear, she left the hair in place. If it was to be used for summer clothing or tipi making, she scraped the hair off. Her tanning fluid was basically a concoction of the brains, liver and fat of the animal. But the softening of the skin was accomplished less by any chemical action than by flexing, stretching and squeezing to work the tanning mixture into the cells and fibers. This she did by tirelessly pulling the hide back and forth over a taut rawhide rope or some-

times through a hole in a buffalo shoulder-blade bone. Finally, after drying, the hide was smoked over a fire to render it water-resistant.

It usually took an Indian woman about six days to complete the tanning. But this might be only the beginning of her work, for the hide was likely to be cut up and stitched into any number of articles, decorated with porcupine quills, beads and other ornaments. The sacred tipi lining shown above—embroidered with dyed cornhusks in horizontal rows and adorned with tufts of red cloth and deer-toe pendants—required nearly a month and a half to make.

113

Seated outside her brush hut, or wickiup, an old Paiute woman weaves a basket of grass. The spatulate object beside her head was used to harvest grain by knocking the seeds into a woven conical carrying basket.

Baskets served an astonishing number of purposes among the Western tribes. For the Paiute woman at left, who endured a precarious existence in the arid Great Basin, the ability to create useful objects out of the sparse desert plants around her was as crucial to the survival of her family as her husband's hunting and fighting skills.

Indian baskets were woven from a wide variety of vegetal fibers—grasses, strips of bark, yucca leaves, bulrushes. Though light in weight, when carefully dried these fibers were surprisingly strong. Using designs and patterns that were modified or embellished with each succeeding generation, Indian women wove platters for serving such foods as dried meat, berries, roots and roasted grasshoppers. The same weaving techniques also produced sandals, pockets for cradleboards and dice trays for gambling. Especially important were the baskets used for the storage of grain and other seeds that could be collected only at certain times of year. Carrying baskets—strapped to the backs of women in tribes that had few horses for burden—held such household necessities as bedding, tools and moccasins. Some objects were purely utilitarian, such as the undecorated Paiute water bottle shown below at right (it was calked with pine resin to make it watertight). More often utility was blended with ornamentation. It took a keen eye for design—and three to four months' work—to turn willow wands and fibers of the devil's-claw plant into the superb Pima grain basket pictured below at left.

A coiled Pima storage basket   A tightly woven Paiute water bottle

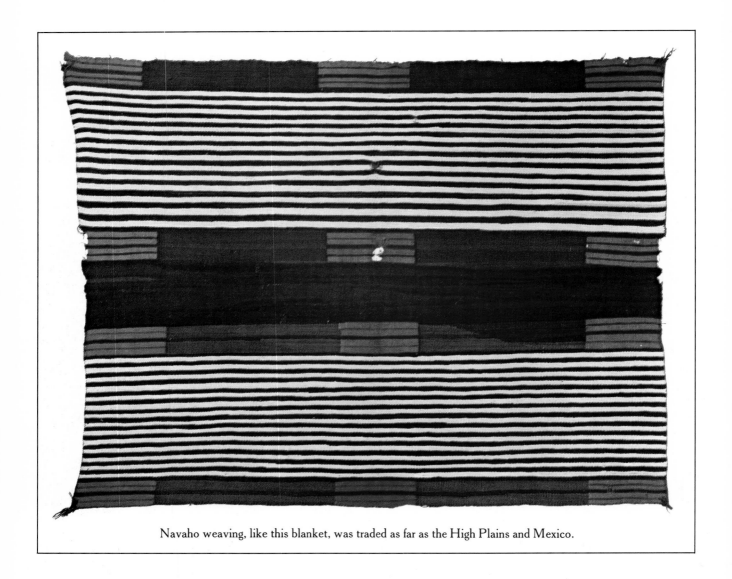

Navaho weaving, like this blanket, was traded as far as the High Plains and Mexico.

Another triumph of the utilitarian artistry of Indian women was woven blankets, a specialty of the Navahos. According to their mythology, Navaho women learned the art of weaving from a supernatural creature called Spider Woman. In fact, they were probably taught by their neighbors, the Pueblo Indians, in the late 17th Century. The Pueblos, sedentary farmers, originally wove with cotton, which they grew. But the Navahos soon began applying their new skill to wool from sheep, recently introduced into the New World by the Spanish and acquired by the men of the tribe when they raided against the white settlements.

Patient and skillful, and having an uncommon eye for inventive design, Navaho women carried the craft of weaving to unsurpassed heights of sophistication. From their looms came such items as dresses, shirts, ponchos, saddle blankets, bedding blankets, sashes and ceremonial rugs. Such was the power and beauty of these works that they became highly prized by other Indians and were traded from tribe to tribe all across the West.

Although the Navahos made their own dyes from roots and plants, the brilliant red color that appears in many of their products came to them in the form of cloth woven in the far-off industrial city of Manchester, England. Acquiring the alien cloth through trade, the Navaho women tirelessly unraveled the threads and then incorporated them into their own magnificent designs.

Using two tree trunks to support the elements of her loom, a Navaho woman in the Canyon de Chelly patiently creates a striped blanket.

4 | Seeking help from the spirits

Four costumed Apaches importune the mountain spirits for success in hunting and war, while a diminutive clown mimics their movements.

To the Western Indians, everything in the world about them was filled with spirits and powers that controlled or otherwise affected the lives of the tribesmen. The sun, the mountains, the beaver, the snake, the eagle—each had its mysterious force, or medicine. To survive and prosper, the Indians believed they must perform a constant round of ceremonies—called making medicine—that would appease these spirits and solicit their aid. Some of these rituals were simple and personal—for example, the warrior's practice of bowing to sky and earth, then turning to the four points of the compass as he lit his morning pipe (*pages 26-29*). Others, like the Apache dance shown here, were elaborate, costumed affairs that could go on for several days or more under the direction of a priest-like leader. He would tell the performers precisely what to do, and woe to the inattentive dancer. According to Apache tradition a dancer who did not don the headdress exactly as he had been instructed would surely go mad.

In observance of a funeral rite common to most plains tribes, the bodies of two Indians, dead of natural causes, rest high in a tree whence the souls can be free to rise into the sky. In some tribes men killed in battle were left on the plains.

A way of life dominated by religion

Some years after the great council on the Arrow-point River, a man named Eagle Chief, a leader of the Skidi band of Pawnees, was in camp in the Platte River area when a troop of Pawnee raiders returned. They brought with them several prisoners who had been captured during an attack on a neighboring tribe. All but one of the prisoners were promptly adopted into the Pawnee band and set free to live normally within the village. The other captive was singled out for a different fate. He was to be sacrificed to Tirawa, principal god of the Pawnees, in the hope that the god would bestow good fortune on the band. Tirawa would be pleased with this man because he was young, stout and brimming with health.

Before the sacrifice, the prospective victim was served the finest food and treated with gentle deference. A succession of women came to eat with him; when each had finished she said, "I hope that I may be blessed from Tirawa that he may take pity on me, that when I put my seeds in the ground they may grow and that I may have plenty of everything."

Years later Eagle Chief related the climax of the rite; what follows is an excerpt from his story.

"At the end of the four days two old men went, one to each end of the village, and called aloud, directing every male person in the village to make a bow and an arrow. For every male child a bow and an arrow was made; for the little boys small bows that they could bend and small arrows. The next day, before daybreak, every one was ready. Every male carried his bow and arrow. Every woman had a lance or a stick. They all went out to the west end of the village and stood there

looking for the prisoner to be brought. Here two stout posts had been set up, and between these had been tied four cross poles.

"As day broke, warriors led the naked captive to the posts, lifting him up, tied first the left hand and then the right to the top cross pole, and afterward tied the feet below. Every one stood there silent, looking and waiting; the men holding their weapons. On the ground under the sacrifice was laid the wood for a great fire which was now lighted. Then a warrior with bow and arrow, he who had taken the captive, ran up close to the victim and shot him through from side to side, beneath the arms, with the sacred arrow, whose point was of flint, such as they used in the olden time. The blood ran down upon the fire below. Then, at a given signal, the males all ran up, and shot their arrows into the body. If any male children were not large enough to shoot, some one shot for them. There were so many arrows that the body was stuck full of them; it bristled with them.

"A man chosen for this purpose now climbed up, and pulled out all the arrows from the body, except the one which was first shot through the side of the sacrifice. After pulling out the arrows, this man took his knife and cut open the breast of the captive, and putting his hand in the opening, took out a handful of blood, and smeared it over his face. When this had been done the women came forward with their sticks and spears and struck the body and counted coup on it.

"By this time the fire was burning up high and scorching the body, and it was kept up until the whole body was consumed. And while the smoke of the blood and of the burning body ascended to the sky, all the people prayed to Tirawa, and walked by the fire and grasped handfuls of the smoke, and passed it over their bodies and over those of their children, and prayed Tirawa to take pity on them, and give them health, and success in war, and plenteous crops. The man who had

Masks, like this Navaho face cover representing the goddess of succor, symbolically transformed Indians into images of the spirits whose powers could help the tribe.

123

killed the captive fasted and mourned for four days, and asked Tirawa to take pity on him, for he knew that he had taken the life of a human being."

Eagle Chief concluded his story with a matter-of-fact comment: "This sacrifice always seemed acceptable to Tirawa, and when the Skidi made it they always seemed to have good fortune in war, and good crops, and they were always well."

The Skidi sacrifice of a healthy young man, or more often a maiden captured from another tribe, represents an extreme of violence in the religious practices of the Plains Indians. But many other tribes had rites that seemed cruel and gruesome to the white man's eyes. To the Indians, however, such acts were natural and necessary in order to avert disaster and maintain their well-being. Despite the plains people's ingenious adaptation to their environment and their iron-willed stoicism, their lives were in many ways uncertain. They were largely at the mercy of the weather, of the waxing and waning of game herds and plants. Death, in the form of hunger, pestilence or marauding enemies, was never far away.

To survive properly in such a world the Indians felt a need for some powerful assistance. They got it from a host of spirits that inhabited the natural world. The spirits were thought to be literally everywhere and were almost always identified with some visible object, animal or phenomenon. They were said to dwell in the sun and earth, in rivers and hills, in thunderstorms and rainbows, and within creatures ranging from the dragonfly to the buffalo. These sacred beings had power to bring success in the hunt and war, protect the young, heal the sick, guarantee fertility, and generally assure the welfare of the tribe and its individuals in whatever they undertook. But this power would be shared or bestowed only if the human beings performed a steady round of ceremonies aimed at enlisting the help of the supernatural forces that shaped and controlled their universe.

These religious rituals took many forms. Some were simply small gestures of respect. When, for example, an Apache hunter skinned a deer, he turned the head of the animal toward the east—the sacred direction where the life-giving sun arose and whence would come new life for other game. When a Comanche sat down to a formal meal he often cut off a tiny morsel of his food, held it up toward the sky as a symbolic offering to a heavenly deity and then buried the morsel in the earth.

Far more complex and demanding were the major ceremonies, such as the Pawnees' human sacrifice, that were supposed to redound to the good of the whole village. These occurred at varying intervals when the bands of a tribe would come together to watch or take part in rites that involved hundreds of formal steps and might take a week or more to complete. It was crucial that each step be flawlessly executed, otherwise the spirits would be displeased and the ceremony would fail to have its intended effect. A typically intricate rite was the *massaum*, or animal dance, of the Cheyennes, performed every few years to propitiate the earth and ensure a continued plenitude of food.

To start, a young cottonwood tree about 25 feet high had to be cut down and trimmed but with a few green branches left at the top so that, in the words of the accompanying prayer, "all the trees and grass and fruits may thrive and grow strong." The chopping was begun by a man who followed a special formula. He swung four times, stopping the ax short of the tree on the first three strokes, then striking it on the fourth (the number four had important spiritual significance related to the four cardinal directions). Women finished the cutting; as they worked they sang an eerie chant, like the sound of wind moaning through branches.

When felled, the tree was carried into the village and erected at the center of a double-sized lodge in which most of the rite took place. There, too, everything that happened was minutely prescribed. The fire could not be built of pine or cedar, which were taboo. When a woman brought a sacred buffalo skull into the lodge she was told to make three false starts and then come in on the fourth; meanwhile, other participants sang four songs. At a certain moment in the rite a wolfskin was painted according to a precise sequence: first the left forefoot, then the right forefoot, then the right hip across to the left shoulder, the left hip across to the right shoulder, and so on.

All of these solemn, painstaking procedures led toward a joyous climax on the fifth day, when men put on the skins of various animals —buffalo, elk, fox, bear, mountain lion, antelope, coyote, blackbird and others. They danced about, scratching, pawing and stampeding like the animals they represented. They were "hunted" by members of the Contrary Society, a special group

said to be affiliated with the Spirit of Thunder, but functioning mainly as comic relief. The Contrary hunters did everything backward, holding their bows in a reversed position, running backward and otherwise acting in an eccentric, clowning manner that delighted the onlookers. When the ceremony was over the tribe was ready to set off on the buffalo hunt, convinced that they would find abundant game.

The Cheyennes had another major ceremony, the arrow renewal, a four-day rite to renew the power of their weapons when their way of life and unity as a people were threatened —during a time of food shortage, for instance, or following a defeat in war. The renewal focused on four sacred arrows (two of which were thought to have supernatural power over men and the other two over buffalo) supposedly given to the Cheyenne long ago by a tribal hero named Sweet Medicine.

In the arrow-renewal ceremony, as in other major rites, all of the steps were followed in exactly the same way each time the rite was held, and everyone had to obey the austere rules. The camp would become solemn and silent, with only the songs and prayers and drumming sounding from a sacred lodge. Women and children stayed inside their home tipis. Men kept secular business to a minimum. A warrior society patrolled the camp to maintain decorum. If a dog as much as growled or whined a warrior would split its skull with a club. The main act, which occurred on the second day, was the opening of the buffalo-skin bundle in which the arrows were kept. If the feathers on the shafts were not in perfect condition, a man of high repute —healthy, good-tempered, brave —was selected to repair them.

At dawn a lone Pueblo Indian standing on a rocky eminence near the Rio Grande tosses a pinch of ground cornmeal to the spirits of cloud and sun, asking them to give rain and warmth for good crops.

On the third day the leaders of the ceremony prepared willow tally sticks to represent each living Cheyenne family, except for any in which a member had murdered another Cheyenne. They passed these sticks one by one through the smoke of incense fires to bless each family individually. On the fourth day the sacred arrows were taken outside and exposed to the view of all Cheyenne males, from the oldest grandfather to the youngest babe in arms.

In appealing for help to the spirit world, some tribes put special emphasis on one power that was considered to be greater than all the rest. To the Cheyenne, the principal spirit was Heammawihio (the Wise One Above), represented by the sun but more powerful than the sun, supreme because he knew more about how nature worked than anyone else. His counterpart was Aktunowihio (the Wise One Below). The two spirits did not represent good and evil, but merely powers thought to reside in different directions. Heammawihio had a great bird, Thunder, who commanded the summer rains and fought against the *minio,* water monsters who lived in lakes and rivers. If a Cheyenne was seized by one of the *minio,* he might hope to be rescued by Thunder. Then there were the *mistai,* or ghosts, who scared people by making noises or tugging on a blanket in the dark. They were not the same as a human soul, *tasoom,* which wafted away from the body at death, to travel up the Hanging Road — represented by the Milky Way — and live in the land of the Wise One Above.

Life in the afterworld was much like that on earth. There, people lived in camps, hunted, went to war and carried on other familiar occupations. The land beyond the grave held no such terrors as judgment or damnation, and, except for persons who committed suicide, everyone could expect to reach it after death.

Thus free from any terrors in the afterlife, the religions of the Indians concentrated on attaining good fortune in the face of the tough practicalities of plains living. "We just knew we were here," commented one old Comanche. "Our thoughts were mostly directed toward understanding the spirits."

Among all the plains tribes, the most useful and frequently called upon of those spirits dwelt within animals. The bull elk, for example, was considered an effective helper in love (Indians were much impressed by the elk's ability to call females). The bear was hard to kill and was thought to heal its own wounds; therefore it was felt that it might help heal human injuries as well. Eagles and hawks with their powerful claws were good helpers in wartime. The skunk was thought to have much supernatural power; its tail was used to hold medicine or was tied to the tail of horses during war, and its image was often painted on lodges and even on the seeds employed by women in gambling.

Some Pueblo farmers of the dry Southwest considered rattlesnakes to have the power of sending rain. In the spring the Pueblos would set out in the four cardinal directions to capture a few live rattlers. In the ceremony that followed, the men danced in pairs, one holding a serpent in his mouth, the other stroking it with a feather whip so that it would not strike. The hypnotic effect of the feather (or perhaps some judicious defanging or milking of venom) prevented serious snake bites. After the dance the Pueblos carried their guests back out in the four directions and deposited them gently on the earth, where, it was hoped, they would fulfill their obligation of sending rain.

The badger could help foretell the future. When a Cheyenne war party was about to set off, the warriors would sometimes kill a badger, rip its belly open, remove the entrails and leave the carcass lying on its back on a bed of sage all night so that blood would collect and congeal in the belly cavity. The next day the men would unbraid their hair and walk naked past the dead badger, staring down into the blood, which acted like a dull mirror. If a man saw a reflection of himself wrinkled and with white hair, he knew he would live to old age; if he saw himself without a scalp and with a bleeding head, he knew it was a bad omen and he turned back from the warpath.

A cricket could also be used for divination. The leader of a buffalo-hunting party would put one of the insects in his hand, wait until it was quiet and then note which way its antennae were pointed. Supposedly buffalo would be found in that direction. The Comanches relied on some other animal helpers in the hunt. They would ask a horned toad to tell them where the prey was located. They thought that the creature would answer their request by running in the direction of the buffalo. They also believed that if a raven circled their camp four times and cawed it would then fly toward the buffalo in order to help its Indian friends get meat.

Trappings from the gods

As visual symbols of their beliefs, Plains Indians created a colorful variety of religious clothes and sacred objects. Most articles were inspired by a vision, which the tribesmen believed to be a contact with the spiritual world. Some visions had occurred in a past so remote they had become traditions; for example, the Blackfeet believed the headdress below was an ancient gift from a bull elk to a beaver medicine man. Certain garments and talismans were a key part of tribal ceremonies. Others, such as the Lord's shirt opposite, were personal, the result of private visions. All were treated with elaborate care so as not to jeopardize their good medicine.

The Apache headpiece above, worn by a *gahe* dancer *(pages 118-119),* represents a shaman's vision of one of the mountain spirits that offered protection to the tribe. The design reflects the tribe's belief that the spirits guarded such game animals as the horn-bearing deer and antelope.

This sacred headdress of a Blackfoot woman *(left)* was a symbol of celebration worn during a sun dance. To qualify as wearer, the woman would vow to sponsor the dance if the sun granted her a wish. If the wish came true, she then had to pay the previous sponsor many horses for the bonnet.

A Piegan weather-dancer shirt imbued its owner with the power to keep the clouds from dropping rain during a sun dance. The shirt wearer would dance first in the direction of the rising sun and then toward the setting sun; finally he might shout a challenge to any lingering clouds.

The Lord's shirt blended Indian beliefs with Christian doctrine. A Blackfoot warrior, lost in enemy territory, had a vision of a white man, wearing a shirt painted with crosses, saying, "I am the Lord, do not fear, you will return home and live to be an old man." The warrior returned and made this shirt to resemble the Lord's; he wore it into many battles and was never wounded.

This dress was worn by a berdache, or homosexual, of the Ponka tribe. Indians believed the moon appeared to boys during puberty and offered a bow and a woman's pack strap. If the boy hesitated when reaching for the bow, the moon handed him the pack strap — symbolizing a feminized life style. Berdaches served as matchmakers and often went into battle to treat wounded warriors.

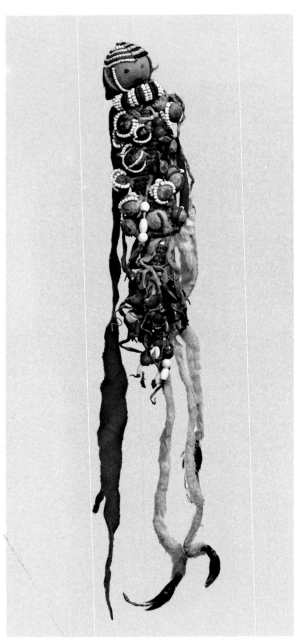

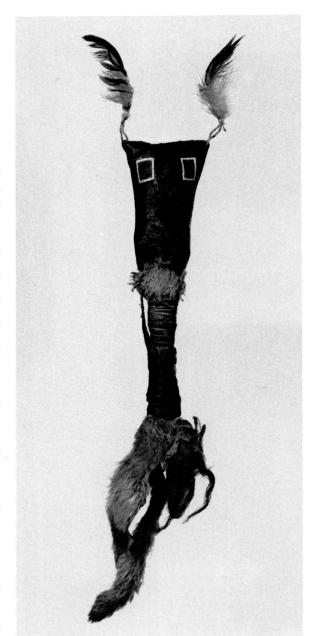

A Crow sun-dance doll had power to grant revenge. When an enemy killed a man's close relative the mourner went to a doll owner and paid for the use of the sacred effigy, often made with animal skin and adorned with beads. Gazing at its face, the man danced until he had a vision in which the doll told him when and where he should slay his enemy.

A Navaho rattle shaken by a medicine man kept the tempo of solemn tribal chants. This one has an outer covering of deerskin decorated with eagle feathers and mountain-lion fur. Religious rattles were so much a part of plains culture that in the sign language common to all tribes the gesture for the rattle was used as a symbol for anything sacred.

This medicine bundle, called the *waxobe,* rekindled the courage of any Osage warrior who viewed it. Belonging to the whole tribe, it was unrolled periodically for ceremonial display. Each article in the bundle is a symbol of bravery: at top the head and shoulders of a hawk, laid out just above the inner straw casing; at center a human scalp with braided hair; and at bottom an eagle's claw and a part of a buffalo's tail.

This Blackfoot medicine man was the custodian of a pipe that the tribe believed had been given to them long ago by the feared thunder spirit. Bear Bull's hornlike hair coil was a symbol of his sacred office.

Within every tribe certain individuals were considered to have exceptional abilities for dealing with the spirits. Major tribal ceremonies, such as the Pawnee human sacrifice and the Cheyenne arrow renewal, were supervised by trained priestlike leaders who had served long apprenticeships and had memorized all the details of the performances. A priest did not wield supernatural powers by himself; he simply guided the participants through the rite, which itself summoned spiritual aid. However, other prestigious individuals were thought to be able to exercise strong supernatural powers on their own. These were the medicine men.

The position of medicine man existed in every Western tribe, but it had no set form or function from tribe to tribe, or even from generation to generation. Although the medicine man sometimes acted as a priest during the major ceremonies, his own personal power could be employed at any time for the good of other people. He (or she, since older, married women could also acquire spiritual power) might use his power to foretell the future, cast love spells, find lost animals or bring about good weather. Some medicine men functioned as tribal physicians, and they might even have specialties, such as curing blood diseases, broken bones or battle wounds.

The spiritual power of a medicine man always came from a dream or trance, usually after long fasting and prayer. In these visions a spirit—perhaps in the form of a bear or bird—gave over great power and told how it was to be used. Many medicine men were exceptionally intelligent and had strong, persuasive personalities. Their personal aura helped to convince other people of the value and reliability of their aid. In return for their services medicine men might charge handsomely—as much as two ponies for a difficult case. But if the spirits failed, the man's medicine was regarded as no good and his livelihood might disappear.

Although the help of a medicine man might be sought for particularly urgent problems, any person was, in fact, free to address a spontaneous plea to the supernatural forces for some favor, and if he proceeded properly he might well be successful. One simple way of getting help was to offer a gift, such as a feather or some fine fur, to a high bluff or to the north wind or the sun or the thunder wherein sacred beings were thought to dwell.

Practically every young man attempted to acquire some personal power that would serve his own interests. As with medicine men, such personal power could be achieved through a vision quest. The young man would go off by himself for several days to a high hill, fasting, searching, seeking some relationship between himself and nature. If he was fortunate, he would have a dream in which a spirit would reveal certain sacred objects or designs that would bring supernatural aid in times of need. The record of one particular vision quest has been preserved in detail—that of the young Sioux Crazy Horse, who would later become one of the most notable warriors of the Western plains.

When he was 12 years old he was still called Curly, on account of a wave in his hair; his father, a medicine man, was named Crazy Horse. Curly witnessed the shooting of an old Sioux chief, Conquering Bear, by white soldiers on the Oregon Trail; it had been a needless shooting over the loss of a cow by immigrants. Seeing the dying chief apparently struck a deep, tender nerve in the boy. He left camp and went to some high gravelly bluffs. There he fasted and put sharp stones between his toes and pebbles under his body to make himself stay awake. Through the day and night he walked around on his high vantage point, trying to make up songs to sing but finding himself without inspiration. His eyes burned. Through the second

An Arikara medicine man cloaks himself in the skin of a bear he has slain to acquire its powerful spirit and to symbolize his membership in the tribe's Bear cult. The Arikaras had nine such tribal orders for medicine men, each with its own animal spirit and a matching costume made of either bird feathers or animal skin.

Carrying branches used for the frame of a sacred sweat lodge, Blackfoot warriors ride into camp wearing white men's hats for decoration. The ritualized building of the lodge, which was part of the tribe's sun dance, required branch bearers to canter, singing, around and around a medicine woman's tipi.

After a sweat-lodge frame was erected it was overlaid by buffalo robes and heated with steam from water sprinkled on hot stones. Before entering, warriors prayed to the buffalo skull shown in foreground.

day he waited for a spirit or a message, feeling unworthy and too young. He persisted through a third day. Then he got sick and dizzy. It was no use. He tried to return to the spot where he had hobbled his pony, but could not make it. He fell delirious under a large cottonwood tree.

A man came riding, light and airy, on a bay, then a yellow-spotted war horse, floating as in a mist. Arrows and lead balls went toward the dream-figure but did not hit him. There was a storm, with dark rolling clouds and thunder; the man rode through the violent storm. He had painted on his cheek a zigzag of lightning; on his body were marks of hailstones. Over his head flew a small red-backed hawk. The man's own people came around him, making a great noise, reaching out their arms toward him. The strangest part of the vision was that Curly knew exactly what was in the man's mind, the wordless thoughts of anguish and pride. Then the lad came awake to rough shaking and

found his father and another man bent over him, angry. They had been hunting him. What a stupid, childish trick, they growled, to be hiding out alone while no one knew whether the Crows or the Pawnees or the white soldiers had got him.

Some years later, when Curly was a young man, his father, old Crazy Horse, took him out for a solemn talk about Sioux religion and the responsibilities of manhood. For the first time Curly told about the vision. His father was surprised but had no doubt that the person in the vision was Curly himself. After that, old Crazy Horse gave his name to his son, and the young warrior made it one to be long remembered among the Sioux. In times of war he called on the personal power revealed in the dream, painting himself with marks of lightning and hailstones and wearing in his hair a red-backed hawk — his supernatural helper.

Personal power of this kind, though originally sought by one individual, was transferable. Thus Curly's father presumably gave over some of his own power by bestowing the name Crazy Horse on the youngster. In another case a warrior who had had great success might actually sell some symbol of his power—a bird's wing or an entire medicine bundle of sacred objects —to another man.

Whether bought or found in a vision, all powers from the spirits were hedged with taboos which, if violated, would render the supernatural aid ineffective. Often the possessor of the power would have to refrain from eating certain foods, such as the entrails or the brain of a buffalo. A man whose supernatural helper was an eagle could not let another person walk behind him when he was eating, for the Indians believed that eagles were disturbed by such an act. Supernatural power also had to be protected from the deleterious effect of grease and menstruating women. Among the Comanches, a shield that was thought to have the power to stop bullets and arrows was often stored at least half a mile from camp so that menstruating women would not pass close to it; when a warrior needed his shield he had to walk in a semicircle to the spot where it was located, then return to camp from the opposite direction, completing the circle.

The breaking of a taboo could have dire consequences. A man whose power guaranteed him good health might become sick or even die if he ate prohibited foods. And a warrior whose spiritual helper protected him in battle would be in mortal danger if he did not fulfill all the conditions attached to his power. This is what happened to Roman Nose, one of the most renowned Cheyenne warriors.

Roman Nose received the power of immunity to bullets and arrows from a medicine man named White Bull, who saw a magical war bonnet in a vision. The medicine man made the bonnet for Roman Nose, following every detail of the vision. It was painted with black pigment made from a tree that had been set on fire by lightning. A single buffalo horn was placed at the front. The skin of a kingfisher was tied to the top (its magical effect would be to close up bullet wounds instantly, just as the water instantly closes up when a kingfisher dives into a pool). A bat was tied to the right side (the bat flies through the dark and cannot be caught; hence the wearer of the bonnet could fight safely at night). When White Bull gave Roman Nose the

war bonnet he listed some taboos. The warrior must not shake hands with anybody, and he must not eat food that was taken from a dish with a metal utensil.

Roman Nose faithfully observed these rules that were attached to the bonnet, and the power seemed to work. Despite the target presented by his great size —he stood six feet three inches tall and weighed 230 pounds—he could lead a charge into withering gunfire and emerge unscathed every time. On several occasions he rode safely back and forth in front of a line of soldiers only 30 yards away.

Before a battle against 48 U.S. scouts at Beecher's Island, Colorado, in 1868, Roman Nose unwittingly ate some food that had been taken from a pot with a metal fork. Realizing his error, he did not join his fellow warriors when they attacked the force of white soldiers. Although the Indians were far more numerous, the fighting went badly, because the soldiers were armed with repeating rifles. One of the Cheyennes rode up to where Roman Nose was watching the battle and said, "Well, here is the man we depend on, sitting behind this hill. Do you not see your men falling out there? All those people feel that they belong to you and here you are behind this hill." Roman Nose was well aware of his value as an inspirational leader and felt that he could not watch his men die. He said, "I know that I shall be killed today." But he painted himself, put on his war bonnet and rode out to lead the Indians against the white position. He charged straight into the line of fast-firing Spencer rifles. When he was almost upon the soldiers, a bullet cut him down. After Roman Nose was mortally wounded, the Indians fought halfheartedly and finally retreated.

The Indians had no doubt that Roman Nose's death was caused not by the white soldiers' superior fire power or the warrior's own foolish bravery, but by his failure to adhere to the ritual taboos. Their confidence in such beliefs reflected and reaffirmed the warrior tribes' conviction that within their religion lay an explanation for every event in the Indians' world, whether it be the death of a warrior, the onset of illness or the changing of the seasons. Their religion even explained how the world itself came into existence. On long winter evenings Cheyenne children would lie around a fire inside a lodge and listen to an old man recite a tale about creation, which occurred, of course, through cooperation between the animals and a spiritual being.

"Long ago all was water and a being floated on the surface. With him were only swimming birds such as the swan, the goose, the duck.

"The being wanted to make land to walk upon, so he called to the swan: 'Dive down through the water and see if you can find earth on the bottom.'

"The swan said that he would try. He plunged down through the water, but in vain; he could not reach the bottom. He came back up and reported to the being on the surface."

The storyteller might enliven the tale with dialogue and many details about birds diving one by one after earth. Finally he would relate how a small duck came up with a bit of mud in its bill. The being worked the mud in his hands until it was dry, then placed it in small piles on the water surface, whereupon it grew and spread, making solid land everywhere. Thus was created the world.

One Cheyenne tale of antiquity was so sacred that it would require the storyteller to mutter a prayer asking for pardon before he began. It reveals the gift of the buffalo to the people by a legendary figure called Yellow Haired Woman. The storyteller would recount how in olden times the tribe had no large food animals and had to subsist on fish, geese and ducks. One time they became so hungry that the chiefs sent two young men out to search for food and told them not to return until they were successful.

The young men took their mission seriously and walked eight days without food, becoming very weak. They saw a high peak and decided to go to it to die, for it would be a marker to show their burying place. But they found a stream between them and their destination, and as they tried to cross, a great water serpent grabbed one of them and held him fast. Out of the peak ahead came a man wearing a coyote skin and carrying a large knife. The coyote was known as a clever and competent fellow, and evidently this coyote man had strong powers. He dived into the water and cut off the serpent's head; then he and an old woman, his wife, took the young men to the peak, where the rocks opened like a door. Inside, the old couple cured the men of their weakness and fed them.

The old coyote man and his wife had a fair-haired daughter, Yellow Haired Woman. Upon the man's sug-

gestion that they take the girl for a sister or a wife, one of the young men agreed to marry her. The coyote man let the girl go with them and he gave them gifts, including a knowledge of corn planting and the use of the buffalo for food; but he cautioned his daughter that she must never express pity for any suffering animal. (This taboo is not explained in the legend; perhaps the idea was that animals lose their usefulness if people think of them in terms of human sympathy.)

The Cheyennes were overjoyed when the two young men and the new bride came, for afterward they were surrounded by many buffalo and were able to get all the meat they needed. But later some boys dragged a buffalo calf into camp and threw dust into its eyes. Yellow Haired Woman said, "My poor calf!" Immediately she realized she had broken the taboo imposed by her father. That day all the buffalo disappeared. She knew she had to go back to her father and mother. Her husband and the other young man went with her, and the three were never seen again. Legend says that much later other mythical figures brought back the buffalo and restored tribal fortunes.

As such myths suggest, the Indians never took the bounty of nature for granted. On the contrary, they believed that nature had a built-in tendency to decline. According to their world view, the underlying energies of nature were expended through activity, and unless man did something to halt the dissipation of the energies, animals would gradually disappear, plants would wither and humans would slowly starve.

Twenty or more plains tribes periodically resorted to a great ceremony called the sun dance to prevent this ultimate disaster. The name of the rite came from the Sioux designation "gazing-at-the-sun dance," but its significance may be more clearly suggested by the Cheyenne name for the structure in which the ceremony was held — "new-life lodge," or "lodge of the generator." The purpose of the rite was no less than to make the whole world over again.

Because the sun dance apparently developed its greatest complexity among the Arapahos, Cheyennes and Oglala Sioux, its origin — or development from more primitive ceremonies — has been attributed to one of these groups. It seems probable that the dance spread from a source in the area of the upper Missouri, for the tribes that practiced it passed through

The medicine man's healing medicine

Although in many tribes the shaman, or medicine man, acted as ceremonial priest or seer, in others his major duty was to be on call to treat any Indian who got sick. In his role as healer the medicine man carried a bag of secret conjures and talismans to drive away the evil spirits and rid the patient's body of bad medicine. Among the tools of his medical trade, used to the accompaniment of chants, were dried fingers, deer tails, drums, rattles and a tiny sack of curative herbs *(below)*.

There was often a genuine physical cure in the herbs. The Dakotas actually relieved asthma with the powdered roots of skunk cabbage, and the Kiowas stopped dandruff with a plant called soaproot. When nauseated, Cheyennes drank a tonic of boiled wild mint, while the Crees chewed the tiny cones of spruce trees to soothe a sore throat.

Some of the Indians' herbal cures were of dubious value; the Hopis, for

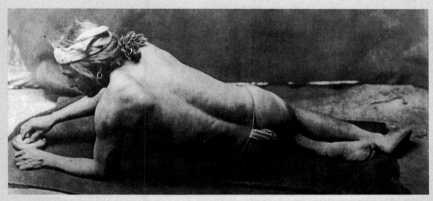

Reclining on his blanket, a Zuñi medicine man concocts a drug with mortar and pestle.

example, believed that the milky juice of the bedstraw milkweed promoted the secretion of milk in nursing mothers. Yet many a white frontiersman, like the Indians themselves, owed his life to a medicine man's cure. A Cheyenne saved William Bent from choking to death of a throat inflammation by snagging and removing the infected membrane with a hunk of sinew strung with sandburs and buffalo

tallow. And in 1834 Prince Maximilian, who was dying of scurvy at Fort Clark, was cured by the Indian remedy — eating the raw bulbs of wild garlic. In recognition of such effective medicine, eventually the authoritative *U.S. Pharmacopeia* and the *National Formulary* officially accepted 170 Indian drugs (including skunk cabbage, mint, yarrow and Indian turnip) for their intrinsic medicinal value.

Black nightshade: Comanche TB remedy

Indian turnip: Pawnee headache powder

Yarrow: Ute salve for cuts and bruises

that region in their migrations or had trading contacts there. The Mandans, who lived in the area during the first half of the 19th Century, had an especially violent version of the ceremony *(pages 142-149)*.

Although there were some variations from one tribe to another, enough overlapping elements existed so that the sun dance may be seen as one ceremony. The ritual was conducted over a period of several days during late summer or early autumn, when the earth seems most bountiful. It was sponsored by a person known as a pledger. He did not have to be a priest or medicine man but was merely an ordinary individual who had some urgent need for a spiritual favor or had been told to take on the role in a dream. A large lodge, facing east, was specially built for the ceremony, and a forked pole was erected in the center. In the fork were placed sacred objects, including a bundle of brush and a buffalo skin. The participants danced facing the center pole for long periods, staring at the sacred objects, perhaps to the point of self-hypnosis.

The most dramatic feature of the sun dance was self-mortification. The participants, usually young warriors, would go without water and food, dance to exhaustion and sometimes slash their flesh or cut off fingers. In certain tribes a young man who had vowed to undergo self-torture in the ceremony would have a medicine man cut two small holes through the skin and flesh of his upper chest on either side. The medicine man would stick wooden skewers through these holes and secure them to two ropes, the ends of which were fastened to the top of the central pole. The young warrior would then begin to dance, straining against the ropes. If he did not break free, the medicine man would finally cut his flesh to release him.

The pain that was experienced in the ritual, whether it involved bloodletting or only hours of dancing, was seen as the ultimate proof of sincerity. A Sioux, Chased by Bears, said, "A man's body is his own, and when he gives his body or his flesh, he is giving the only thing which really belongs to him." But the sacrifice and supplication in the sun dance were well invested. When the ceremony was over the Indians could again count on enjoying health, fertility and food. The world was renewed, its complex harmonies restored, its many supernatural powers revived and ready once again to work for the welfare of the tribe.

Curative art for a bed of pain

In some Southwestern Indian tribes when special help was needed from the spirits medicine men prepared beds of sand decorated with mystical designs, such as the one at right reconstructed from 19th Century reports of a secret Navaho ceremony. Crowds of tribesmen came to watch the ritual and to feast on corn meal, soup and roast mutton—all supplied by the patient. The rite began with the medicine man spreading a light layer of sand across the floor of the patient's lodge. Then, from a traditional repertory of symbols varying in size from one foot to 20 feet in diameter, he decided on the suitable motif. The one here symbolizes the gods of planting and harvest, and would have been executed in spring or fall to help bring abundant crops as well as to heal the patient. Using pigments ground from rocks, charcoal, root bark, crushed flowers and pollen, the shaman created his design by trickling the colored powders between his thumb and forefinger. When the picture—called a sand painting, or dry painting—was done, the shaman and his assistants put the patient in the middle of it, while they chanted exhortations to drive evil spirits from the body. Spectators picked up handfuls of sand to keep as talismans. When the ceremony was over, the shaman erased the last traces of the design with a long wand.

This dry painting pays homage to the Navaho gods of the four main compass points. The principal god of the east, at top, is painted white. Like the others, he suspends from his right hand a number of magic symbols, including a rattle, a Y-shaped good-luck charm and a swastikalike basket symbolizing the harvest; and he raises his relatively unencumbered left hand to protect a sacred plant, in this case the corn. The god of the south and his beanstalk are blue-gray, the god of the west and his squash plant are yellow, while the god of the north and his tobacco plant are black. If this were a true ceremonial medicine painting, the god of the east and the opening of the encircling rainbow would be at the sacred right-hand, or easterly, side of the painting. But in keeping with tribal tradition that no outsider should ever see a perfect dry painting, the shaman altered the design.

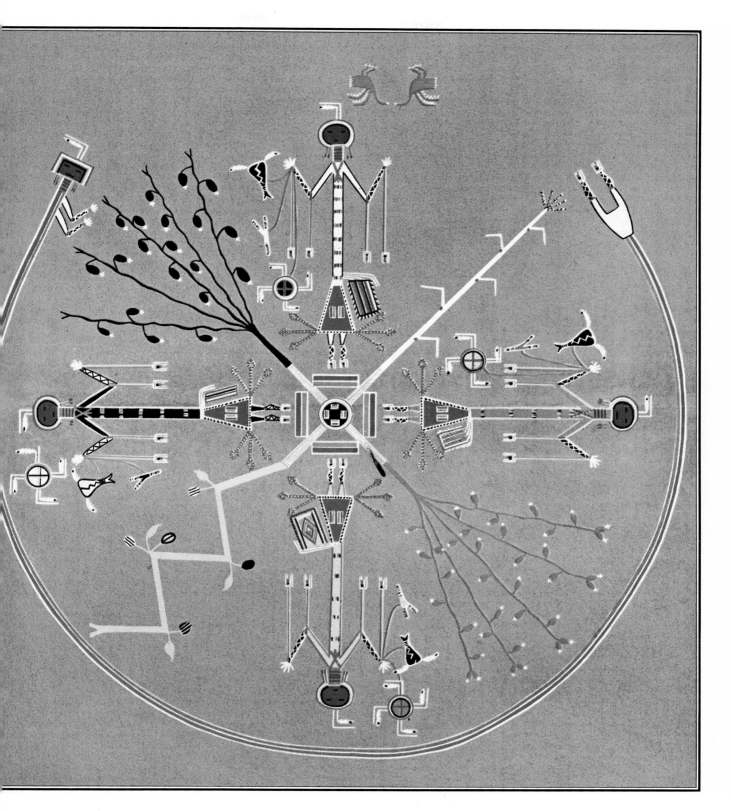

Mandan tribesmen wearing buffalo skins dance to ensure a year's supply of buffalo.

A spectacular ceremony of prayer and sacrifice

The supreme ceremony in Plains Indian culture was a festival held each summer as a renewal of the life of the tribe and its relationship to nature. One such ritual was the Mandan's *o-kee-pa,* vividly shown on the following pages in paintings made during the 1830s by Philadelphia artist George Catlin. While the so-called sun-dance ceremonies of the other plains tribes focused on fertility and the sun, the emphasis in the *o-kee-pa* was on placating the spirits of the waters, which the Mandans believed had once flooded the earth. In common with most other tribes, however, the Mandans also conducted dances to the buffalo *(below).* The elaborate *o-kee-pa* rites ended in an agonizing climax, when young men offered their flesh to the spirits in an ordeal of torture and amputation. Catlin's paintings provided whites with their first real look at the Western tribes. And his representations of some parts of the *o-kee-pa (pages 146-149)* were so shocking to Victorian eyes that they were attacked as morbid fantasies.

During the *o-kee-pa,* tribe members impersonated animal spirits whose favor the Mandans sought. The snake spirit was the source of rain, and the beaver, sometimes called the little buffalo, represented food.

Other Mandan dancers, painted to symbolize night and day, re-created through the motif of their body decorations the tribal myth of a time long ago when the earth was born and light replaced darkness.

In the *o-kee-pa* torture rite two young men hung from rawhide ropes attached by pegs skewered under their flesh. Buffalo skulls attached to their legs increased their weight, while older warriors prodded them. During this gruesome test of courage, most men fainted within 20 minutes. When they regained consciousness they dragged themselves to the masked warrior at lower right, who chopped off one or two fingers.

As a final test, the mutilated young men were expected to run a circle outside the medicine lodge. Most initiates collapsed and had to be dragged, while the thongs holding the buffalo skulls tore out of their legs. Spectators followed the rites closely, for the men who had best withstood the pain and exhaustion were candidates for future leadership.

5 | The white man's invasion

In 1829 Chief Speckled Snake of the Creeks addressed his tribe after President Andrew Jackson had urged the Indians to leave their ancestral lands in the South and move beyond the Mississippi: "Brothers! I have listened to a great many talks from our Great Father. But they always began and ended in this—'Get a little farther; you are too near me.' I have spoken."

The chief clearly foresaw the future. All Indians to the west would soon share his outrage. In 1841 the first train of covered wagons brought pioneers across the plains. Within two years more than 1,000 whites had made the journey, disrupting Indian life even though most of them continued on beyond the Rockies. Then, after the Civil War, the iron horse pushed across the West. Settlers came in torrents —eight million in two decades. Finally the Indians could not get a little farther. There was nowhere farther to go.

Civilization in the iron guise of a Northern Pacific train thrusts across Indian lands.

CIRCULAR.

TO THE OREGON EMIGRANTS.

GENTLEMEN:

It being made my duty, as Superintendent of Indian affairs, by an Act passed by the Legislature of Oregon, "to give such instructions and directions to Emigrants to this Territory, in regard to their conduct towards the natives, by the observance of which, they will be most likely to maintain and promote peace and friendship between them and the Indian tribes through which they may pass," allow me to say in the first place, that the Indians on the old road to this country, are friendly to the whites. They should be treated with kindness on all occasions. As Indians are inclined to steal, keep them out of your camps. If one or two are admitted, watch them closely. Notwithstanding the Indians are friendly, it is best to keep in good sized companies while passing through their country. Small parties of two or three are sometimes stripped of their property while on their way to this Territory, perhaps because a preceding party promised to pay the Indians for something had of them, and failed to fulfil their promise. This will show you the necessity of keeping your word with them in all cases.

There is another subject upon which I would say a few words. A number of the emigrants of 1845 took a cut off, as it is called, to shorten the route, leaving the old road; the consequence was, they were later getting in, lost their property, and many lost their lives. Some of those who reached the settlements, were so broken down by sickness, that it was some months before they recovered sufficient strength to labor.

A portion of the emigrants of 1846 took a new route, called the southern route. This proved very disastrous to all those who took it. Some of the emigrants that kept on the old road, reached this place as early as the 13th of September, with their wagons, and all got in, in good season, with their wagons and property, I believe, except a few of the last party. While those that took the southern route, were very late in reaching the settlements—they all lost more or less of their property—many of them losing all they had and barely getting in with their lives; a few families were obliged to winter in the Umpqua mountains, not being able to reach the settlements.

I would therefore recommend you to keep the old road. A better way may be found, but it is not best for men with wagons and families to try the experiment.

My remarks are brief, but I hope may prove beneficial to you.

Dated at Oregon City, this 22d of April, 1847.

GEO. ABERNETHY,
GOVERNOR OF OREGON TERRITORY AND
SUPERINTENDENT OF INDIAN AFFAIRS.

Earth Mother becomes real estate

The year was 1859, and a number of local citizens gathered at the new Blake and Williams Hotel in Denver to hear a few remarks by Little Raven, a leading chief of the Arapahos. The chief did not speak long, and some of the nuances of his statement are forever lost; the interpreter, apparently having imbibed too much firewater, fell off his chair at an early stage in the proceedings. But the import of Chief Little Raven's speech remains clear. He liked his white brethren, he said, and was glad to see that the miners were finding gold in the vicinity. But, more important, he expressed the hope that the whites would not remain too long, reminding them that all the land around young Denver belonged to the Arapahos.

The city fathers shook Little Raven's hand and gave him presents. They rather liked him; the chief was an affable and courteous man, and one of his hosts somewhat patronizingly remarked that he "handles knife and fork and smokes his cigars like a white man." But the chief's hope for the imminent departure of the whites was no more effective than a bit of down from a cottonwood tree blown in a prairie whirlwind. The whites were there to stay, and certainly the Denverites were not overly concerned with the chief's assertion that the land "belonged" to the Indians. It is to be doubted, in fact, that they paid much attention to that part of his speech. Yet the concept of land ownership was the nub of the conflict between Indians and white men as the whites increasingly encroached upon the territories that had been the exclusive domain of the Indians.

To the white Americans land was real estate — property to be sold, bought and exploited — to be tilled,

mined, grazed or lived on. Moreover, it was private property, to be held and worked by individuals. This was not what the Indians meant when they said the land belonged to them. The Indians' land belonged to all of them. A man could own horses, bows and arrows, and other pieces of hunting equipment. Similarly, his wife could own horses, or the hides that made the tipi or cooking utensils. But the land was community property. Broadly, the land was jointly held but not owned, in the white sense, by the tribe. The land was an entity to be cherished by all of the tribe's members, not something to be exploited by individual tribesmen. Protesting white incursions on tribal lands in 1806, Shawnee Chief Tecumseh defined the Indian attitude: "The way, the only way to stop this evil is for the red men to unite in claiming a common and equal right in the land, as it was at first, and should be now — for it was never divided, but belongs to all. No tribe has the right to sell, even to each other, much less to strangers. *Sell a country! Why not sell the air, the great sea, as well as the earth?*"

Indian feeling for the land ran deep. The Western Indian found himself a part of nature, subject to her rather than her conqueror. He felt the burning sun and the dust, the gentle rain, the severe blizzard. He could do nothing against the threatening thunderstorm. Above all, he saw the heights and the vast distances to be traversed only by making footprints or hoofprints on the land. The earth contained much solitude, and man did not seem a powerful factor in it; clearly the earth bore fruit after being fertilized by seed, rain, sunshine — without man's intervention. The land, to the Indian's way of thinking, was the Earth Mother, and that was one reason he did not believe that he owned her, nor that anyone else could.

As Luther Standing Bear, a Lakota Sioux, wrote: "The Lakota was a true naturist — a lover of nature. He

---

A guide to conduct on the Oregon Trail offers well-meaning but often ignored advice on getting along with the Indians. The circular was posted at points along the route.

loved the earth and all the things of the earth, the attachment growing with age. The old people came literally to love the soil and they sat or reclined on the ground with a feeling of being close to a mothering power. It was good for the skin to touch the earth and the old people liked to remove their moccasins and walk with bare feet on the sacred earth. The soil was soothing, strengthening, cleansing and healing."

While Indian love of the land was undoubtedly sincere, it was as often based on practical concerns as upon religious beliefs. To be restricted in tribal territory might require a change in the warrior way of life: the proud life of the plains, the exhilarating gallop after the buffalo, the dawn raid on an enemy's camp, the recital of brave coups before the evening fires, the women and children listening admiringly — and respectfully — at the shadowy edges of the flickers of flames.

At the Medicine Lodge council in southern Kansas in 1867, Kiowa Chief Satanta, or White Bear, said to the U.S. commissioners: "I have heard that you intend to settle us on a reservation near the mountains. When we settle down, we grow pale and die. A long time ago this land belonged to our fathers; but when I go up the river I see camps of soldiers on its banks. These soldiers cut down my timber; they kill my buffalo; and when I see that, my heart feels like bursting; I feel sorry. I have spoken." White Bear was a brilliant diplomat and a political thinker who could be described as militant-progressive. He had welcomed white traders into his country and had himself learned to play an army bugle. He was being clever when he said that "a long time ago this land belonged to our fathers," for the Kiowas, a historically minded people, well remembered that they had migrated from the North. But White Bear's wiliness was of no avail. The lands of the Kiowas and those of dozens of other tribes passed into federal hands between 1840 and 1870 under pressures fair or foul. From 1853 to 1857 alone, the peak period of acquisition, 174 million acres, for example, were transferred by the Indians.

Certainly not all Indians realized what they were selling. Some of them understood perfectly that they were relinquishing possession totally. Others believed that they were granting only hunting, fishing or grazing rights, sometimes retaining their own rights to such uses of the same territory. Still other Indians thought that they were merely giving rights of passage over the land.

Whatever the Indians believed, the push upon their ancestral territories was increasing at a geometric rate. Since 1840 white movement into the West had been accelerating. Steamboats raised their clouds of white smoke up the Missouri. Trains of ox-drawn wagons wound out along the Platte, across Wyoming and through South Pass in the Wind River Range, heading toward Oregon and California. Other trains moved out along the Arkansas and up the Canadian, through Kiowa country.

To protect the emigrants the federal government dotted Army posts throughout the West. The Indians hoped that these were temporary establishments, but the soldiers rode across the land year after year, and the brisk tattoo of "Boots and Saddles" became as much a part of the Western landscape as the cooking fires of Apache and Kiowa women — and a much-resented part. Moreover, the bluecoats were not the only permanent white riders on the plains. In 1857 the Butterfield Stage Line, carrying the overland mail, began the first regular schedule of trips across the continent, down out of Missouri, across Indian Territory, through the center of Comanche land in West Texas, through the heart of Apache country in New Mexico and Arizona, and on to Los Angeles. Aboard the stages and steamboats, as well, came added numbers of missionaries eager to convert the Indians to the ways of a Greater Spirit.

The search for gold remained as powerful a lure as the desire to win souls for the love of God. The California strike in 1848 brought thousands westward — and unforeseen tragedy. Earlier, traders had brought smallpox to the plains; now cholera, carried to the East Coast from Europe by German immigrants, traveled westward with the forty-niners and brought painful and frightening death to entire bands of Indians. An estimated half of the Cheyenne tribesmen of the upper Arkansas River area were wiped out.

Moreover, California and Colorado were not the only places where gold was to be found in the West. In the early 1860s prospectors made strikes in Bannack City and Virginia City, Montana, and fresh hordes of whites descended on the area. They still thought of the High Plains as the Great American Desert, something there solely to be crossed, and in their passage they marked it with wagon ruts and destroyed game and timber on

A chronology of broken treaties

Almost as soon as the white man set foot in America, Indian tribes began ceding tracts of their land through treaties *(below)*, in a process that quickened when the colonies became a nation. The first of 370 treaties between the United States and Indian tribes was signed in 1778 — this one with the Delawares, whose land had once stretched from Ohio to the Atlantic. In return for the Delawares' agreement to side with the U.S. against the British the treaty provided for the organization of an Indian state, with the Delaware tribe as its head.

But over the next century the presumably binding contract was rendered meaningless by a succession of 18 new treaties that pushed the Delawares into and out of Indiana, into and out of Missouri, into and out of Kansas, and finally into Oklahoma, where the few remaining tribesmen ended up with 160 acres apiece.

Further treaties also turned out to be worthless. The last one in the long series was signed on August 12, 1868, with the Nez Percés. Having given up seven eighths of their land by earlier treaties, including their beloved Wallowa Valley in Oregon, the Nez Percés agreed to yield part of their reservation to the U.S. Army in return for the right to reclaim parts of the Valley. When pioneers began to swarm into the region, the Indians begged the Great White Father to intercede, and President Ulysses S. Grant obliged with an executive order barring settlers. Then gold was found nearby. The President's order was promptly rescinded, and the Wallowa Valley was again taken away.

In 1871, with Indian power waning, Congress declared that the U.S. would no longer view Indian tribes as separate nations and would sign no more treaties. Such a declaration was hardly necessary. The Indians, who once had held all the land in America, retained only about 200,000 square miles. And the whites, who started out with no land at all, now held about three million square miles.

Dismemberment of Indian territory by treaties was underway as early as 1682 when William Penn traded goods for Delaware lands.

155

One of many missionaries who sought to harvest souls among the plains tribes, Methodist J. J. Methvin is shown in Indian Territory with some Kiowa children and the bicycle that he preferred to horses.

every road west. Raw frontier towns sprang up west of the Mississippi from Minnesota down to Arkansas, and homesteaders staked out claims. From the Southwest, ranchers—Californians, Texans, Mexicans—drove their longhorn cattle out upon the land, asserting that it was free range, open to grazing herds by any rancher who wished to use it. From the East in the mid-1860s the whites brought noisy iron monsters, puffing smoke and spitting fire, running on an iron trail. The white tide was on the flood, and it represented a fearsome challenge to the way of life of the warrior Indians of the prairies, plains and mountains.

The push of white pioneers was accompanied by impressive speeches on the floor of Congress and by ringing statements on the editorial pages of Eastern newspapers. It was, trumpeted the New York *Democratic Review* as early as 1845, "our manifest destiny to overspread the continent allotted by Providence for

the free development of our yearly multiplying millions." The *Review's* editor, John L. O'Sullivan, was writing of the proposed annexation of Texas, but the phrase manifest destiny and the thinking behind it were echoed by expansionists. "Our great mission," announced Senator John C. Calhoun of South Carolina, "is to occupy this vast [continental] domain."

Manifest destiny was in fact more a rationalization than a driving force. The frontiersman wanted land, gold, opportunity, elbowroom, the chance to show what he could do if he were not restricted by the established social and economic patterns back East. He was following a long-established principle, one taken for granted—that the native people of the Americas had no moral right to stand in the way of the expansion of European civilization.

As far back as 1516, when Europeans still had only scant and vague knowledge of the New World, the English philosopher Thomas More had coined the word Utopia and made it the title of his book about a wise socialistic people who lived in an ideal state in the newfound lands across the ocean. More described many practices of the Utopians, among them a custom they followed when their lands became overpopulated. They migrated and built a new town "under their own laws in the next land where the inhabitants have much waste and unoccupied ground."

More, ironically considered a liberal thinker, wrote further: "But if the inhabitants of that land will not dwell with them, to be ordered by their laws, then they drive them out of those bounds which they have limited and defined for themselves. And if they resist . . . then they make war against them. For they count this the most just cause of war, when any people holds a piece of ground void and vacant, to no good or profitable use, keeping others from the use and possession of it."

Nearly a century later the Dutch jurist Grotius concurred with More: "If within the territory of a people there is any deserted and unproductive soil, this also ought to be granted to foreigners, if they ask for it. Or it is right for foreigners even to take possession of such ground, for the reason that uncultivated land ought not to be considered as occupied." But Grotius added a significant reservation. Title to the land in question, he went on to say, should remain "unimpaired in favor of the original people."

To a large extent this was the policy followed by the federal government. As a general rule from the very beginning the U.S. attempted—on high administrative levels, at least—to take proper note of the Indians' rights. The government recognized Indian title to the land, and acknowledged Indian sovereignty in treaty after treaty (box, page 155). The "basis of our proceedings with the Indian nations," wrote George Washington, "has been, and shall be *justice*," a sentiment later echoed by Thomas Jefferson. If Indian lands, he declared, "had not yet been ceded by the Indians, it was necessary that the petitioners should previously purchase their right." Jefferson was enunciating the U.S. policy established by the Northwest Ordinance of 1787, the document that set the ground rules for the westward movement. It, too, declared a benign policy. "The utmost good faith," read the historic ordinance, "shall always be observed toward the Indians; their

land and property shall never be taken from them without their consent; and in their property, rights, and liberty, they shall never be invaded or disturbed, unless in just and lawful wars authorized by Congress."

These were high-minded goals, to be sure, but to the Indians it often appeared that the Great Father, as they came to call the incumbent President, tended to say one thing and do quite another. Still the feeling lingers that the disparity between lofty ideals expressed in Washington and actual procedures in the West came not so much from devious intentions on the part of the whites as from the near-impossible complexity of the problem. The nation had, after all, begun in 1789 as a small collection of people—some four million in all —strung out in a relatively thin line along the Eastern Seaboard. By the time of the administration of Andrew Jackson in 1829 the population numbered 12.5 million. The westward pressure for more land was enormous, and thus, as the years went on, the pressure upon the Indian became ever more inexorable.

The government had already been drawing up legislation dealing with Indian affairs and making treaties with the tribes before Congress set up the office of Superintendent of Indian Trade in the War Department in 1806. The new Superintendent's duty was to operate the Factory System, under which the United States supplied basic trade goods at cost to all Indians under its jurisdiction. It was a noble experiment, but commercial interests anxious to sell goods to the Indians at a profit forced its abandonment in 1822. In 1824 the Secretary of War created within his department a Bureau of Indian Affairs charged with handling, through a superintendent and agents, all matters relating to Indians. This bureau was transferred to the Department of the Interior in 1849. By this time the federal government had developed most of the policies and methods it would henceforth use in dealing with the native inhabitants.

One policy, that of removal—the purchase of Indian lands and the transposition of their former owners to new territories to the west—dated back to Colonial times. The Southeastern Indians, including the bulk of the Cherokees (box, page 164), were moved west of the Mississippi through agreements coerced by white power. Some whites, even some Indians, thought that

the tribes would actually be better off farther west, away from the bad influences of unprincipled white men, and located on reservations where they could build and develop at their own pace. There was in fact considerable merit in that argument.

The experience of the Creeks in Alabama was typical. They had agreed to submit to state laws; in 1831 a Creek chief lodged an official complaint that 1,500 settlers were laying out farms on their lands. Washington's response was that the Creeks would be removed to a reservation in the West, and in 1832 they signed a treaty surrendering their Alabama territory. The treaty included a provision that individual Creeks might remain on small holdings in the state. Whites rapidly swindled these remaining Creeks out of their land with a classic bag of tricks: getting the owner drunk and having him sign a contract of sale; bribing an Indian to impersonate the owner of a particular plot and to make his mark on papers of sale; outright forging of documents; rigging procedures in the state courts. By 1835 there were virtually no Creek landowners left in Alabama and, after an uprising, the remnants of the tribe were forced to join their brothers in Indian Territory.

The reservation was far from an ideal solution. A reservation in its original concept was in no sense a concentration camp, for an Indian might leave it at will. In fact, he had to leave it, and frequently did, in pursuit of game. The reservation was land set aside, guaranteed as a homeland, supposedly free of white pre-emption or trespass. Often in a treaty or agreement setting up a reservation a tribe would cede other land to the United States. In 1861, for example, the Arapahos, Chief Little Raven's tribe, gave up virtually all their lands in Nebraska, Kansas, Colorado and Wyoming and retained only a reservation tract in eastern Colorado. Certain other considerations, in addition to cash payments, were often proffered by the government. These might include the government's providing blacksmiths, millers, schoolteachers and farming teachers, as well as appropriate equipment. Such agreements frequently specified that a money consideration would not be paid in a lump sum but as an annuity of food and supplies, plus small amounts of cash to spend with a licensed trader.

In theory, the policy was benevolent; in practice, many felt, the annuity system encouraged indolence on the part of the Indians. This was in a measure true, and

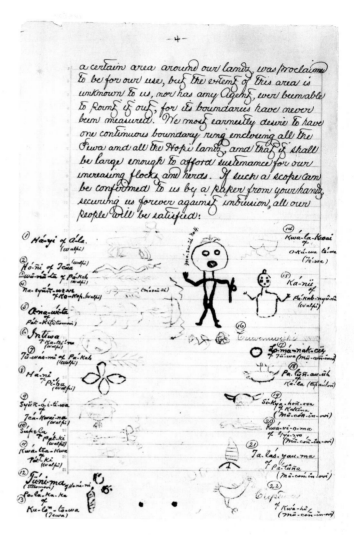

scarcely surprising. The Indians, wrote the Superintendent of Indian Affairs for Oregon Territory, "are not inclined to industry and economy while their wants can be otherwise supplied." For that the Indian could hardly be blamed, but there were other flaws in the system as well. The supplies shipped under the annuity plan were frequently of poor quality, or ill-adapted to Indian needs. Moreover, if the annuities failed to arrive, either through bureaucratic mismanagement or outright theft by white officials or traders, Indians starved.

Underlying all these procedures was the conviction that the only way to pacify the warrior Indians was to transform them into farmers. Peaceful husbandmen were what they should become, turning away from the red man's ways of hunting and war to the white man's

At a site appropriately known as Camp Supply a tribe in the Indian Territory gathers its horses in a circle to await the government annuity — a regular issue of flour, sugar, coffee, dried fruit and vegetables. These handouts were intended to discourage the roaming life style of the buffalo hunters.

These two somber Mandans were among 31 survivors from their tribe of 1,600 that had been ravaged by smallpox in 1837. The same disease killed about half the 4,000 neighboring Arikaras and Hidatsas.

plow and furrow. But the policy was never going to work. Few warriors were interested in farming; it was woman's work. Moreover, even if they had been willing to farm, the East Coast agricultural techniques the government attempted to teach the Indians were rarely viable on the arid plains.

A key figure in U.S. policy was the Indian agent, an employee of the Bureau of Indian Affairs charged with the sometimes dangerous task of issuing supplies and annuities to tribes that might be hostile, and of trying to see that both sides lived up to treaties. If the Indians trusted the man, and if he in turn sympathized with them, the ideals of policy might on occasion mesh with reality. But good agents were rare; William Bent *(box, page 169)* was one of the great ones. His kind were few; those mediocre or worse were all too common.

Another of the good agents, on a par with Bent, was a former mountain man named Thomas Fitzpatrick, whom the Indians called Broken Hand. Appointed in 1846 as agent for the tribes of the Arkansas, Platte and Kansas Rivers, Fitzpatrick was one of the few men in the country who knew the seriousness of his job; the tribes in question included many of the most warlike Indians in the West: Sioux, Snakes, Arapahos. At his advice the government established a fort at Laramie, the site of an old fur-trading post near the junction of the Laramie and the North Platte Rivers in what is now southeastern Wyoming.

In the spring of 1850 Fitzpatrick saw more than 50,000 gold seekers move past Fort Laramie en route to the lodes of Oregon and California, leaving in their wake devastation on the plains: dying grass, thousands of dead buffalo, deaths among Indians and whites alike from hunger and from the cholera that the wagon trains brought with them. The Sioux nonetheless remained quiet. "I have had no reason to complain of the Indians or their conduct for the past two years," Fitzpatrick reported. But the Indians' complaints were numerous, and even the normally peaceful Cheyennes, who were also in Fitzpatrick's charge, were beginning to harass the emigrant trains. It was only a matter of time, Fitzpatrick feared, before the tribes would rise in wrath against the white settlements and one another; moreover, he felt that the Indians deserved compensation for the damage to their lands and the decimation of the buffalo herds, that the "justice" of which George Washington had

spoken little more than 50 years earlier should be done.

Fitzpatrick persuaded Congress — somewhat to his own astonishment — to authorize funds to hold a conference at Laramie of all the tribes in his jurisdiction. His object was to ensure the safety of the emigrant trains by winning from the Indians a right of passage across their lands and, equally important, to define the boundaries of their own territories to prevent warfare that might inflame the entire plains. Amazingly, representatives of most of the tribes came to Laramie in the autumn of 1851, including bands from the Sioux and the Crows, who were deadly enemies. Even a delegation of Shoshoni, enemies of the Sioux as well as of the Cheyennes, traveled from their hunting grounds to the west. The Comanches and Kiowas refused to come from their territory to the south, saying that they owned many horses and there were too many horse thieves in the Fort Laramie country. But 10,000 representatives of nine nations were present; it was the greatest assemblage of Indians ever seen on the continent. One white observer understandably sighed for the presence of a "painter or daguerreotypist." It was nothing short of a miracle that the Indians of the central and northern plains, each tribe vaunting its bravery and power, did gather and did sign a treaty with sincere intentions.

Equally miraculous, the tribes did accept boundaries for their various hunting grounds — this in the face of the fact that no Sioux or Crow had ever before admitted that the other tribe had any right to exist at all anywhere on earth. Thus the United States apparently established peace on the plains by delimiting the land-use rights of the tribes. Among other provisions, the Indians agreed that the government might establish roads and Army posts in their territory, and as recompense they would receive annuities to the value of $50,000 per year for 50 years. The Senate, during the ratification process, later reduced the 50 years down to 10 (or 15 at the discretion of the President).

There was good faith on both sides. Yet even such a treaty as this could not work for long. The whites still thought of the lands of the Plains tribes as territory to cross; they did not anticipate how many thousands of whites would cross it in the years ahead — and, indeed, how many would finally decide to settle on it. Nor did the Indians. They were willing to tolerate a few Army posts and a few travelers, but not the onrush of great

A lesson in civilization from the Indians

One of the most sweeping eviction proceedings in all history began in 1829, when President Andrew Jackson asked Congress for legislation to remove the Indians of the South to "an ample district west of the Mississippi . . . to be guaranteed to the Indian tribes as long as they shall occupy it." Jackson's generous phraseology could not in any way conceal the misery implicit in the plan. By fiat 60,000 Indians would lose their wooded homeland and be consigned to the unknown. Their destination was a section of the treeless southern plains that came to be known as Indian Territory and would eventually be the state of Oklahoma.

Ironically, the very Indians suffering this expulsion had already shown a willingness to accept white culture and to live in peace. For good reason the Cherokee, Chickasaw, Choctaw, Creek and Seminole Indians were known as the Five Civilized Tribes. At that time many of them were living in log cabins, wearing homespun clothing, tending livestock and plowing fields with oxen. Considerable intermarriage with whites was steadily furthering acculturation, and most tribal leaders could read and write English and comprehend the law.

But since Jackson felt — and Congress agreed — that assimilation was impossible, all of the Southern tribes had to go, even the Cherokees, the most advanced of all. In 1838 the bulk of the Cherokee Nation was rounded up at gunpoint from their farms in Tennessee and Georgia, herded into camps, and moved west under a military guard. During the

The Cherokee Female Seminary outside Tahlequah sent graduates to white colleges.

forced march westward, one out of every four Indians died of dysentery, measles, whooping cough or some other ailment. An eyewitness reported "even aged females, apparently nearly ready to drop into the grave, were traveling with heavy burdens attached to their backs."

When they reached northeastern Oklahoma, only 14,000 Cherokees had survived. They should have been a broken people. But miraculously they rallied and renewed their efforts to build a society based on the best features of white civilization. Establishing a capital in Tahlequah, they restored their three-part government, with an executive branch, a legislature and courts of law overseen by a five-man supreme court. They continued their former practice of publishing a

newspaper in both English and their own language (unique among Indians, the Cherokees had developed their own alphabet). They also set up a system of elementary schools and seminaries—equivalent to high schools —for men and women *(above)*.

But even as the plains began to seem like home, the whites moved closer, eyed the fertile prairie and demanded that the Indian Territory be opened to white settlement. It would not be long before the Cherokees' land would, in the words of their own newspaper, the *Cherokee Advocate,* once more "excite the cupidity and moisten the lips of those who have not failed to filch by fraud or rob by superior power of their native inheritance, every Indian community with whom they have come in contact."

crowds of people onto their beloved Earth Mother.

It took no more than three years and a minor incident to rend the Laramie treaty asunder. In the summer of 1854 the tribes assembled outside Fort Laramie for the distribution of the annuities. A Sioux brave shot and slaughtered a lame cow that had either strayed from an emigrant train or had been abandoned. Its owner, hoping for recompense, complained to the Laramie commander and a hotheaded young lieutenant, John L. Grattan, eagerly set forth to arrest the offending Indian. This was something the Army had no right to do under the Fort Laramie treaty, which provided that both whites and Indians were required to punish their own malefactors. The Indians, after much parleying and protesting, refused to turn over the Sioux warrior to the soldiers. Grattan ordered a volley fired; a major chief was mortally wounded, and in the battle that followed Grattan and his entire 30-man party were wiped out. Grattan was found with 24 arrows in his body. The Army naturally sent punitive expeditions, the Indians naturally retaliated, and the peace brought by the Fort Laramie treaty was destroyed.

The Laramie experiment, a genuine effort at establishing mutually agreeable boundaries among equals, was of course not the only government effort to fail. One of the saddest experiments tried under the reservation-and-removal policy was that at Bosque Redondo, New Mexico, with the Navahos during the Civil War. A key figure in this series of events was Christopher (Kit) Carson, perhaps the best-known combination scout, guide, trader, hunter, trapper and soldier in the early West. At the time, Carson was a soldier, serving under the command of Brigadier James Carleton, a hardfisted officer of the old school.

The Navahos, cousins of the Apaches, were fighters, but had learned small-scale farming, sheep raising and weaving from the Pueblo Indians and the Spaniards. In 1861 and 1862, seeing the whites engaged in a bloody struggle, they began to raid and loot American and Mexican settlements. The United States government, having little success in its greater war east of the Mississippi, and with its patience consequently limited, determined to dispose of the Navaho problem harshly and decisively. The troops would drive them out of their rugged desert country in northern Arizona and New Mexico and force them east to a reservation on the Pecos River at a place called Bosque Redondo (meaning round grove of trees), where Fort Sumner was established and where a band of dissident Apaches had already been concentrated.

Colonel Kit Carson, at the head of the 1st Cavalry of New Mexico Volunteers, took the field against the Navahos in the summer of 1863 and marched out into the high plateau country, which is cut with canyons and dotted with rocky peaks. The hinterland had been little explored by whites and poorly mapped. Carson hired Ute spies and scouts to guide him and in the process came up with an ingenious idea for helping to alleviate the Navaho problem. He proposed to General Carleton that his Utes be allowed to keep some of the Navahos they captured. These could be sold to citizens of New Mexico as domestic or farm help and thus "civilized" would be no more trouble to the government. Fortunately, the idea was vetoed.

In fact, Carson had badly misjudged the nature of the campaign that lay ahead of him. He did not realize how vulnerable his opponents were, nor did the Navahos themselves. The land on which they lived barely furnished the needs of human existence, and an invasion by a white army meant their doom.

Carson established his troops at Fort Canby, at the mouth of Canyon Bonita, near the present Arizona-New Mexico line. And at another post farther west, called Pueblo Colorado, he began to execute a scorched-earth policy. "When about two hours from Camp," Carson reported on his first major foray, "we found and destroyed about seventy acres of corn. Three hours afterwards encamped in Wheat and Corn fields. The Wheat (about fifteen acres) we fed to the animals and the Corn (about Fifty acres) was destroyed." On that trip he laid waste several more fields, killed a few Indians, captured several, took 43 head of horses and mules, captured one herd of a hundred sheep and goats, and another of a thousand head.

Later the same month he swept through the Navaho homeland destroying crops, including, he reported, "large quantities of pumpkins and beans" and in a large bottom "not less than one hundred acres of as fine corn as I have ever seen." The Navahos were too scattered and ill-organized to oppose him. They knew that they were beaten, but they were reluctant to surrender, fearing that the United States intended to exterminate them.

Buffalo carcasses, brought down by long-range rifles, litter the prairie. When the hides were stripped off, the meat often would be left to rot.

"The buffalo is gone, and the red hunters must die of hunger"

To the Plains Indians, supplying buffalo hides to the white man seemed like good business at first. They always had hunted for their own needs, and merely by killing more buffalo they could obtain guns, tobacco, whiskey and other goods. By the 1840s they were delivering at least 100,000 hides a year to traders, who shipped the pelts to Eastern markets to be sold as lap robes.

This increase in hunting by the Indians began to whittle down the total number of buffalo, though there were still an estimated 50 million at midcentury. Soon, however, white men took over the bulk of the hunting and began to kill the animals with devastating efficiency. Approaching a herd downwind and hiding 200 to 600 yards away behind a rock or shrub, they could pick off the animals without alarming the grazing herd. One hunter might bag 150 buffalo in a day. Then the skinners stripped the animals and pegged the pelts to the ground to dry *(below)*. The tongues were smoked and sent East to be sold as a delicacy.

By the 1860s the large-scale destruction of the herds by professional hunters, as well as the steady but less systematic shooting of the animals by pioneers traveling westward in covered wagons, was beginning to disrupt the migration patterns of the buffalo. This in turn forced the Plains Indians to move away from their traditional hunting grounds in order to follow the animal that was crucial to their very lives. But no matter where they went the Indians were almost immediately followed by hunters, soldiers and pioneers. As Sioux Chief White Cloud lamented, "Wherever the whites are established, the buffalo is gone, and the red hunters must die of hunger."

At a hunting camp in Texas buffalo hides are stretched out to dry on the ground, and the animals' tongues are hung from the rack at right.

Through that fall Carson continued his campaign, not only taking livestock and destroying crops, but burning villages as the Indians fled before him. He chopped down many orchards of peach trees. As cold weather came, the Navahos began to surrender, still highly suspicious. Then more and more gave up and came in. They were destitute, some almost naked. They had been living on piñon nuts and had been afraid even to build fires for warmth lest the soldiers discover them. Carson, whose command had destroyed two million pounds of Navaho grain by the end of the year, seems suddenly to have understood what he had done; he began to write back East almost frantically for warm blankets and rations for the Indians.

In January 1864 he invaded the last great Navaho stronghold, Canyon de Chelly, which had seemed inaccessible and formidable, but proved to be defenseless. Some of Carson's command had frozen feet; the Navahos had a number of frozen corpses. There was nowhere now for the Indians to go, and they surrendered in large groups, as soon as they became convinced that they would not be killed.

What came to be known to the Navahos as the Long Walk began—southeast through the Tunicha Mountains and the Zuñi Mountains, through the rough country to the Rio Grande, up the river to Santa Fe, thence southeast again and out on the plains into strange country. The Army took them in convoys, with a few wagons for the old and sick, the rest walking. Food and clothing were inadequate. One group of 2,500 lost 126 members from cold and malnutrition before they left Fort Canby and lost 197 on the march. Other convoys lost people from the same causes and even had some stolen into slavery by other Indians, whites or Mexicans with old grudges against the Navahos. At the end of the trek was Bosque Redondo, where Carson had been appointed supervisor.

The reservation might have been adequate for the Apaches already there; it would not support the added burden of more than 8,000 Navahos. The situation proved hopeless. The Navahos were too crowded. They felt exiled in a strange land. They did not wish to live with the Apaches. Basically pastoral, they could not adapt to the sedentary routine of soil tilling.

Under the watchful eyes of guards, the captives dug 30 miles of irrigation ditches and plowed and planted 2,000 acres of land, mostly with corn. Their efforts were fruitless. Cutworms attacked their corn, and the entire crop was killed the first year; nearly as much was lost the second year. Then the Pecos River overflowed and destroyed their irrigation system.

Failing to grow their own food, the Indians had to depend on rations for survival. These were often scarce and unpalatable; the Navahos were unaccustomed to a diet based on wheat flour. Nor could they find the acorns, wild potatoes and cedar berries of their native land. The Indians also hated the alkaline Pecos water.

To add to these miseries there was not enough firewood on the reservation. Whatever the weather, the Indians walked 12 miles to find mesquite roots for fuel and then lacerated their backs carrying them on the return trip. If days were hard, nights were little better. The wind whipped through their flimsy shelters of brush and canvas; at times they were huddled in holes dug in the ground. The Apaches meanwhile raided Navaho camps and stole their blankets and clothing.

They dreamed of their canyons and mountains. In the fourth year they planted almost nothing and began to slip away. To its credit the government admitted the failure of this reservation experiment; finally it allowed the Navahos to go back to their homeland.

North of Navaho country the white settlers continued to invade Indian territory in droves, hungry for cheap land and the freedom of the big sky. Invasion of the plains was already threatening the free life of the warrior tribes, and now the tribes were not prepared to stand still for the destruction of their way of life. Inexplicably the whites were blind to the portent of the smoke rising on the plains. After a purchase of tribal lands President Millard Fillmore had confidently addressed Congress: "A large tract of valuable territory has thus been opened for settlement and cultivation, and all danger of collision with these powerful and warlike bands has been happily removed." That optimistic statement was in total contrast to one by Sioux Chief Red Cloud, who would play an important role in the coming tragedy on the plains: "What voice was first sounded on this land? The voice of the red people who had but bows and arrows. What has been done in my country I did not want, did not ask for it; white people going through my country. When the white man comes in my country he leaves a trail of blood behind him."

The most thankless job in the West

No man was ever more caught in the middle than the Indian agent. Appointed by the federal government to live among the Indians, he dispensed annuities that often did not arrive on time. Singlehandedly, he was supposed to restrain the legions of traders who cheated the Indians and illegally sold them whiskey. He was expected to teach the Indian how to farm in areas that were often too arid for agriculture—and where, in any case, the government often supplied the wrong kinds of farm implements. It was also the agent's job to keep white settlers off Indian land. But in this capacity, too, he was practically powerless, since the government steadily undermined his role by giving in to the demands of land-hungry pioneers. For all this he was paid less than a village postmaster. Not surprisingly, most agents were ineffective or plain dishonest, and the few who were committed to the job ultimately failed.

No one sensed the paradoxes of the position more keenly than William Bent *(above)*. He was unusually well-qualified to be an Indian agent, for he had lived among the Cheyennes and Arapahos as a respected trader for years (the great Indian peace council on the Arkansas River had been held near his fort in 1840). He spoke their languages and was married to a Cheyenne woman. When the Pikes Peak gold rush of 1858-1859 brought thousands of miners into Cheyenne and Arapaho territory, the Indians appealed to Bent as the one white man they really trusted. To Bent's surprise government officials responded to his concern for

William Bent sits with Arapaho Chief Little Raven (left) and the chief's three children.

the Indians by appointing him agent to the tribes. In this post he fervently pleaded the Indians' cause, writing to Washington that "a desperate war of starvation and extinction is imminent and inevitable, unless prompt measure shall prevent it." But Bent came to realize that the power of the white man was too great to be resisted. After arranging for a new treaty that would greatly reduce the Indians' lands he resigned in frustration.

For every Bent there were many more corrupt agents. Samuel Colley, a Cheyenne agent, had his son join him on the reservation. The young man arrived with about 30 cows to his name and, presumably following the example of his father, amassed a small fortune of $25,000 within two years by selling goods that rightfully

belonged to the Indians. At another reservation a new agent arrived in 1869 to take up his post and found that his predecessor had not been seen for a month. There was no money, and there were $14,000 worth of unpaid bills. None of the annuities promised to the Indians in return for their land had been distributed to them in four years.

William Barnhart, the agent at the Umatilla Reservation, had to be replaced for killing an Indian. His successor, Timothy Davenport, was surprised to find a salaried schoolteacher but no school. This enterprising fellow had been acting as a private secretary to Barnhart; he openly admitted to Davenport "the place of agent at Umatilla is worth $4,000 a year." An agent's salary was $1,500.

The Minnesota Massacre: Sioux on the warpath

Bishop Henry B. Whipple

Colonel Henry H. Sibley

In 1862, when North and South were locked in Civil War, the frontier state of Minnesota felt the fury of an even more fundamental internal conflict. The Santees, an eastern branch of the Sioux Nation, having endured a decade of traumatic change on a narrow reservation along the upper Minnesota River, launched the first great attack in the Indian wars that would rack the West for many years to come.

Eleven years earlier the tribe had ceded 24 million acres of hunting ground for a lump sum of $1,665,000 and the promise of future cash annuities. Some genuine attempts had been made to ease the Indians into the society of whites. Indian families were offered brick houses (right) if they would agree to give up their hunting way of life and begin farming. Many of those who accepted this option continued to live in tipis, however, and used the brick houses for storage. In addition to the disruption of their culture the Sioux gradually found themselves dependent on trade goods, which made them easy prey for white merchants, who gave credit and then collected di-

rectly from the government. Thus the Indians saw little of the annuities for which they had sold their birthright. Their anger finally reached the flash point when, following a winter of near starvation, the annual payment failed to arrive on time.

Bursting from their reservation, they killed more than 450 settlers in the region before they were defeated by a hastily assembled force of raw recruits led by Colonel Henry Sibley (above, right). Even the Episcopal Bishop of Minnesota, Henry Whipple (above, left), a man of compassion and understanding who later pleaded with President Lincoln to spare the lives of most of the defeated miscreants, described the killing as "the most fearful Indian massacre in history."

After the uprising many horrified whites adopted the precept that naked force was the only law Western Indians could learn—while others like Whipple argued for peace. There followed alternate fighting and truce, which the U.S. Cavalry set out, once and for all, to end in 1876 in a great battle with the Sioux at Little Bighorn.

The Sioux warriors spared some whites, among them a settler named Myers (waving in the background) who had been friendly to them.

Momentous events often have trivial beginnings, and the Minnesota Massacre was no exception. On Sunday, August 17, 1862, four Sioux braves —named Killing Ghost, Breaking Up, Brown Wing and Runs Against Something When Crawling— were walking back to their reservation after a hunting trip. They spotted some hens' eggs in a nest near the cottage of a settler named Robinson Jones. When one of the braves picked up the eggs another told him to leave them alone because they belonged to a white man. Angered, the first smashed them on the ground and accused the other of cowardice. "I'm not afraid of whites," was the reply, "and to prove it I'll kill one." By the

time that boast had run its course Jones, his wife, his daughter and two neighbors had been shot dead, and the braves were headed pell-mell toward the reservation on stolen horses.

After they told what they had done, a council was hastily called from among several Sioux villages. All night the chiefs deliberated. Either they could meekly turn the murderers over to the whites or they could mount a general war. Arguments were advanced on both sides. Little Crow, the most prominent of the tribal leaders, warned that there was no way to beat the whites. "Kill one, two, ten and ten times ten will come to kill you"—a prophetic warning, but it was not heeded. Per-

suaded by the other chiefs, Little Crow ordered an attack for the following morning on the government agency near Redwood Falls. According to later testimony, "Parties formed and dashed away in the darkness to kill the settlers." With surprise on their side the Indians met little resistance. Although they took some prisoners and even spared a few settlers whom they regarded as friends, nearly every white they could find was killed on the spot.

After the uprising was put down lurid tales of terror and cruelty were chronicled by a local artist, John Stevens, in a panorama of crudely executed paintings that traveled around the country. These pictures are from that series.

While threshing wheat, a homesteader is surrounded by a party of warriors. He was killed and scalped and his horses ridden off.

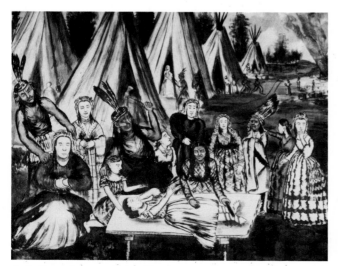

As Indians threaten their white captives, one squaw slashes open the legs of a young girl in the presence of her mother (left).

Captured by a band of the rampaging Sioux, Julia Smith tries to protect her mother from being shot. Both died from the same bullet.

Refugees of the onslaught, a party of missionaries, teachers and their families rests in the grass during the dash eastward on the fifth day of the massacre. Warned by friendly warriors, they got away just in time.

174

A mother and her children are reunited after a harrowing escape. Eleven-year-old Merton Eastlick carried his baby brother 50 miles to safety after his father and two brothers were killed and his wounded mother had told him to flee. Miraculously, Mrs. Eastlick lived to rejoin her sons.

Many victims of the Minnesota Massacre were those who bore no guilt for provoking the Sioux other than that they were white and they were there. For those teachers and missionaries *(left)* who had devoted their lives to helping the Indian the uprising was a particularly cruel setback. The women and children of many families were unprotected because the men were off fighting for the Union cause. But the wrath of the Indians fell most heavily on persons who had flagrantly abused them in the past. One prime target was Andrew Myrick, a detestable storekeeper who earlier in the summer had refused the Indians further credit with the remark, "If they are hungry, let them eat grass." His corpse was found with its mouth crammed with grass.

Four weeks after the rampage began, the Sioux were decisively beaten by troops and local militiamen led by Colonel Sibley. Among the 2,000 Indian men, women and children who surrendered, 392 prisoners were quickly tried and 307 sentenced to death. Sibley favored execution at once. But Bishop Whipple of Minnesota went to Washington to plead for clemency—an act that earned him general condemnation from his white parishioners. "I ask," wrote the distraught clergyman in a formal appeal, "that the people shall lay the blame of this great crime where it belongs, and rise up with one voice to demand the reform of an atrocious Indian system, which has always garnered for us the same fruit of anguish and blood." After weighty appraisal, President Lincoln commuted most of the sentences but sustained the death penalty for proven rapists and murderers.

On the day after Christmas 1862, 38 Sioux warriors were brought to a specially built gallows and hanged simultaneously. "As the platform fell," reported an eyewitness, "there was one not loud but prolonged cheer from the soldiery and citizens." However, three of the leaders of the massacre were absent. Little Crow himself had escaped into North Dakota. Two other chiefs, shown at left, fled to Canada and were later kidnapped and returned to the U.S., where they were duly executed. Little Crow returned to Minnesota the next summer and was shot from ambush by a farmer while picking berries.

Captured Sioux Chiefs Shakopee (*top*) and Medicine Bottle await the gallows in Minnesota. After the massacre they sought sanctuary in Canada but were drugged there and smuggled back across the border tied to a dogsled.

Shakopee and Medicine Bottle hang on the gallows at Fort Snelling. As he went to his death, Shakopee is said to have heard a train whistle and to have declared, "As the white man comes in, the Indian goes out."

A mist shrouds the walled compound beside the Minnesota River, where 1,700 Sioux who did not participate in the massacre spent a desperate winter before being driven onto a reservation farther west.

In the aftermath of the Civil War, Indian policy was in utter disarray. On the frontier, troops were combating plains tribes, who fought an intermittent but ferocious guerrilla war against white encroachment. Atrocities and massacres by both sides ignited passions and troubled consciences, splitting whites and Indians alike into war and peace factions. In Colorado a mass meeting of citizens subscribed $5,000 to pay for Indian scalps, specifying a bounty of $25 for those "with ears on." In Washington a strong political coalition favored appeasement, for humanitarian reasons and because they felt the nation could not afford a war. To this end, in 1867, Congress voted to create a peace commission. Its membership —divided between civilian humanitarians and military hardliners, like General William Tecumseh Sherman (below, third from left)—reflected its conflicting approaches. If the commission could not secure peace by negotiation, four regiments were authorized "for the purpose of conquering the desired peace."

Peace commission members pose for a picture with an Indian woman during treaty talks at Fort Laramie in 1868.

Cheyenne Village Aug. 29th/64.

Maj. Colley.

Sir

We received a letter
from Bent. wishing us to make peace.
We held a consel in regard to it all
came to the conclusion to make
peace with you providing you make peace
with the Kiowas, Commenches Arr—
opahoes Apaches and Siouxs.
We are going to send a messenger to the
Kiowas and to the other nations
about our going to make with you.
We heard that you some prisoners
in Denver. We have seven prisoners
of you which we are willing to give
up providing you give up yours
There are three war parties out yet and
two of Arropahoes. they been out some
time and expect now soon.
When we held this counsel there
were few Arropahoes and Siouxs
present. we want true news from
you. in return, that is a letter

Black Kittle &
other Chiefs

Brought to McLean Sunday Sept
4th 1864 by One Eye —

The bloodstained road to war

During the early winter of 1864 white men in Denver were celebrating a great military victory. Headlines in the city's *Rocky Mountain News* of December 8 trumpeted the exciting story.

GREAT BATTLE WITH INDIANS!

THE SAVAGES DISPERSED!

500 INDIANS KILLED

OUR LOSS 9 KILLED, 38 WOUNDED

Under one final headline — "Full Particulars" — the paper gave an account of a battle that had taken place nine days before on Sand Creek in eastern Colorado. The primary source of the news was a brief report by Colonel J. M. Chivington, a former Methodist minister, now commander of the Military District of Colorado. In it he said: "I, at daylight this morning, attacked a Cheyenne village of one hundred and thirty lodges, from nine hundred to one thousand warriors strong. We killed Chiefs Black Kettle, White Antelope and Little Robe, and between four and five hundred other Indians; captured between four and five hundred ponies and mules." For his own troops, he had praise: "All did nobly."

On December 12 the newspaper noted that Colonel Chivington, whom it now called the "old war horse," would be in town that very evening. The 3rd Regiment, which had made up the larger portion of his forces, would soon follow. A letter from one of the troopers, printed the same day, exulted: "We have met the enemy and they are ours. The 'Bloodless Thirdsters' have gained the greatest victory, west of the Missouri, over the savages." The writer added this

comforting opinion: "We have completely broken up the tribe, and think the settlers will not be further molested by them." When the men of the regiment paraded through Denver they were cheered as the saviors of the frontier. Some of them appeared between acts of a performance at the theater, where they showed off Indian scalps and described their brave deeds to applause.

But the "particulars" provided by the *Rocky Mountain News* turned out to be far from full. Missing from the story was a curious addendum that Colonel Chivington had passed on to the commanding general of the Department of Kansas: "I cannot conclude this report," wrote Chivington, "without saying that the conduct of Capt. Silas S. Soule, Company D, First Cavalry of Colorado, was at least ill-advised, he saying that he thanked God that he had killed no Indians, and like expressions." The final word did not seem at all in harmony with the exultant tone of the original report. And that was not the only jarring thing omitted from the original story. A few officers and men were in anguish over the part they had played in the engagement; some of them wrote to officials in Washington. From their letters and those of sympathetic traders and agents a different picture of the battle began to emerge. And before the month was out the pioneers of the Colorado Territory were stunned to learn that the Sand Creek affair would be the subject of investigations by Congress and the Army. The charges: Chivington's men had murdered Indians who thought they were under Army protection; most of the Indian dead were women and children; Indian bodies had been mutilated.

As it turned out, Chivington's report proved to be both incomplete and, said eyewitnesses, in most other ways an outright lie. Two traders, John Smith and Edmond Guerrier, who had been in the camp at the time of the attack, stated that the village had between 80 and 100 lodges with no more than 500 people. Two

On August 29, 1864, Cheyenne Chief Black Kettle dictated the letter at left proposing peace. Three months later 123 Cheyennes were massacred at Sand Creek.

thirds of them were women and children. The weight of other testimony showed that most of the Indian casualties were not warriors. Gradually the Indian side of the story began to emerge.

Black Kettle and his Cheyennes had indeed come in peace, were attempting to live and camp according to the soldiers' instructions and believed themselves to be under the guardianship of the government. In fact, for several years Black Kettle had been foremost among plains chiefs in trying to persuade his own people not to go on the warpath against the whites. It was no easy position for him to take, nor had it been very successful. Only two years before, the Sioux in Minnesota had gone on a bloody rampage *(pages 170-179)* in anger against white encroachments and promises broken. Since then more and more settlers had followed the miners into Indian lands and built roads and farms on the old buffalo ranges as far west as Colorado.

Beginning in the late spring of 1864 peace seekers like Black Kettle were pushed into the background, and the war faction of the High Plains Indians prevailed. They swooped down on isolated settlements, emigrant caravans and supply trains. For over a month they closed down the main road between the East and Denver; mail had to go south by ship, across Panama and back from San Francisco. The people of Denver heard true stories of atrocities — attacks, rapes, mutilations, the capture of women and children. In June a settler named Ward Hungate, his wife, a 4-year-old daughter and a baby were killed on Box Elder Creek, only 30 miles southeast of the city. Their bodies, scalped and cut up, were brought into Denver, and many townsmen saw them. Emotions ripened and anger mounted. With such hostile preliminaries the tragedy of Sand Creek became almost inevitable.

Even some of Black Kettle's own Cheyennes had been raiding. Yet many other Cheyennes had done no killing, and Black Kettle himself had remained a spokesman for peace. In September, only two months before the Sand Creek Massacre, he had gone with six other Cheyenne chiefs to Camp Weld, near Denver, to meet in conference with Territorial Governor John Evans, Colonel Chivington and other officials. Black Kettle, one of the most important among the Indians at Camp Weld, admitted to the white men that he had been unable to control the young warriors, but he asserted that

Indian chiefs ride a wagon into Denver to negotiate peace in 1864. Despite months of Indian raids in the area, many citizens turned out to greet them. This was two months before the Sand Creek Massacre.

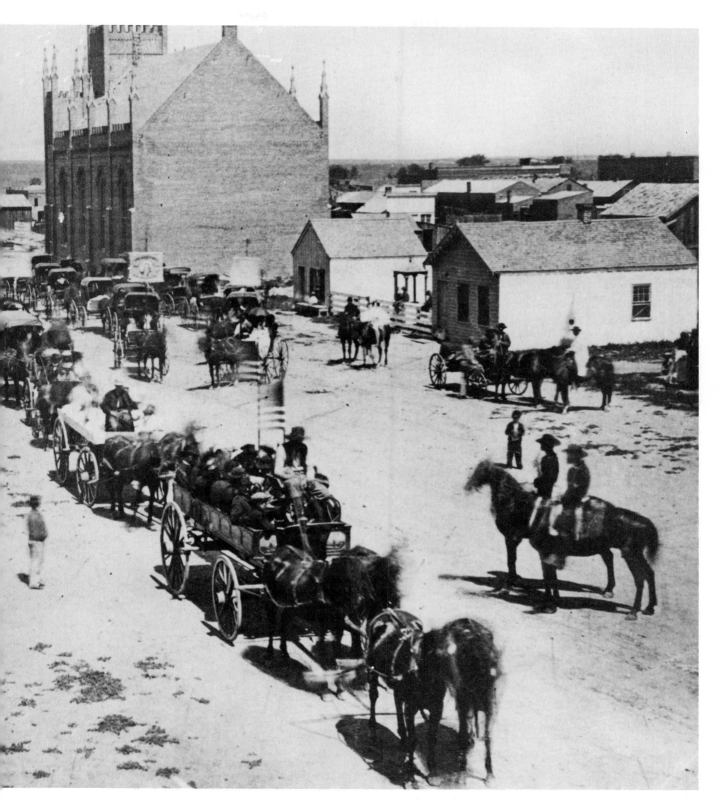

A U.S. officer and a frontiersman examine the scalped corpse of a hunter caught by Cheyennes. So bloody was Indian revenge for Sand Creek that 8,000 troops were pulled from the Civil War and sent West.

he would try to do so and sincerely wished for peace.

Some of the other pacifist chiefs at the Camp Weld conference led their bands to Fort Lyon on the Arkansas River as a token of surrender. The post commander gave them rations for some days, then ordered them to move on to a location where they could support themselves by hunting. The Indians could sense no threat of war in what the white soldier said, no clue for the Indians to what Chivington really had in store. They camped on Sand Creek along a large bend in the course of the stream. Black Kettle and White Antelope discussed the matter in their own bands, where warminded warriors still prevailed, and persuaded some families to join the peace faction at Sand Creek.

The attack came at dawn of a cold morning, between first light and sunrise. When Black Kettle ran from his tipi and saw troops approaching he hoisted an American flag above his lodge and raised a white flag

below it. Nevertheless, the soldiers cut off the Indian horse herd and began firing. Black Kettle called for the awakening camp to remain calm; possibly he thought that some of the warriors had recently been raiding, and that the show of force was meant only to frighten them and to take some prisoners. It soon became clear, however, that the attack was deadly serious. The soldiers set up cannon on high ground beyond the creek and began to fire into the tipis.

Chief White Antelope ran toward the troops with his hands raised shouting in English, "Stop! Stop!" When he saw the hopelessness of it he halted and stood with folded arms. They shot him down. Women and children screamed and cried. They ran from the camp to scatter in the sandy hills. The warriors began to offer resistance, covering a retreat up the stream bed, where the high creek banks offered some protection and firing pits could be quickly dug in the soft sand. Black

186

Kettle remained under his flags at first; then, with his wife, he joined the movement upstream. She would be shot nine times during this day of savagery, yet would live. Black Kettle, contrary to the report of the white commander, would also survive.

The battle lasted into the afternoon, but it was more an Indian hunt than a military engagement. White officers either would not or could not maintain discipline over the troops. Robert Bent, a half-Cheyenne who had been forced to guide the expedition, later described the things he witnessed. Here are some of his comments: "I saw five squaws under a bank. When troops came up to them they ran out and showed their persons to let the soldiers know they were squaws and begged for mercy but the soldiers shot them all. Some thirty or forty squaws, collected in a hole for protection, sent out a little girl about six years old with a white flag on a stick. She was shot and killed. I saw one squaw cut open with an unborn child lying by her side. I saw the body of White Antelope with the privates cut off, and I heard a soldier say he was going to make a tobacco pouch out of them. I saw one squaw whose privates had been cut out." One observer, who claimed he had counted the Indian dead, put the total at 123, of whom 98 were women and children.

Black Kettle fled north with the remnants of his half-naked band, where he fell in with another, more warlike, encampment on the Smoky Hill River. There he found food, clothing and shelter against the pitiless plains winter. He was deeply angry at the slaughter, yet still he did not advocate all-out war. He continued to believe that the destiny of his Cheyennes would be accommodation with white people. But his influence in the council was weakened, as, once again, was that of other would-be peacemakers among the Indians.

The reaction of the other plains chiefs to Sand Creek was quick and violent. By late December, 2,000 Cheyenne, Northern Arapaho and Sioux warriors had gathered in villages on the Republican River. Said one chief to a placating fur trapper: "What do we have to live for? The white man has taken our country, killed our game, was not satisfied with that, but killed our wives and children. Now no peace. We have now raised the battle ax until death." And death to the whites it was, in another fierce spate of raiding. In January a war party lured a cavalry detachment out of Fort Rankin

and slaughtered some 45 troopers. In quick succession the Indians then ravaged every white man's ranch west of Fort Rankin for 80 miles, killed eight more people, stole some 1,500 head of cattle and ended with an orgiastic sacking of Julesburg itself, during which masses of chanting warriors danced to the light of a bonfire made from torn-down telegraph poles.

While the frontier trembled and raged at these retaliations, elsewhere in the country a deep and very different kind of white reaction to Sand Creek was taking shape. The testimony taken at the Congressional investigations on the "great battle" set off a wave of revulsion across the country, and led more and more people to take a deeply searching look at the confrontation that had plagued all the West in the second half of the 19th Century. Just after the slaughter, none other than Ulysses S. Grant admitted to Governor John Evans of Colorado, according to one source, that Sand Creek was nothing more or less than a murder by Federal troops of Indians who thought they were under the protection of the Army. Joseph Holt, the Army's Judge Advocate General, branded it a "cowardly and cold-blooded slaughter, sufficient to cover its perpetrators with indelible infamy, and the face of every American with shame and indignation."

A number of Western editors continued to espouse the traditional hard-line frontiersman's attitude ("exterminate the whole fraternity of redskins," recommended the *Nebraska City Press* of January 16, 1865). But Senator Lot M. Morrill reflected more accurately the awakening conscience of the United States and its government when he said in the Senate, "We have come to this point in the history of the country that there is no place beyond population to which you can remove the Indian, and the precise question is: Will you exterminate him or will you fix an abiding place for him?"

Finally the white man as well as the Indian was facing up to the basic choice between accommodation and war. Heretofore the United States had been substantially able to postpone its Indian troubles by the hardhanded but basically simple expedient of moving the Indians westward. Now, with the Civil War drawing to a close and the West fast filling up with settlers, there was nowhere else to move them. Some other solution would have to be sought. And Americans, confronted with the barbarous reality of Sand Creek and its bloody aftermath, were becoming far less cavalier about warring with them.

In the East, especially, religious leaders and a number of top government men espoused a fundamentally humanitarian approach — although in some cases what appeared to be humanitarianism was also a milder form of pragmatism. As Secretary of the Interior James Harlan noted in 1866, the old concept of extermination was "manifestly as impracticable as it is in violation of every dictate of humanity and Christian duty." Behind his words was the hard fact that to support a single Indian fighting regiment cost as much as two million dollars per year. At those prices it seemed cheaper to keep an Indian alive on a reservation than to kill him in the field. And Congress, with the treasury drained by the Civil War, was of a mind to go for bargains.

Beyond that the country was still full of a crusading spirit, the same humanitarianism that had fired the Abolitionists. One reformer who had long agitated for a more enlightened approach to Indian relations was Henry B. Whipple, the Episcopalian bishop who spoke for the Sioux after the Minnesota uprising. He asked the government to fulfill its promises and to administer the Indian Bureau through persons of temperance and integrity. Partly in response to Whipple's urgings the Episcopal Church combined with the Quakers — who had a 200-year tradition of friendship with the Indian — and later with other denominations to lobby for better treatment of the Indians. The basic solution of the church people and other reform groups was to assimilate the Indian, to house and feed him through annual allotments of food, stores and money, to Christianize him, to introduce him to modern agriculture and to teach him a trade.

Through such methods, they argued, the Indian problem would disappear, since there would be no more Indians in the tribal, free-roaming sense of the traditional plains bands. These reformers, wrote historian Robert Mardock, envisioned for the Indians a "new way of life that would be based on the values of idealized, middle-class, nineteenth-century Easterners — law-abiding, morally Christian, and politically democratic. The new Indians would be industrious, self-supporting landowners who had all the rights and duties of citizenship."

The clergymen found some surprising allies in their campaign. General Alfred Sully, after an expedition into Dakota Territory, reported to his superiors that, indeed, the easiest way to exterminate a wild Indian was to civilize him. The general favored a partnership between the government and the Christian missionaries, who would work among the tribes to see that justice and fair trading and honesty replaced the shenanigans at most Indian agencies (box, page 169). While such ideas were clearly worth a careful hearing, still at issue was the question of what was possible. General William T. Sherman, the greatest power in the post-Civil War Army, was a pragmatist who would put up with Indians as long as they behaved, but some of his writings and public statements made it clear that he favored extermination of the fighting tribes.

The great debate would continue through the 1860s. It culminated in a famous peace policy proclaimed by Ulysses S. Grant after he became President. Essentially the policy was an expanded version of General Sully's program for using men nominated by various churches as Indian agents. Though much debated and discussed, and even widely tested, the policy was never clearly successful or unsuccessful, and was eventually abandoned; the problem ran too deep for the clergymen to eradicate — even when they were aided by government intentions to reform.

However, one result of the soul-searching was a peace commission set up by an act of Congress to treat with hostile Indians. The stated purpose of the commission was to "remove the causes of war; secure the frontier settlements and railroad construction; and establish a system for civilizing the tribes."

In October 1867 the commission took a huge wagon train of annuities — food, clothing and other supplies — to a place called Medicine Lodge in southern Kansas. There the commission hoped to negotiate fresh treaties with the Cheyennes, Arapahos, Comanches and Kiowas. In exchange for rations, clothing, housing and vocational training programs, the tribes would agree to remain on large reservations, leaving them only for buffalo hunting. They would not raid, and in return white supervision would be benign.

The projected treaty was a complicated one, and the commission's expedition was a large undertaking, involving tons of supplies and hundreds of people. Nine newspapermen came along to report the proceedings to the nation. In the great gathering held at Medicine

A white Indian and her tragic saga

On a May day in 1836 in northern Texas, a 9-year-old frontier girl was abducted by a raiding band of Comanches, who swooped down on the family home and killed her father. The child was Cynthia Ann Parker, favorite niece of Isaac Parker, rancher, soldier and legislator. The story of her 25-year captivity and her subsequent return is one of the most poignant of all the frontier tales.

As Cynthia Ann toiled at the work of a Comanche woman, her complexion darkened from the sun and dirt, and her flaxen hair, clipped short, became greasy. Yet as a white she remained an alluring prize. The chief, Peta Nocona, chose her as his bride when she was 18, and she bore three children—two sons, Quanah and Pecos, and a daughter, Topasannah. For 15 years she cared for her family as the tribe staged forays into Parker County, named after her uncle.

Cynthia Ann's return to white society occurred the way she had left it, through a raid. While camped near the Pease River in 1860, her tribe was surprised by a detachment of government Indian hunters. Her husband and her teen-age sons escaped into the prairie. Quanah later would become a noted Comanche warrior and chief (*pages 192, 194*). During the skirmish Cynthia Ann's short hair and buffalo robe gave her the look of a brave, but just as she was about to be shot by a white man she held up her baby, Topasannah, as a sign that she was a woman. Closer inspection revealed her blue eyes—the conclusive evidence that she was white.

Certain that they had found the

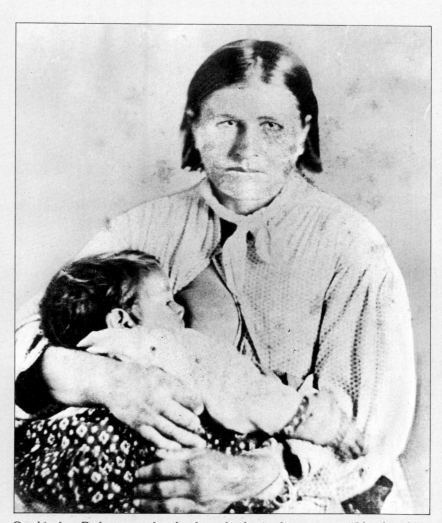

Cynthia Ann Parker nurses her daughter after having been recaptured by the whites.

long-lost lady of the Parker family, the soldiers summoned Isaac Parker. He tried to talk to the blue-eyed woman, but she spoke little English. Finally Parker said, "Maybe we were wrong. Poor Cynthia Ann." On hearing the name the 34-year-old woman remembered it from her childhood: "Me Cynthia," she replied simply.

Cynthia was welcomed back by the whites, who even voted her a pension and some land. But she never smiled. Several times she stole horses and lit out in quest of her sons. After about four years back with the settlers, Cynthia Ann's little girl died from a fever. Devastated by grief, Cynthia Ann starved herself to death.

Lodge, one man was particularly noteworthy—Chief Black Kettle, still searching for peace three years after the massacre at Sand Creek.

During those three years, while other Cheyennes had engaged in intermittent guerrilla war with the whites, Black Kettle had regained control of his band. He had brought his people to Medicine Lodge determined to negotiate for peace. He camped at the designated peace site; the other bands camped a short day's ride away on the Cimarron River, keeping at arm's length, as it were. If things went badly they could attack. When some of their leaders came from the Cimarron to the Medicine peace meetings they appeared to be scouting the layout of the whites.

The peace commission hearings concerned various skirmishes and raids that had gone on since Sand Creek. After the hearings these leaders, instead of returning straight to their camp on the Cimarron, evidently went over to Black Kettle's camp and held a hearing of their own at which only Indian witnesses gave testimony. A great soul-searching was going on within the tribe. At the meeting Black Kettle was threatened by the other chiefs when he apparently had reacted against the warlike mood. The Cheyennes kept the white officials waiting almost two weeks with the excuse that they were having a big medicine ceremony that could not be interrupted. Then they arrived at the peace site in a mock charge, shouting and firing guns. But they signed the new treaty, and it was clear that Black Kettle had won the day with his people.

As it turned out, the Medicine Lodge treaties utterly failed to keep the peace. The same Congress that set up the peace commission would not appropriate the provisions needed to meet the pledges of its own commission. On the other side, there were some plains warriors who probably had no intention of observing a permanent peace, regardless of signatures and X's on treaties. Among both whites and Indians, even before the end of the 1860s, the currents of cultural conflict had grown too strong to be reconciled. One of the first victims was that long-suffering peacemaker Black Kettle. And his story, together with that of three other plains chiefs—Quanah of the Comanches, the Kiowa named Sitting Bear (page 34) and the shrewd Sioux Red Cloud—illustrates the fickle and often tragic consequences for those Indian leaders who operated

within the shifting tides of accommodation and war.

On November 27, 1868, only a year after the conference at Medicine Lodge, Black Kettle was camped on the upper Washita River in what is now western Oklahoma. Snow blanketed the plains and the cottonwood groves along the river. The day before, a party of raiding warriors had come into camp from the north, leaving a clear trail in the snow.

In the chilly dawn, just as first light made the tipis of the quiet camp visible among the trees, there was the sound of a shot, followed by the notes of a bugle. The

U.S. 7th Cavalry, led by the officer the Indians called Long Hair (George Armstrong Custer), was charging in from four different directions.

As he sprang to wakefulness, Black Kettle must have thought of Sand Creek. It could not be happening to him again, but it was. Quite possibly in those first moments of awareness—as he armed himself, as the frightened screams began—he must have thought: I don't want to live through it this time. He did not; this time he died alongside his wife, near his tipi, and Custer's Osage scouts scalped him. Some 40 Indian women and children were also killed in the engagement. Yet this time no white officials came from Washington to ask why another camp had been ravaged, why once more women and children had been killed. In fact the cavalry's leader, Custer, already a hero in the great war in the East, was commended by his own chiefs, Generals Sheridan and Sherman. From now on, apparently, the white man would hold no more councils. Instead, he would strike hard at any Indian tribe or band that showed the slightest semblance of armed resistance and would force any survivors onto the reservations.

JAMES M. CAVANAUGH

QUANAH PARKER

RED CLOUD

SATANTA

WILLIAM TECUMSEH SHERMAN

COLONEL JOHN M. CHIVINGTON

The advocates of war

JAMES M. CAVANAUGH, a delegate to Congress from the Territory of Montana, epitomized the frontier attitude toward the Indian, and used a notorious phrase, when he declared before the House of Representatives, "I have never in my life seen a good Indian (and I have seen thousands) except when I have seen a dead Indian."

QUANAH PARKER was a subchief and renowned warrior of the Quohada band of Comanches. He refused to sign the 1867 Medicine Lodge Treaty, saying, "Tell the white chiefs that the Quohadas are warriors and will surrender when the blue coats come and whip us." When they finally did, Quanah was the last chief to give in.

RED CLOUD, an Oglala Sioux, carried on such a fierce war across the northern plains that the U.S. government temporarily agreed to peace on his terms. Later, when he realized further war meant extermination, he turned negotiator, but only reluctantly: "I suppose I must in time go to farming, but I can't do it right away."

SATANTA, or White Bear, a Kiowa chief, signed the Medicine Lodge Treaty of 1867 but continued raiding white settlements. Seized by General Sherman, he was tried and sentenced to death but later pardoned and released. After another raid he was sentenced to prison, but committed suicide rather than submit.

WILLIAM TECUMSEH SHERMAN, Civil War hero and later U.S. military chief on the High Plains, concurred with Cavanaugh's judgment on Indians. "The more we can kill this year, the less will have to be killed the next war," said Sherman, adding, "they all have to be killed or be maintained as a species of paupers."

COLONEL JOHN M. CHIVINGTON, a former minister who turned down a military chaplaincy to become a fighting soldier, made his place in history by leading the infamous Sand Creek Massacre of Cheyennes in 1864. "I am fully satisfied," he had written, "that to kill the red rebels is the only way to have peace and quiet."

WASHAKIE

SAMUEL TAPPAN

VINCENT COLYER

WENDELL PHILLIPS

CHIEF JOSEPH

SPOTTED TAIL

The partisans of peace

WASHAKIE was a Shoshoni chief noted for his friendliness toward whites, despite an earlier reputation as a fighter in wars with rival tribes. In a move rare among chiefs, who generally resented the white incursion, Washakie, in the 1850s, actually ordered his tribe to help the whites passing through his territory in Wyoming.

SAMUEL TAPPAN, an abolitionist during the Civil War, transferred his egalitarian passions to the Indians after Appomattox. He was president of a military commission that censured Chivington for the Sand Creek Massacre and in 1867 was in the presidential Peace Commission that negotiated the Medicine Lodge Treaty.

VINCENT COLYER, a successful artist, steadily argued that honest dealings with the Indians would bring peace. He volunteered to become secretary of the Board of Indian Commissioners, a government-sponsored body of unpaid philanthropists that supervised the disbursements of annuities promised the Indians by treaty.

WENDELL PHILLIPS, another former abolitionist, became a fiery advocate of Indian rights. He demanded that the U.S. abandon the transcontinental railroad and give the Indian "a department in the Cabinet which shall watch his rights." A war-hawk editorial in *The New York Times* blasted him for his "sickly sentimentality."

CHIEF JOSEPH of the Nez Percés in Oregon preached forbearance: "Better to live in peace than to begin a war and lie dead." His tolerance was futile. Driven off their land, the tribe under Joseph tried to flee to Canada, fighting off pursuing cavalry. Close to the border, the tribe was finally cut off, and Joseph surrendered.

SPOTTED TAIL, a Brûlé Sioux, gave himself up as a hostage to spare his tribe, which was to be punished by the Army for a raid on settlers. In 1877 he negotiated the treaty with the government by which his nephew, Crazy Horse, surrendered to the Army. Spotted Tail was later killed in reprisal by one of his own tribe.

One man who had resisted whites from the first was the renowned warrior, Chief Quanah, most dynamic leader among the Comanches. Quanah's mother was a captive white woman named Cynthia Ann Parker *(box, page 189)*, who in 1845 bore Quanah after a chief had taken her as his wife. The child grew up as a normal Comanche, with the broad cheekbones and appearance of his father's people. But at the age of 15, when a boy of any race may be at his most sensitive and vulnerable, he suffered a traumatic loss. A force of U.S. Cavalry, Texas Rangers, Tonkawa Scouts and civilians attacked the Comanche camp on Peace River; one of the results of the engagement was the recapture of Cynthia Ann Parker.

The effect of the loss upon Quanah is suggested in the fact that he kept his name the rest of his life. While his young companions on the warpath took names like Big Horse and Fighting Wolf and Wild Bear, he retained his name, Quanah (meaning fragrant), because that is what his mother had called him. If the other braves teased him about his name, they soon learned better, for he became the epitome of the oldtime, fiercely aggressive Comanche warrior.

While still in his early 20s he began to lead raids. At the age of 26 he led a successful night charge through the cavalry camp of Colonel Ronald Mackenzie, who had been sent specifically to subdue Quanah and his band. The warriors captured many horses, first stampeding the animals by shooting, yelling and dragging buffalo hides along the ground. Quanah acted as a leader in other raids among the white man's settlements in Texas, driving off cattle and horses and taking plunder of every kind.

But the power of the Comanches was fast crumbling. Their population was reduced partly by diseases, partly by a lower birth rate and partly by war. Inevitably they faced the basic Indian decision: accommodation to the white man's arrangements or continued war. Most of the bands agreed to live on a reservation, but the Kwahadi Comanches, who had never signed a treaty with the whites (they had refused even to attend the great treaty conference at Medicine Lodge), remained free for a time, with Quanah as one of their most effective war leaders. On the Comanche reservation, the other bands heard his name again and again, and remembered the days when they were lords of the southern plains.

But finally even the fierce Kwahadis came to realize that their cause was hopeless, as the U.S. Army used a brutal technique to "pacify" recalcitrant Indians; namely, the destruction of their winter food supplies and the capture or killing of their horses.

On a clear, cold day in late September 1874, the same Colonel Mackenzie whom Quanah had defeated three years earlier attacked a camp of Comanches, Kiowas and Cheyennes in the heart of Palo Duro Canyon on the headwaters of the Red River. The site had seemed a safe refuge to the Indians. Though they had seen soldiers in the area, they were unprepared for the assault. They retreated. Before they could organize a counterattack, Mackenzie burned their lodges and food supplies, and drove away more than 1,400 Indian horses and mules. Knowing the difficulty of holding on to the stock in Indian country, the colonel had the animals driven back to shallow Tule Canyon and killed.

The shooting of 1,400 horses and mules is a violent and bloody business. The Comanches, for whom the animals were god dogs, must have felt a great shock as they spied upon the slaughter or saw the acres of bodies later. Although only a few Indians had been killed in the attack, the immediate loss of food and horses, together with the long and ruinous depletion of buffalo by white hunters, convinced Quanah that even the wild Kwahadis would have to surrender. And so, in 1875, Quanah rode into a reservation with the remnants of this last fighting band of what had once been a powerful Indian nation.

The Kiowas, who finally settled on the reservations at about the same time, never found such a man around whom they could rally to salvage a little pride after surrender. Their most influential and trusted leaders died or were killed during the final years of confrontation with the whites. In fact, one of the most famous of their chiefs, unable to endure even the notion of surrender, chose death instead. His name was Sitting Bear. In 1871, at the age of 70, he left the Kiowa reservation in southwestern Oklahoma Territory to join a raid into the Texas settlements. The raiding party attacked a train of 10 grain wagons, killed the wagon master and six teamsters, and captured 41 mules. Sitting Bear, as leader of the Kiowa Kaitsenko, Society of the Ten Bravest, had been one of several chiefs at the head of the plundering expedition. After the raid the Indians blandly rode into Fort Sill to pick up their allotment of rations. Astonishingly, one of the chiefs began bragging about the recent massacre — whereupon soldiers arrested Sitting Bear and two others. The three men were to be sent back to Texas to stand trial for murder.

The soldiers fitted the three chiefs with irons, shackling both wrists and ankles, and held them about a week in a dungeon under a barracks. On one of those days Sitting Bear acquired a hunting knife, probably from an Indian visitor, and hid it under his blanket.

On the morning the cavalry was ready to escort the prisoners south, two wagons pulled up to the dungeon. Sitting Bear was put in a wagon by himself, for he was acting strangely and chanting in a shrill, doleful voice. Horace Jones, the post interpreter, said, "You had better watch that old Indian. He means trouble." Two soldiers armed with carbines got in the wagon with him.

The wagons and soldiers of the 4th Cavalry began to move. Double-ironed, Sitting Bear must have appeared to be only a whining old man, his loose hair and his thin mustache the color of cotton twine. One wonders what he remembered of his long life as the wagons lumbered south on the road toward Texas. Did he think of the day, so long ago, when he walked along the river sand in front of the rows of erstwhile enemies, passing out counting sticks to symbolize the 250 horses he was giving them? One thing he certainly remembered, that he was the leader of the Society of the Ten Bravest, for his chant, or song, consisted of these words.

Kaitsenko ana obahema haa ipai degi o ba ika.
Oh, sun, you remain forever, but we Kaitsenko must die.

Kaitsenko ana oba hemo hadamagagi o ba ika.
Oh, earth, you remain forever, but we Kaitsenko must die.

Again and again as he sang he ducked his head under his blanket, stripping the flesh from his hands with his teeth until he could slip through the handcuffs. A short distance south of the fort he got them free. He retrieved the hunting knife from under his blanket and stood up, no more a whining old man but an armed Kiowa warrior.

He slashed into one of the guards and wrenched the man's carbine. Both soldiers tumbled head over heels out of the wagon into the dusty road. Sitting Bear struggled to get a cartridge into the chamber, but perhaps the old man simply did not know how to work the gun. In any case it would not fire, but that did not matter much. He screamed his war cry and pointed the useless gun while soldiers' bullets cut into him.

The panicky cavalrymen fired so wildly that they seriously wounded the teamster riding one of the mules. Sitting Bear jerked at the bullets' impact and went down. But he rose again in the swaying wagon, staggered to his feet and thrust his empty gun at them, with his bleeding hands — gnawed to the bones — pointing the gun in his last gesture of total war. One does not take the leader of the Society of the Ten Bravest to be tried by foreigners in something called a court. And so the white soldiers cut him down again with a frightening volley, exactly as he wished.

It had been a decidedly one-sided battle — five troops of cavalry against one man, double-ironed, surrounded, 70 years old. But it had been, in its way, a real battle. Sitting Bear had grown up in a world where white men were rare, traders mainly, certainly not the arbiters of anyone's destiny. He had led a full and highly honored life, and he probably did not wish to live on and to witness the destruction of the old ways. Behind him he left a memory valuable to his people, the memory of a man with a kind of ultimate integrity.

Another great chief, Red Cloud of the Sioux, was judged more harshly by his people for in the end negotiating with the whites. Yet it should not have been so, for he was a man of great courage, who had been the cleverest war strategist among the Sioux. The whites named an entire campaign after him — Red Cloud's war — during which he was an architect of a Sioux triumph known as the Fetterman Massacre.

Red Cloud was beginning to emerge as a major leader in 1863, when settlers and miners began to pour over a new road they called the Powder River Trail, or the Bozeman Trail (after the scout who had blazed it). On its way toward the mines around Virginia City, Montana, the new road, which was a branch of the Oregon Trail, left the old route in Dakota Territory and headed northwest through the best of all the Sioux hunting grounds. The Indians under Red Cloud's leadership harassed travelers on the trail with such determination that in the summer of 1866 white leaders arranged a council at Fort Laramie.

To the council, along with Red Cloud, came such noted Sioux chiefs as Red Leaf, Old Man Afraid of

His Horses and Spotted Tail, also a number of their people. At the outset of the council it appeared that peaceful use of the Bozeman Trail might be negotiated as long as travelers would not disturb the game. But as serious talk got underway, a Colonel Henry Carrington marched into Fort Laramie with a large body of troops and plans to establish forts to protect the trail against Indian raids. Carrington attended the council and made no secret of his intentions.

Red Cloud exploded. He said the peace commissioners had treated the chiefs as children. "The Great Father sends us presents and wants us to sell him the road," he asserted, "but before the Indians say yes or no White Chief goes with soldiers to steal the road." He walked out, and half of the chiefs went with him.

The negotiations proceeded with Spotted Tail and other chiefs, and a treaty was signed. Carrington thereupon went ahead with the rebuilding of Fort Reno and the establishing of Forts Phil Kearny and C. F. Smith to protect the road through Sioux country. But soon after Carrington arrived at Fort Reno with his troops Sioux warriors swooped down upon the post and ran off a band of horses. Red Cloud's war had begun.

The war amounted to a series of harassments. As in Denver four years earlier, the Indians cut off the mail routes, attacked wagon trains and either destroyed them or forced them to turn back. They set upon details of soldiers sent out from the various posts to gather hay or wood. Camps of the Sioux war faction were strung out along the Tongue River, and the restless warriors under Red Cloud's direction constantly raided the trail and the posts.

Among the officers stationed at Fort Phil Kearny, Carrington's headquarters, was a headstrong young captain named William J. Fetterman, who had become particularly angry about the raiding. He had no respect for the fighting ability of the Plains Indians and was frustrated that they were permitted to get away with such harassment without being punished. On one occasion he boasted, "Give me 80 men and I would ride through the whole Sioux Nation." Already some Sioux warriors were planning a battle tactic designed to take full and deadly advantage of the captain's cocky attitude.

Fort Phil Kearny nestled on a slight plateau in the forks of Little Piney and Big Piney Creeks, surrounded on all sides by hills and ridges, molded by the elements.

The high ground was bare of timber, tan with sun-dried grass, often covered or spotted with snow in the winter, though the creases in the land had strings of choke-cherries and other brush running along them. The Bozeman Trail ran northwest past the fort and led up behind a long hill known as Lodge Trail Ridge.

On the morning of December 21, 1866, a party of soldiers, sent out for logs and firewood, was working its way along the Big Piney. About 11 o'clock a lookout on a hill near the fort signaled with a flag that the loggers were under attack and might need help. Immediately Captain Fetterman demanded and got command of the relief force, with orders not to press a fight unnecessarily and under no circumstances to venture beyond Lodge Trail Ridge. As he prepared to ride out, he had under his command 78 officers and men, cavalry and infantry. At the last minute, as if fate remembered his boast, two civilians joined him, making up exactly the number of 80 men he had claimed he needed to ride through the Sioux nation.

The attack against the logging train was not pressed by the Indians, but a smaller band, led by a brilliant young warrior named Crazy Horse, had come close to the fort itself. Crazy Horse had the feathered skin of a red-backed hawk pinned in his hair and a streak of jagged lightning painted on his cheek. If the red hailmarks of his characteristic war paint were on his body, they were hidden under his belted blanket, for the weather was cold. He was mounted, as were a few others of his small group; the rest walked. They moved along the edge of the brush, pretending to hide but in reality preparing to execute perfectly one of the simplest battle tactics ever devised.

Two canister shots from the fort's howitzers burst over the Indians. One of the decoys was knocked from his horse. The others howled and scrambled north as if they were all afraid. As awkwardly as he could manage, Crazy Horse made a show of covering the retreat. Since the log-and-wood detail was already returning safely toward the fort, Fetterman's force went after the small group of fleeing Indians.

Crazy Horse and the other mounted warriors stayed just outside rifle range of the whites, and one or another of the mounted men kept charging briefly at the oncoming soldiers as if to drive them back. Crazy Horse must have been praying, "Come on! Come on!" He led

In an effort to pacify the Indians — subtly encourage warriors to turn to farming — the government awarded them medals like this one featuring President Grant and a globe surrounded by farm implements.

his pursuers through the hills, across the Big Piney and up onto Lodge Trail Ridge. "Come on! Come on!" Once he dismounted as if to tighten the war rope about his pony's chest, once as if frantically digging at the pony's hoof, possibly to remove a stone. Meanwhile the Indian scouts lay on their bellies along the gullies, waiting for the moment to signal the main force of mounted warriors hidden behind the hills. Steadily Crazy Horse led the white soldiers over Lodge Trail Ridge, down along the wagon road and on toward the forks of Pano Creek. Suddenly he screamed his war cry.

Out of sight of the fort, out of the reach of its howitzers, Fetterman was swarmed over by hundreds of whooping Indians. His men scattered like quail, tried to regroup, tried to escape, tried to form firing lines. The warriors charged straight through the soldiers from every direction, swinging war clubs. A few Indians fell before the cracking rifles, but the others kept on coming. They showered the knots of soldiers with arrows. Fetterman and the remnants of his command, horses dead or wrenched away from them, retreated up a knoll beside the Bozeman Trail, where a few flat rocks offered scant protection. Here they made their last stand. The captain had left the fort just after 11 a.m.; by 12:45 p.m. he and his 80 men were dead, stripped of guns and clothing, and scalped.

Fetterman's Massacre was not a major engagement, but it was like an exclamation point in the war of harassment that Red Cloud had pursued and would continue to press for months to come. Like Sand Creek, the Fetterman Massacre pointed up the grim failure of the government's Indian policy and caused many people to examine their basically bellicose attitudes. Now, both Western and Eastern whites wanted peace. Red Cloud would not grant it. The Sioux chief was adamant; he demanded that the whites take their forts out

of Sioux country. And, finally, the United States government yielded to him.

In May 1868 Army authorities ordered the abandonment of Forts Reno, Phil Kearny and C. F. Smith. In late summer of that year, as the soldiers marched out from the posts, the Indians burned them to the ground. Then, in November, Red Cloud came into Fort Laramie and signed a treaty of peace. He was the first and only Western Indian chief to have won a protracted war with the United States.

A short time after the signing of that peace treaty a traveler talking with Red Cloud expressed surprise that the government had given in. To the chief, it turned out, the matter was simple. He said, "I have more soldiers than the Great Father, and he cannot take my lands against my will."

Of course, the Great Father had more troops than Red Cloud had seen — indeed he had more of everything, a fact that Red Cloud and his brothers were soon to learn. Trouble still threatened on the northern plains; there was disagreement over such questions as where traders might deal with the Sioux and where the tribes must report to receive annuities. Therefore, in the spring of 1870, 16 chiefs, including Red Cloud, were invited to Washington, D.C., ostensibly for a conference. While in Washington, however, these Indians — like others before them — were given a revealing look at the white man's world and strength.

Red Cloud did a manly job of concealing the fact that he was impressed. His itinerary included a visit to the U.S. Arsenal and Navy Yard, where he was shown a Rodman gun with a 15-inch bore almost big enough for a man to crawl into. He visited the Senate while it was in session and must have remembered the councils that he himself had attended in crude surroundings. He stared out over the city from the dome of the Capitol and must have thought about numbers — the numbers of the Sioux people and of the white people. He met twice with President Grant.

It had undoubtedly been Red Cloud's intention to tell the whites once and for all that they could not control the destiny of the Sioux. He had tried to defend that position in discussions about the provisions of the treaty he had signed less than two years earlier. He probably thought that exact treaty provisions did not matter much — that the Sioux under his leadership would

197

In 1857, as part of a campaign to impress—and to pacify
—the Indians, leaders of the Pawnee, Ponca, Potawatomi,
Sioux and Winnebago tribes were invited to Washington.
This photograph of the chiefs with their top-hatted hosts
at the White House is attributed to Mathew Brady.

be able to interpret the provisions as they wished. Now, despite the evidence of white power, he continued to demand that still another fort on the northern plains be abandoned, that his people be paid liberally for railroads passing through their land, that they be allowed to continue their free life and not have arbitrary boundaries drawn around them.

Speaking to the Secretary of the Interior and the Commissioner of Indian Affairs, he set down a series of demands and accusations against the white man's actions. But he ended his angry speech by admitting that his people were only a handful compared with the whites. His words were marked by a characteristic Indian simplicity and eloquence, surpassed by few men of any race: "Our nation is melting away like the snow on the sides of the hills where the sun is warm, while your people are like the blades of grass in the spring when the summer is coming."

Despite Red Cloud's apparent discouragement, the Washington officials sensed that the Sioux chief was still deeply angry. Therefore they arranged with various Christian leaders and other humanitarians for Red Cloud to make a speech in New York City where widespread pro-Indian sentiment had arisen. They were hopeful that a favorable reception might change his mood. Reluctantly, Red Cloud agreed. At the Cooper Institute in New York he attended a great rally, and his speech was the highlight of it. He sensed the sympathy of the audience and spoke of the brotherhood of man under the Great Spirit, of wrongs done to Indians, of the need for help and understanding. They wildly applauded nearly every sentence as it was translated from his lips. It was one of his finest hours.

The idealists who gave him that welcome in the nation's largest city had established a committee to draw up "a plan for the settlement of all our Indian difficulties." They did not lay the plan in detail before Red Cloud and the other chiefs. But had they done so it is doubtful the chief would have found in it much hope or solace. The plan included, among other provisions, that all Indians of the West would be concentrated on not less than four nor more than seven reservations, that each individual Indian should get 80 acres of good land and that the red men should be moved immediately toward "civilization." But the well-meant plan only showed once again that many of the reformers and idealists were almost as limited in their views as the white war hawks whom they despised. To put the numerous distinct tribes of the West on so few reservations would inevitably have caused frustration and confusion; much Western land was so arid that 80 acres would not support a person equipped with only the farming implements and methods of the time; and, most important of all, many Indians simply did not want to be civilized or to accept the whites' definition of civilization.

Heading west, Red Cloud and the chiefs with him got off the train at Omaha and received gifts of horses to take home with them. The great chief would never be the same again. He would never lead his people in war again. He would journey to Washington seven more times and would continue to do his best in negotiating for Sioux interests, but his faith in his superiority and in that of his warriors was gone. His power of leadership declined, too.

The ultimate effect of the Eastern humanitarians on the frontier crisis was difficult to assess with any accuracy. Undoubtedly they did some good. Without their idealistic pressure, the proposal for exterminating the last free fighting Indians might have been put into action. Yet it was clear that the humanitarians did not understand all of the realities of the Plains Indians' way of life. The Sioux were a proud, conquering people. What warrior would follow a plow or do woman's work because some white man said he should?

And what white gold seeker would let savages stand between himself and riches? Rumor had said there was gold aplenty in the Black Hills of the Dakota Territory, the homeland of the Teton Sioux. In 1874 George A. Custer, the leader of the Washita Massacre, was sent with a large expedition to examine that area with its fertile, green valleys and its promise of mineral wealth. Custer reported gold deposits, and almost immediately prospectors rushed toward this last stronghold of the Sioux. The federal government wanted to buy the land; the Sioux refused to sell it. Red Cloud was willing to negotiate, but other powerful leaders were arising among his people. There was the war chief Gall, the medicine man Sitting Bull. Above all, there was a war chief of the Oglalas — still young, but with a strange, oldtime magic in war and already challenging Red Cloud for influence. His name was Crazy Horse.

An Indian betrayed by civilization

A classic case of what can happen when a man is taken from a simple life and dazzled by undreamed-of grandeur occurred with the Assiniboin Ah-jon-jon, one of the first Western Indians to get a close-up view of the white man's world. In 1830 American fur traders of the upper Missouri prevailed on the United States government to help them woo the allegiance of the tribes in their area away from the powerful Canada-based Hudson's Bay Company. Their idea was to give Indian leaders a tour of the glittering civilization of the United States, show them forts, cannons, ships and towering cities crowded with tens of thousands of people. And while the Indians were being impressed by the white man's might, they would receive proof of his goodwill through parties, presents and even a visit with the Great White Father.

In the fall of 1831 the first delegates, including Ah-jon-jon, were chosen and sent off down the Missouri. En route, Ah-jon-jon kept a record of the number of houses in the white man's land by notching a pipestem for each one he saw. When the pipe was covered with notches he used the handle of a war club, then a long stick. By the time he had reached St. Louis he gave up and threw the counters in the river.

In January they reached Washington, where they met the President. Ah-jon-jon and President Andrew Jackson took an immediate liking to each other and in a spontaneous ceremony of goodwill exchanged names and clothing. But what was only a symbolic act to the white President became real to Ah-jon-jon. From that day forward the Assiniboin called himself Jackson and often wore a general's uniform. An instinctive showman, he went on to receive an almost doting welcome at receptions in Bal-

Before-and-after portraits of Ah-jon-jon show how much he had changed in three months.

timore, Philadelphia and New York.

In the spring the Indians returned to St. Louis and went back up the Missouri on a steamboat. On board was the painter George Catlin, who had met Ah-jon-jon in St. Louis the previous winter. Catlin was so struck by the change in the Indian that he painted the dual portrait above, showing the transformation of Ah-jon-jon from a somber-faced man of the plains into a strutting dandy.

When Ah-jon-jon landed at Fort Union, near the present Montana-North Dakota border, his family was

aghast and pretended at first that they did not know him. Some of his tribesmen were afraid of him. Others, on hearing his fantastic stories, decided that he was a brazen liar, and when one man dared to question his account of the height of a shot tower in Washington, Ah-jon-jon did what he had seen a man there do to someone who had questioned his word: he beat him in public with a cane. But now he was back in an Indian world, and Ah-jon-jon paid the highest price for his haughty act. The man he had beaten returned and shot Ah-jon-jon dead.

While scouts keep watch from the hilltops, a war party marches single-file on a raid along the upper Missouri.

The fierce ritual of the warpath

Though Plains Indians could earn respect for skill in hunting, the real heroes of a village were warriors like the ones marching to battle in this Catlin painting. From the time they were boys waving handfuls of buffalo hair as simulated scalps, male Indians prepared for combat. At about 14 they were initiated into a young men's society as embryo warriors, and from then on their standing in the eyes of the tribe depended mainly on their conduct in war.

For Plains Indians the honor to be gained in the battle was more important than the overt reasons for fighting. These might range from an imagined insult to decade-long rivalries between tribes for possession of a favored hunting territory. But even when there was no real provocation, hot-blooded braves would invent one and stage a raid on another tribe, which might be camped nearby or hundreds of miles away.

On a typical horse-stealing raid some five to 25 warriors would leave their village during the night and travel for as long as two or three weeks before reaching their objective. Once near the enemy camp they would sneak up just before dawn, make the strike and then ride for home on the plundered horses. If pursuers from the aggrieved camp caught up with them, a battle took place. Afterward, if the raiders won, they would ride whooping into their village crying, "I made a kill and took their horses." That night the entire village would dance jubilantly, while the warriors related their heroic deeds, telling of rival tribesmen cut down and sometimes even showing off women and children whom they had captured.

Indians dabbed on war paint both before and after a battle. This portrait shows a Pawnee warrior after a victory, with hands painted on his chest as a sign that he had killed an enemy in hand-to-hand combat.

Since war was the climax of the Indian's life, he brought to it all the supernatural aids that he could muster. War paint sometimes symbolized past deeds; the hands adorning the chief at left are an example. But more commonly a warrior decorated his face and torso with designs intended to protect him as he went into battle. In fact, according to some sources, it was the warrior's red paint that originally caused the Europeans to call the Indian a red man.

Probably the most fascinating insight into the warrior mentality was the act of touching a live or dead enemy; this act was called counting coup, after the French word for blow. To the Indian, contact with a live enemy was the supreme act of his existence as a man. In Comanche tradition the first warrior to touch a fallen foe would cry, "A-he!" meaning, "I claim it." A second and a third warrior could also count coup on the same body, each earning a lesser honor. Some warriors carried special coupsticks like the one at right. Others used guns, whips or their bare hands. However it was done, the man who counted coup most often and most daringly was the hero of the battle.

Magic charms, like these stuffed kingfishers decorated with beads and feathers, were worn into battle. The agile kingfisher symbolized quickness, and the warrior hoped this charm would help him dodge arrows.

Some warriors used coupsticks like the one at right to touch the enemy during a fight. If the owner survived this bit of symbolic derring-do, he re-enacted the scene during a celebration with fellow tribesmen.

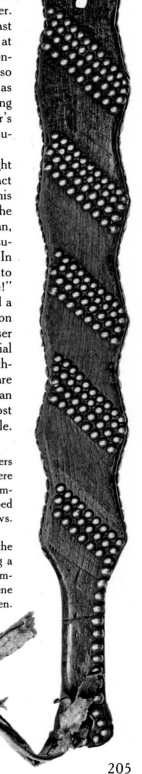

The five-foot-long war bonnet at right was made of bear-skin and eagle feathers. The Crow warrior who made it believed that the grizzly was his personal guardian, while the eagle feathers symbolized that fierce bird's predatory qualities. The Blackfoot headdress below was worn by senior tribesmen at warrior society meetings and at victory fetes.

Besides painting his face and body for battle, the Indian dressed for the occasion. But except for his shield, most of the things he wore or carried were of little practical use as armor. Rather, they were part of his personal medicine, or spiritual armor. For example, he believed that a war bonnet *(right)* conferred on him the superhuman powers needed to survive. Even a shield like that shown on the opposite page was thought to embody more magical than physical protection. Yet its physical qualities were impressive. Made of one or two heavy layers of hide from the shoulder of a bull buffalo, and sometimes reinforced with a padding of feathers or animal hair, it could deflect an arrow or a low-velocity musket ball.

206

The Mandan tribesman who owned this shield painted a stylized turtle on its surface; he had dreamed that the turtle, with its defensive shell, should be his personal symbol of protection. In battle the warrior strapped the shield onto the same arm with which he held his bow so that his hands were free for shooting arrows or using other weapons.

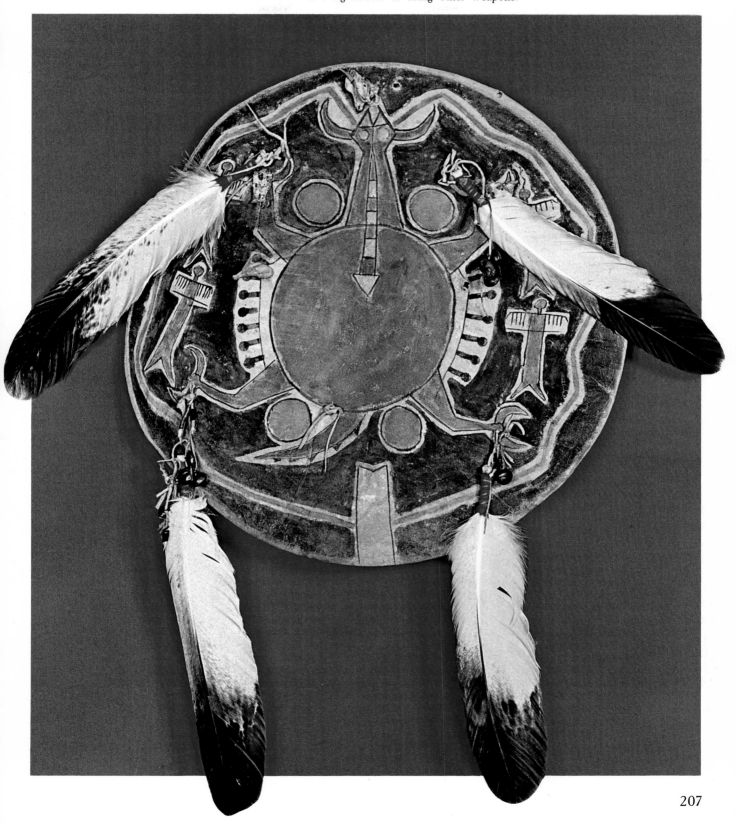

This 1869 model rifle, either bought or stolen from a white man, belonged to a Sioux or a Cheyenne warrior who carried it during the battle of the Little Bighorn.

For all the Indian's trust in his spiritual protection, in the heat of battle every warrior bet his life on the effectiveness of his weapons. The classic battle instruments were bows and arrows, clubs and tomahawks, like those at right and below. And they were still used in combat during the late 1860s and 1870s, the climactic period of the plains warrior tribes. By the 1850s, however, the rifle—especially the late-model repeaters—had begun to replace the bow and arrow as a preferred weapon for horseback and long-range fighting. The scalping tool, too, had changed from a piece of finely honed stone to a butcher knife, bought from white traders. In fact, some explorers who traveled among the Plains Indians were bemused to find them carrying knives that had been made in Sheffield, England.

Indians often modified factory-made weapons to their own tastes. The warrior who owned the single-shot Springfield infantry rifle above shortened the barrel, changed both the rear and front sights, and replaced a worn-out metal barrel band with rawhide lacing. He also decorated the stock with the brass tacks the Plains Indians so fancied. By the close of the period of the plains wars, the Indians had come to rely on guns as weapons to such an extent that the expression for war honor in the Blackfoot language had become *namachkani,* meaning "a gun taken."

Every warrior owned a knife, which he usually wore under his belt. In battle the knife was used for close combat and to cut off scalps. After a Chippewa had taken the scalp at left from a Sioux, he presented it to a dead comrade's mother or wife.

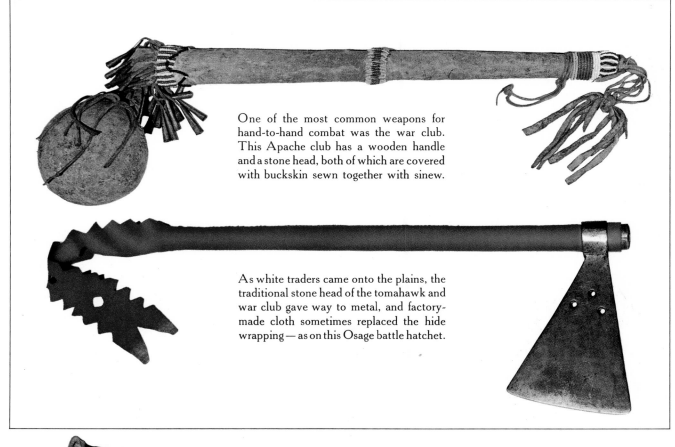

One of the most common weapons for hand-to-hand combat was the war club. This Apache club has a wooden handle and a stone head, both of which are covered with buckskin sewn together with sinew.

As white traders came onto the plains, the traditional stone head of the tomahawk and war club gave way to metal, and factory-made cloth sometimes replaced the hide wrapping — as on this Osage battle hatchet.

A Sioux warrior's bow was made of carefully selected ash and strung with two buffalo sinews twisted together. Shown here in its buckskin case with attached quiver, the war bow was accurate at over 100 yards — and could be fired more rapidly than muskets or single-shot rifles.

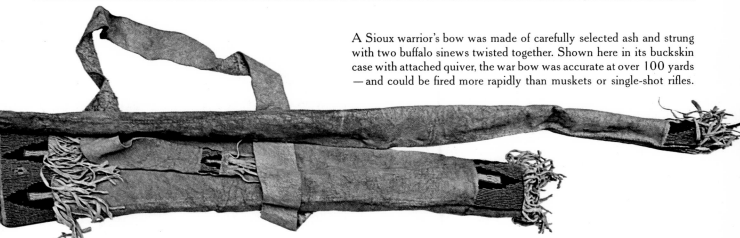

7 | Confrontation on the plains

In 1874 George Custer, on a reconnaissance mission with his cavalry, reported the discovery of gold in the Black Hills, the last stronghold of the warlike Sioux. Prospectors poured onto Indian land, and angry warriors raided and harassed white settlements. Finally, in December 1875, the Commissioner of Indian Affairs sent an ultimatum to agents on the Sioux reservation west of the Missouri. It read, in part: "Sir, I am instructed by the Hon. Secretary of the Interior to direct you to notify Sitting Bull's band and other wild and lawless bands of Sioux Indians, residing without the bounds of their reservation who roam over Western Dakota and Eastern Montana, that unless they shall remove within the bounds of their reservation (and remain there) before the 31st of the next January they shall be deemed hostile and treated accordingly by the military force." The agents dispatched runners through the snow to bring word to the tribal chiefs. But the Indian leaders refused to move their people upon this demand. By the next spring many Sioux bands had collected into a single, mobile body, mustering upward of 1,500 to 2,500 men. Together, still free and in a fighting mood, they would show the whites for all time what it meant to be an Indian warrior.

Mounted and in full battle regalia, a chief and two warriors look out across the mountains near the Little Bighorn.

A bold warrior's brilliant victory

Custer. Sitting Bull. The Battle of the Little Bighorn. For a century the names have echoed in the American consciousness. Yet the story most of us know is based on misconception and myth. The Battle of the Little Bighorn was not an Indian ambush, it was an Indian defense against a white soldiers' attack. Sitting Bull did not fight that day. The Indian who triumphed was a warrior chief of the Sioux, a brilliant tactician and a brave fighter named Crazy Horse. And he did not even call it the Little Bighorn. To him it was the Greasy Grass River. No one can ever know precisely what Crazy Horse thought and felt during the battle; white men wrote the history books. But from the events that are known it is tempting, and perhaps permissible, to reconstruct that fateful day of Indian glory as it may have been seen through the eyes of the most venerated fighter among the Western Sioux.

He was young for an "old man" chief, still in his early 30s, about five feet eight inches tall, not as large as many of his fellow tribesmen, but lithe and sinewy, quiet and dignified, with a reflective, melancholy face. When he rose to leave, the men of the council circle paused in case he had any final words to say. But it had all been said. Some of the older men were inclined to go on talking, but the war chiefs would not tarry long after he left. He ducked out of the giant tipi and walked toward the camp circle of his tribe, the Oglala Sioux.

It was midday and hot, though thin clouds hung in the sky. If he went up into the hills lining the valley he would be able to see, far to the south, the dim snow-striped peaks of the Bighorn Mountains, with clouds piled over them. The valley was spotted with sunlight and cloud shadows, a beautiful place in this early summer month of June, the Moon of Making Fat. The Greasy Grass River, timber-lined in places, wound along the east side of the valley, its clear waters fed by snow and springs. A boy of six or seven winters could throw a stone across it. It was only stirrup-deep at the fording spots, but the people loved to swim and bathe in its cool water. On the outer sides of the river bends the banks were high bluffs—in some places rising as bare brown earth, in others grown over with such wild plants as rose vines, now blooming tender pink. Out on the gray hills the Spanish dagger blossomed, its stems heavy with green-white petals. Here and there blue flowers revealed the scattered hiding places of prairie-turnip roots to women diggers.

Set in this peaceful scene were the camp circles. In one sweeping view lay at least six camps of Sioux, large and small, and one of Cheyennes. Altogether they extended almost three miles up and down the river. In addition to the camps' many willow and brush shelters, the wickiups of independent warriors were scattered along the stream. Most of them had come here relying on their leaders and on their old faith that bravery and ability in war were the ultimate answer.

Through the Brûlé camp of the Sioux a crier made his rounds, droning out the orders that had come from the council: "Send for all the women diggers up on the hills; they must come to their lodges! Drive all horse herds into the camp circle! Women, be ready to move quickly, but be calm! You will be protected! Warriors, prepare yourselves to fight!" Downriver in the other camps, the criers repeated the same instructions: "Horse herds into the camp circle! Women, be calm! You will be protected! Warriors, make ready to fight!"

The camp was huge—too large to stay together for many days at one location because the enormous herd

Medicine man Sitting Bull, thought to have commanded the Sioux at the Little Bighorn, actually did not take part in the fighting, but stayed in the hills making medicine.

of ponies ate off the grass. But it was well that they were many. The *wasichus* might come this very day. Sioux scouts had reported some 650 of them half a day's ride away, coming over the divide from Rosebud Creek. Many of the chiefs thought the column was no more than a reconnaissance in force; however, no one could read the mind of a *wasichu* war chief.

Perhaps the bluecoats were the ones the *wasichus* called the 7th Cavalry—led by Long Hair, whom they called Custer, the one who had protected the railroad surveyors along the Yellowstone, invaded the Black Hills and brought the gold hunters. It was he and his men who had killed Cheyenne Chief Black Kettle down south on the Washita River. If they came now while this great encampment still held together, before the bands had to split up, this would be a good day and a good place to meet them, here along the beautiful Greasy Grass, the stream called the Little Bighorn by their enemies the hateful Crows, who sometimes had helped the *wasichus.*

In the large camp circle of the Oglalas most of the horses had been brought in and were now loose herded by the boys. Crazy Horse's yellow pinto, one of his two best war horses, was saddled and tied to a tree near his lodge. Crazy Horse ducked through the entrance of the tipi and squinted in the semidarkness at Black Shawl, his wife, and the old woman, her relative, who lived with them.

His wife was a good woman. She had borne him a child some years past, a little girl who had lived just long enough to laugh and dance and talk. Then she caught the disease that white men called the whooping cough and died. Their common grief had brought Black Shawl and Crazy Horse even closer together.

Without a word the warrior walked to his war bundle. He stripped off his buckskin shirt and leggings, leaving only his breechclout, and knelt on a buffalo robe. He untied the war bundle and laid out his paint, thinking of the many lives already lost this year.

The fighting had started early this spring, more than three moons ago, when the cold still held the north plains in its grip. Having given the arrogant, impossible order that all Indians must go on reservations in midwinter, the whites had struck a sleeping Sioux and Cheyenne camp on the Powder River. Only eight days ago Crazy Horse had led an attack on another column

of white soldiers that was out looking for the Indians along Rosebud Creek. After an all-day battle the soldiers had turned back. The Indians felt very strong.

Now, as he readied himself for battle, he remembered the dream of Sitting Bull. At the sun dance this spring the great medicine man had offered a painful sacrifice. Fifty bits of skin were cut from each arm; then for two days he danced, staring at the sun, until he was exhausted and fell unconscious. When he awoke he told of his vision. Many soldiers would fall upon the camp. Perhaps now the dream would be fulfilled.

Crazy Horse painted a lightning streak across the side of his face and hail marks on his body, and pinned the red-backed hawk in his hair. Then he stepped outside, drew a small piece of boiled meat from the cooking pot and began to eat. The chiefs and subchiefs of the Oglala Sioux came to him to talk. He reminded them that if the *wasichus* had come to fight, they would not fight like Indians. They would be here to conquer and to kill. And so today the Indians must fight the same way. Counting coups would not be enough, the warriors must also strike to kill.

Crazy Horse himself had struck many a coup without counting or even seeming to remember it. If he had put an eagle feather on his bonnet for every enemy he had struck, one would not be able to see the man for the feathers. But this was not a time to be thinking only of such honors.

Suddenly, even as they spoke, they heard the distant crackle of guns far upstream, like the sound of a prairie fire rushing through dry brush. They saw the dust of running horses beyond the farthermost circle of tipis —the circle of the Hunkpapa band of Sioux. Quickly Crazy Horse chose a party of warriors to go with him. In a few moments they were mounted and ready to ride. He took no shield, just a bow, a quiver of arrows, a war club and a rifle; around his neck he hung his eagle-wing-bone war whistle.

He led the warriors galloping up the valley between the camps. The people were excited now and fearful. As he raced by, they recognized him and cried, almost in a frenzy, "Crazy Horse! Crazy Horse!"

He was studying the action ahead at a bend of the river—the dodging warriors, mounted and afoot, operating across the valley and up onto rising ground. The first gunfire must have broken out as soon as the enemy

Indian scouts for the U.S. Cavalry

According to the renowned Indian fighter George Custer, one way to beat the plains warriors was to "fight the devil with fire." By this he meant using Indians to scout for other Indians the cavalry could then destroy. The idea was not to divide and conquer; the plains people were never unified. The Army merely capitalized on long-standing animosities between tribes. Most scouts came from so-called reservation Indians, mainly of the smaller, pacified nations such as the Osage and Kansa, who long had been pushed around by their more powerful neighbors. These men were anxious to get off the reservation, earn $13 a month and get a little safe revenge on their old blood enemies.

Although Indian scouts formally enlisted in the Army, the white soldiers did the actual fighting. All the scouts had to do was apply their intimate knowledge of the plains to trail the enemy and locate his camps. Once a battle erupted, the scouts' only further duty was to cripple the enemy by stampeding his horses.

In his war with the Sioux, Custer used Crow and Arikara scouts. If he had taken their advice, he never would have rushed after the Indian forces at the Little Bighorn. Days before the famous battle, his scouts knew they were on the trail of the bulk of the Teton Nation. Bloody Knife, an Arikara chief and Custer's most trusted scout, repeatedly warned him that there were too many Sioux. But Long Hair, as Custer was called by his scouts, pushed on, fearing only that the Sioux would escape. That was the one thing he need not have feared.

On their first campaign together, in 1873, Custer and his chief scout, Bloody Knife, consult a map of Sioux country. Three years later both would fight at the Little Bighorn.

215

George Armstrong Custer, named a brevet general at 23 during the Civil War, felt by 1876 that the magic of his "boy general" reputation was fading. He hoped to recoup with a spectacular victory over the Sioux.

had come near the wickiups scattered along the river. The attackers had stopped within rifle range of the Hunkpapa camp.

The defenders cheered him as he came among them, thinking that he would lead a charge. But he merely waved at them and veered left into the timber, where he saw Black Moon and some of the other chiefs. They held a hurried war council while bullets whipped through the cottonwood trees above them, dropping twigs and leaves. Black Moon had seen the attack. The bluecoats had charged, but they had stopped when the Indians came out to meet them.

Crazy Horse rode over to where he could see the battle line better, and at that moment a curious event occurred. From the line of white soldiers a horse ran away —straight toward the Indians. Some of the Indians thought it a daring show of bravery, but Crazy Horse saw the panicked horse—white-eyed, new to battle —and the anguished rider trying desperately to hang on and control his mount.

He kicked his pinto and went after the runaway, yelling to make his pony run, aware that he was in the gun sights of many bluecoats. He whipped alongside the white man's horse and swung once with his heavy, stone-headed war club. There was consternation in the enemy's eyes and then squirting blood. He pulled his pony away, leaving the others to catch the frightened horse and to strip the weapons and ammunition from the sagging blue bag that had been a human being.

Now he urged the yellow pinto in a jagged course between the battle lines, turning the trained pony right and left and making a small target of himself on the shoulder of his mount. As he rode he could study and count the enemy: the kneeling cavalrymen; the horse holders scrambling back, each with four horses; and the hated Ree scouts. But the enemy was giving way; Black Moon was turning their flank.

Crazy Horse swerved away from the line until he was out of range, then made a large circle back to a stand of trees where some chiefs were waiting. Gall, a leader of the Hunkpapas, had also joined them.

As he sat for a few minutes letting his horse catch its wind, Crazy Horse watched the fighting. It seemed to him that there were very few soldiers to have attacked such a large Indian camp alone. Perhaps there were more of them out there somewhere. This flurry could be a diversion. The other chiefs agreed. It was certain these soldiers could not hold out long against so many warriors. Meanwhile, the Indians must be watchful for an attack from another direction.

Soon these white men did begin to run, falling back first on the river, where there was cover in a clump of scrub willows and buffalo-berry thickets. But the wind favored the Sioux. They started fires in the drying buffalo grass and bottom brush, destroying the cover and laying a smoke screen in the valley. The smoke was thick from half-green weeds, bitter and spicy with the scent of sage.

The whites broke; they remounted and retreated pell-mell toward a bad ford over the river, where the east bank and the hills above were steep. The Sioux swarmed around them as they fled, clubbing some in the river, showering them with arrows and bullets as the retreating horses scrambled up the gray slopes to a defensive position. The fleeing force of whites left at least 30 men dead or dying. The Sioux recognized two of the enemy who would never fight again: a Ree scout named Bloody Knife and a paleface scout called by the whites Lonesome Charley Reynolds. Another dead one was a black-skinned man with tightly curled hair, the same kind of hair that down in the southern plains had won such men the name of buffalo soldiers from their Indian opponents.

Crazy Horse held back many of his Oglala warriors and waited, consulting with other leaders, sending and receiving messages from the camps. Then his caution and patience were rewarded. Scouts east of the river signaled to them with blankets and mirrors; an attacking force was behind the ridges and headed north. Now Gall pulled back, too, leaving only enough men to pin down the cavalry that had taken position on a hill east of the river.

Crazy Horse and Gall turned down the valley. Gall and his warriors would gallop downriver between the main enemy force and the Indian camps, crossing the river before the enemy could attack. Crazy Horse would keep going straight through the camps, taking hundreds of warriors with him, and cross beyond the bluecoats so that he could hit them from behind.

He forced his tiring pinto back through two and a half miles of the camps, motioning as he went to the warriors still in camp to join him. By the time he came

Custer on Indians

In battle against the Plains Indians, George Armstrong Custer was impetuous, merciless and intent on personal glory. Yet when he wrote about them he showed a subtle, reflective side and even some occasional — though grudging — flashes of insight into their predicament. The following quotations are excerpted from his autobiography of 1874, *My Life on the Plains.*

If I were an Indian, I often think I would greatly prefer to cast my lot among those of my people who adhered to the free open plains, rather than submit to the confined limits of a reservation, there to be the recipient of the blessed benefits of civilization, with its vices thrown in without stint or measure.

Stripped of the beautiful romance with which we have been so long willing to envelop him, the Indian forfeits his claim to the appellation of the "'noble' red man." We see him as he is, a "savage" in every sense of the word; not worse, perhaps, than his white brother would be similarly born and bred, but one whose cruel and ferocious nature far exceeds that of any wild beast of the desert.

When the soil which he has claimed and hunted over for so long a time is demanded by this to him insatiable monster [civilization], there is no appeal; he must yield, or it will roll mercilessly over him, destroying as it advances. Destiny seems to have so willed it, and the world nods its approval.

to his own Oglala circle, an army of Sioux fighters was following him, cheering and yelling war cries. Black Shawl had his other war horse, the bay, tied close by and waiting. In a moment he was up on his new mount.

It was time for the traditional call to battle — rifle held high as the words resounded across the camp:

"Hoka hey, Lakotas! It's a good day to die!"

"Hoka hey!" came the answering war cry. "It's a good day to die!"

He led them north at a fast gallop along the valley floor, picking up Cheyenne reinforcements as he went. Off to his right he had seen a troop of cavalry mounted on gray horses at Medicine Tail Coulee. But the ford was well defended, and Gall was charging toward the spot with a mass of warriors. The hoofs of his own warriors' horses sounded like thunder rolling down the valley floor. The main battle was being joined at last.

Upon this day when the government sent its most renowned cavalry regiment—led by its most flamboyant Indian fighter—against the great Indian encampment, many bands of the Western Sioux were there, along with some Eastern Sioux, Northern Cheyennes, some Southern Cheyennes and a few Arapaho friends. Not only chiefs and warriors were in the encampment; women, old men and children were there. Some were standing by, excited, cheering, scared. Others were moving out onto the low hills to the west in readiness to escape. Among those who rode out to fight were three teen-age boys. Each of them survived to live a long life and later to remember and recount how it was to be a boy, reared in the warrior ethic, on that day on the Greasy Grass. Their stories are as much a part of the day as that of Crazy Horse himself.

Black Elk, an Oglala Sioux and a cousin of Crazy Horse, was 13 years old that summer. He had gone to the social dances around the camps the night before, staying till he got too sleepy; then he had gone home. His father wakened him at daybreak to help take the horses out to graze. Concerned for the safety of the horses, his father cautioned him to leave a long lead on one so that it could be easily caught; it could then be used to gather the others. He told the boy to hurry the horses home if anything happened.

As the day grew hot, the appeal of the clear river became too great for Black Elk; he left the herd in charge of a young cousin and went swimming with some other boys. While they were playing in the water, the cousin brought the horses to the same spot for a drink. At that moment the herald of the Hunkpapa circle cried out: "The cavalry is coming! The cavalry is coming!" Black Elk's older brother dashed away toward the attackers without even a weapon. Soon the boy's father came, bringing weapons for each of his sons. The father's instructions to Black Elk were to take one of the guns to his brother, then come straight home. But after Black Elk got to the place where Black Moon and the others were turning back that first diversionary attack, he could not help remaining. When Crazy Horse rode up, the boy took great pride in the cheers for his cousin.

When the whites broke and ran Black Elk followed in the wake of the counterattack. A Sioux warrior pointed to a blue-clad soldier kicking on the ground. "Boy, get off and scalp him," he said. Black Elk dismounted and began the job, but he was not an expert and his knife was dull. The dying man ground his teeth, so the boy shot him in the forehead with his revolver, then finished cutting away the hair.

He remounted his buckskin pony and soon rode straight back to his lodge in the Oglala camp to show his mother the scalp. When his mother saw the scalp she sounded a tremolo, a shrill yell of triumph made by crying out while patting the lips. Black Elk was not punished or criticized for his disobedience that day. After all, at 13 he had taken his first scalp.

Iron Hawk was a Hunkpapa Sioux, 14 years old. He had stayed up nearly all night watching the dances, had slept through the morning and was eating his first meal of the day when the criers warned of the approaching white soldiers. Iron Hawk ran out toward his family's horses and caught his pony. But the other horses stampeded briefly from the sounds of firing and the excitement, and it took some time for him and his brother to round them up in the Hunkpapa camp circle.

Then Iron Hawk ran into the family tipi to dress for battle. His hands were so shaky that he had difficulty in braiding the eagle feather into his hair and rubbing his face with red paint. He grabbed his arrow quiver and heavy bow, mounted and rode out.

The first attack had already been repulsed, and everyone was riding toward the ford opposite the middle of the encampment. Iron Hawk followed, yelling war cries to bolster his courage. He crossed the Greasy Grass and headed toward the rising dust and smoke in the hills. It was all confusion to him. He saw the fighters, Indian and white, dashing here and there, mounted and afoot, doing brave deeds, taking risks, falling. He himself did not actually join the battle until a small group of troopers moved in his direction. He began to jerk out arrows and shoot them.

Almost immediately he put an arrow through a mounted trooper; the point stuck out on one side, the feathers on the other. The trooper screamed and grabbed hold of his saddle; his head sank and his body wobbled, and the boy struck him a mighty blow on the back of the neck with his bow. The trooper tumbled off his horse. The boy sprang off after him and began to beat him with the bow, beating and beating even after the man was dead. Each time he struck he yelled "Hownh" because, as he said later, he was angry thinking about the women and little children back in camp, scared and running. Of course, Iron Hawk may have been in a frenzy because he was afraid himself; it's difficult to be calm in battle when you are 14 years old.

Another teen-age defender was Wooden Leg, an 18-year-old Cheyenne whose name, far from implying that he was crippled, came from the treelike strength of his limbs. In fact, he had danced at the social the night before, going with other young men to a Sioux camp where the girls asked them to dance, for it was the Sioux custom that the women at social dances ask the men. The young warrior, already over six feet tall, was popular with the girls; he danced until dawn, then wearily returned home. Instead of disturbing the family in his lodge, he lay on the ground outside and slept a few hours. Then he ate and went with his brother to the river for a bath. Under a shady tree near the water the two of them lay down again to catch up on their sleep. They were awakened by the commotion when the fight began much farther upstream.

Wooden Leg's elderly father had already caught and saddled his warrior son's favorite horse, and Wooden Leg had only to prepare himself for battle. He put on his best breeches, a good cloth shirt and beaded moccasins. Then he painted a blue-black circle around his face and filled it in completely with red and yellow. If the Great Medicine called him this day

This Indian battle standard, lined with hawk feathers, belonged to an unknown Sioux chieftain. Carried into a fight, it was a rallying point for fellow warriors and a symbol of its bearer's bravery.

he wanted to be dressed for the occasion. He felt that he should oil and neatly braid his hair, but his father told him to hurry, so he simply secured it with a buckskin thong and let it hang loose. His weapon was an old revolver; he gathered up his caps and balls and powder horn and rode upstream toward the battleground.

Wooden Leg arrived at the point of first attack as the cavalry gave way on its left flank, and he joined a group of Sioux warriors that was circling clear around the whites. Thousands of arrows and many bullets flew toward the enemy; many bullets came back. When the whites broke out of the bushes and trees in which they had taken refuge Wooden Leg was in their path. He lashed his horse and fled; then he realized that they were on the run and turned to chase them. He fired his revolver four times, but saw no result. Racing after the soldiers whose horses were badly tired, he caught up with a trooper and clubbed him with the elk-horn handle of his pony whip. As the wounded man fell from his horse, Wooden Leg wrestled his gun away. Then he joined the other warriors in the pursuit to the river, where he clubbed at the fleeing whites with his new weapon.

Later Wooden Leg returned to the west side of the stream to help hunt for hidden enemies through the smoking, smoldering brush. From the pockets of a dead soldier he took some tobacco, and from the man's waist he took a cartridge belt; in the saddlebags of a dead horse he found two small boxes, each containing 20 cartridges that fitted his new cartridge belt and gun. At this moment, as he later recalled it, he felt brave indeed.

He rode back down through the camps to his lodge for a fresh horse. He gave the tobacco to his father, who told him that he had been brave enough for one day and should not join the new fighting in

Proof of daring in battle is everywhere visible among this war party of Oglala Sioux, the tribe to which Crazy Horse belonged. Although some of the warriors have guns, most are carrying coupsticks to strike an enemy directly. The eagle feathers in their war bonnets signify their past coups.

the hills to the east. But Wooden Leg wanted to go. His father saddled a fresh mount for him and made the medicine to protect it. But he reminded Wooden Leg that his older brother was already fighting in the battle; he did not want to risk losing both his sons. He instructed his younger son to remain as far as he could from the soldiers. Wooden Leg rode east toward the main battle but stayed at a distance from it, just as his father had asked him to do. Wooden Leg fired his gun and watched the progress of the struggle from afar.

When Crazy Horse swept downstream through the camps, gathering warriors behind him, he began to comprehend the enemy's strategy: attack the upper end of the encampment with a small force to draw off the warriors, then hit the undefended camp downriver with the main force of bluecoats. But the whites were laboriously maneuvering in the horse-killing hills, while he had the valley floor. In a matter of minutes he had come well past the camps, beyond any of the fighting. Now he turned eastward across a ford in the river, which slowed them slightly. Then he led them up a broad ravine, which was deep enough to conceal the warriors from the enemy.

The hills out here, gray-tan in color, were dotted with sagebrush, each plant like a tiny tree with a twisted trunk hardly large enough to hide a rabbit. The soil supported an occasional Spanish dagger plant thrusting up its spike of tender green flowers; in some spots lonely thistles held up powder-puff flowers of lavender. The prairie pea vines, hardly noticeable unless one looked carefully, had already bloomed and were growing seeds in their small pods. But in spots the plants did not conceal the adobe earth, which was bare to the erosion of rain and wind, and to the crushing hoofs of horses. Farther upriver the draws were softened by clumps of juniper or chokecherries; here they were mostly barren washes. There were no cliffs or steep banks or outcrops of rock. It was as if the land had giant wrinkles, but the slopes were steep enough to labor horses mightily. This place was appropriately naked and raw. If men were gathering to kill each other, why not do it here?

Crazy Horse had no difficulty in locating the battle. Gall and his force had already struck. Gray dust rose in a cloud beyond the ridge, and Crazy Horse turned up out of the ravine toward it. The bay gelding took the slope eagerly; it had gained its second wind. He raised his hand to stop the broad train of warriors behind him, then proceeded with half a dozen of the chiefs not to the cap of the ridge, but only high enough to see the panorama of battle. Their view extended two miles to Deep Coulee and Medicine Tail Coulee beyond. Almost a mile off to the right was the Greasy Grass.

The nearest whites were only an arrow's flight away, but their forces stretched about half a mile along a ridge and down a ravine. Attacked from two sides, they were trying to regroup. A bugle repeated and repeated an insistent call, but the troops were half mounted and half dismounted, many of them kneeling in firing lines. Crazy Horse could identify the leaders, consulting, yelling at their men. They knew they were in trouble. Striking quickly, before they could decide what to do, should completely rout them.

A contingent of warriors scrambled farther up the ravine in order to surround the enemy. Then Crazy Horse, with one slender brown arm, waved the remaining warriors toward the center of the scattered U.S. Cavalry. Putting the eagle-wing-bone whistle to his lips, he blew a shrill blast and kicked the bay up and over the top. He did not look back. For two long breaths he could not even hear the mounted men behind him, for horses on an uphill slope dig silently in the dirt as they come; but as the horses hit the more level downhill footing, their hoofbeats grew to a roar. He guided his own horse with his legs and held up his rifle and his stone-headed war club; he was the symbol of all Sioux bravery, leading his warriors against the enemy.

The troopers turned erratically toward the charge, some of them late because of their single-minded attention to Gall's warriors coming at them from the opposite direction. Crazy Horse saw one blue-clad figure hesitating, trying to hide on both sides of a tiny sagebrush hummock. The chief's magnificent bay, almost a part of him, picked his footing like a dancer in a dead run, and Crazy Horse guided him straight into the center of the enemy, straight into the muzzles of their guns. Behind him he could hear the others blowing their piercing war whistles and yipping like coyotes.

Now the dust rose thicker, mixed with the darker, dirty powder smoke. The midafternoon seemed like twilight; under the pall gunflashes winked like fireflies. At times, for some short heartbeats, the blasts of rifles and

TACTICS AT LITTLE BIGHORN

This map traces the action of the Battle of the Little Bighorn, which the Indians called the Greasy Grass River. By noon of June 25, 1876, Custer was advancing on an Indian encampment protected by 1,500 to 2,500 warriors. His small force had been split three ways. He had sent Captain Benteen with 125 troopers on a probe, then dispatched Major Reno with about 140 men straight toward the Indian village. Confronted by a massive enemy concentration, Reno made a brief stand. But the Indians drove him back, and he and his men barely escaped across the river. Soon Benteen reinforced him, and they dug in against a heavy attack. Meanwhile Custer, with about 215 men, raced north along a route thought to be as shown here, until he ran into the warriors led by Gall and Crazy Horse. By charging ahead so impetuously, Custer disobeyed all instructions and ignored the warning of his friend, Colonel John Gibbon, who had called out as Custer first started off, "Now don't be greedy, Custer, as there are Indians enough for all of us."

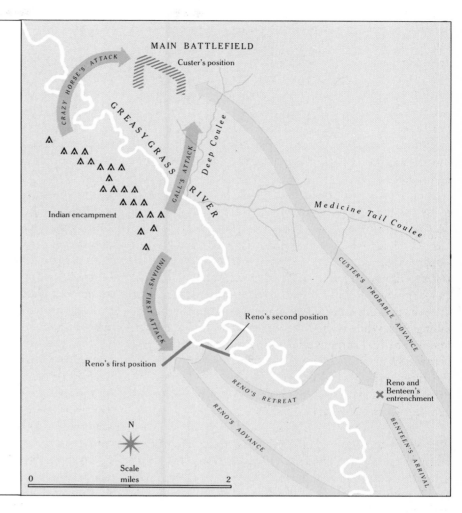

MAIN BATTLEFIELD
Custer's position
CRAZY HORSE'S ATTACK
GREASY GRASS RIVER
Deep Coulee
GALL'S ATTACK
Medicine Tail Coulee
CUSTER'S PROBABLE ADVANCE
Indian encampment
INDIANS' FIRST ATTACK
Reno's second position
Reno's first position
RENO'S RETREAT
RENO'S ADVANCE
Reno and Benteen's entrenchment
BENTEEN'S ARRIVAL
N
Scale miles
0   2

carbines sounded like the ripping of a giant canvas down the wrinkles of the hills.

Crazy Horse pulled down his rifle, which he had held like a banner as high as he could thrust it, and began to fire it, one-handed. The whites reeled away from the charge on either hand, their shying horses jerking their aim awry. And meanwhile Gall's warriors had risen up to take full advantage of the enemy's suddenly divided attention.

The white men's horses screamed above the din. They clawed at the gray slopes like cats; they whinnied as the arrows and bullets entered their bodies, as they bled, as they struggled against the weight of the troopers on their backs or dragging from the stirrups. Their necks and sides and flanks were flecked with dirty white sweat, their mouths were marked with bloody foam from the wrenching by the soldiers on cruel bits.

The genius of a leader is that he thinks well in the midst of the sounds and confusion of a battle. Crazy Horse did not pursue single running soldiers. He and his warriors bore down on concentrations of white troops, forcing them to yield and split or be overrun. They thrust between the whites and their horses, killing horse holders when they could, stampeding the animals with their saddlebags of ammunition. The charge was like a great arrowpoint cutting through the enemy forces. And when Crazy Horse pulled up at the end of his run the military forces of the white men were in utter disarray.

To one side a small group of Sioux were chasing a lone soldier; he fled in front of them for a desperate mile and, finally realizing that the flight was hopeless, put a

Custer's last message was this plea, later transcribed more legibly by Benteen, the recipient: "Bring packs," meaning bullets. His men had only 124 rounds apiece, leaving more than 24,000 in the pack train.

On July 6, 11 days after the battle, the *Bismarck Tribune* ran this "first account." But the *Bozeman Times* had scooped it with an extra on July 3; by July 4 telegraphers had wired the story to New York.

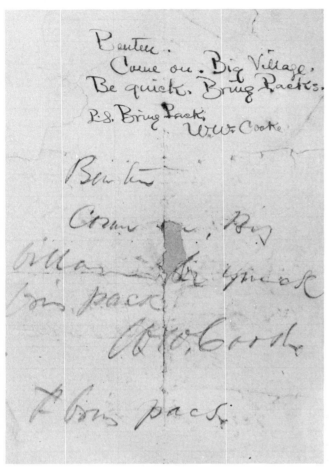

bullet through his head. There would be no regrouping for the whites, no escape. The warriors had moved up to better and closer positions all around them. The only protection was an occasional swell of ground or the carcass of a horse, and every small group or line of cavalry found itself defending in one direction as an attack came from another. There were short charges and pursuits. At the last, most of the work was done with lances or war clubs, as the whites' guns jammed or their ammunition ran out. It was over in minutes.

As the fighting ended, one may picture Crazy Horse sitting on his tired pony, on a ridge where he could see the last white resistance being wiped out. Soon the moaning women would come with their travois to pick up their warriors, wounded and dead, and to strip the whites and slash futilely at their remains. This moment belonged to the Sioux chief. Custer, his will, his energy, lay still. Crazy Horse must have been deeply stirred.

He surely knew that the victory was not decisive, that it was a battle he had won, not a war. But it may be that he did not philosophize, though he was an intelligent man. It may be that the sense of the rightness of what he had done lay deep in his bones rather than on his tongue, that he would have said, "If you want to talk to a wise old medicine man go hunt up Sitting Bull at his prayers or go back to the reservation and talk to Red Cloud and his white friends. I have done what I have done."

As for those who have followed, it seems that we cannot let that bloody day alone. Writers multiply the monographs and books about it; they probe it, search it; they seem compelled to tell the story again and again. Some believe that the Battle of the Little Bighorn — with Crazy Horse tall on his pony and Custer lying in the dust amid the ruins of his crack regiment — was a symbol around which Indians might have banded together against their white enemies. There are objections to this view. The Crows and Arikaras were on Custer's side. Could the Crow people have renounced their history of conflict with the Sioux, the beliefs and traditions of their ancestors, to rally behind a Sioux victory over the white man? United, the Plains Indians might have held out longer against the encroaching white man. But they were not united.

Perhaps the clearest meaning of the battle was that the Plains Indian still had his dignity and would fight for his freedom. He would lose the war, but he could still win a battle — especially this one. The white commander's big mistake was in not understanding this. By his acts Custer had asserted: I will meet you on your own terms, I will give you numerical odds and I will beat you. He had the option of bringing along Gatling guns and additional cavalry, but did not. He might have waited a day for other troops to come up, but did not. He challenged on the basis of manliness as he knew it, of bravery, of horsemanship, of fighting spirit, of complete, blind devotion to one's cause. On that fateful Sunday, June 25, 1876, Custer renounced the advantages of his white background and in doing so he meant to leave the Indians nothing.

At that moment, when he sat motionless on the ridge above the battleground, Crazy Horse might well have said in quiet exultation: "Today, white soldiers, you were mistaken. But it *was* a good day to die."

FIRST ACCOUNT OF THE CUSTER MASSACRE

TRIBUNE EXTRA

Price 25 Cents.

BISMARCK, D. T., JULY 6, 1876.

MASSACRED

GEN. CUSTER AND 261 MEN THE VICTIMS.

NO OFFICER OR MAN OF 5 COMPANIES LEFT TO TELL THE TALE.

3 Days Desperate Fighting by Maj. Reno and the Remainder of the Seventh.

Full Details of the Battle.

LIST OF KILLED AND WOUNDED

Bismarck Tribune's Special Correspondent Slain.

Squaws Mutilate and Rob Dead.

Victims Captured Alive. Tortured in Fiendish Manner.

What Will Congress Do About It

Shall This Be the Beginning of the End?

It will be remembered that the Bismarck Tribune sent a special correspondent with Gen. Terry, who was the only proffessional correspondent with the expedition. Kellogg's last words to the writer were: "We leave the Rosebud tomorrow and by the time this reaches you we will have

MET AND FOUGHT

the red devils, with what result remains to be seen. I go with Custer and will be at the death." How true! On the morning of the 22d Gen. Custer took up the line of march for the trail of the Indians, reported by Reno on the Rosebud. Gen. Terry, apprehending danger, urged Custer to take additional men, but Custer having full confidence in his men and in their ability to cope with the Indians in whatever force he might meet them, declined the proffered assistance and marched with his regiment alone. He was instructed to strike the trail of the Indians, to follow it until he discovered their position, and report by courier to Gen. Terry who would reach the mouth of the Little Horn by the evening of the 26th, when he would act in concert with Custer in the final wiping out. At four o'clock, the afternoon of the 24th, Custer scouts reported the location of a village recently deserted, whereupon Custer went into camp, marching again at 11 p. m., continuing the march until daylight when he again went into camp for coffee. Custer was then fifteen miles from the village located on the Little Horn, one of the branches of the Big Horn, twenty miles above its mouth, which could be seen from the top of the divide, and after lunch Gen. Custer pushed on. The Indians by this time had discovered his approach and soon were seen mounting in great haste, riding here and there, it was presumed in full retreat. This idea was strengthened by finding a freshly abandoned Indian camp with a deserted tepee, in which one of their dead had been left, about six miles from where the battle took place. Custer with his usual vigor pushed on making seventy-eight miles without sleep, and attacked the village near its foot with companies C, E, F, I, and L seventh cavalry. Reno having in the meantime attacked it at its head with three companies of cavalry which, being surrounded, after a desperate hand to hand conflict, in which many were killed and wounded, cut their way to a bluff about three hundred feet high, where they were reinforced by four companies of cavalry under Col. Benteen. In gaining this position Col. Reno had to recross the Little Horn, and at the ford the hottest fight occurred. It was here where Lieutenants McIntosh, Hodgson and Dr. DeWolf fell; where Charley Reynolds fell in a hand to hand conflict with a dozen or more Sioux, emptying several chambers of his revolver, each time bringing a red-skin before he was brought down—shot thru the heart. It was here Bloody Knife surrendered his spirit to the one who gave it, fighting the natural and heriditary foes of his tribe, as well as the foes of the whites.

The Sioux dashed up beside the soldiers in some instances knocking them from their horses and killing them at their pleasure. This was the case with Lt. McIntosh, who was unarmed except with a saber. He was pulled from his horse, tortured and finally murdered at the pleasure of the red-devils. It was here that Fred Girard was separated from the command and lay all night with the screeching fiends dealing death and destruction to his comrades within a few feet of him, and, but time will not permit us to relate the story, through some means succeeded in saving his fine black stallion in which he took so much pride. The ford was crossed, the summit of the bluffs, having, Col. Smith says, the steepest sides that he ever saw ascended by a horse or mule reached, though the ascent was made under a galling fire.

Companies engaged in this affair were those of Captains Boylan, French and McIntosh. Col. Reno had gone ahead with these companies in obedience to the order of Gen. Custer, fighting most gallantly, driving back repeatedly the Indians who charged in their front, but the fire from the bluff being so galling, forced the movement heretofore alluded to. Signals were given and soon Benteen with the four companies in reserve came up in time to save Reno from the fate with which Custer about this time met. The Indians charged the hill time and again but were each time repulsed with heavy slaughter by its gallant defenders. Soon, however, they reached bluffs higher than those occupied by Reno; and opened a destructive fire from points beyond the reach of cavalry carbines. Nothing being heard from Gen. Custer, Col. Weir was ordered to push his command along the bank of the river in the direction he was supposed to be, but he was soon driven back, retiring with difficulty. About this time the Indians received strong reinforcements, and literally swarmed the hill sides and on the plains, coming so near at times that stones were thrown into the ranks of Col. Reno's command by those unarmed or out of amunition. Charge after charge in quick succession, the fight being sometimes almost hand to hand. But they drew off finally, taking to the hills and ravines. Col. Benteen charged a large party in a ravine, driving them from it in confusion. They evidently trusted their numbers and did not look for so bold a movement. They were within the range of the corral and wounded several packers, J. C. Wagoner, among the number, in the head, while many horses and mules were killed. Near 10 o'clock the fight closed, and the men worked all night strengthening their breastworks, using knives tin cups and plates, in place of spades and picks, taking up the fight again in the morning. In the afternoon of the second day the desire for water became almost intolerable. The wounded were begging piteously for it; the tongues of the men were swolen and their lips parched, and from lack of rest they were almost exhausted. So a bold attempt was made for water. Men volunteered to go with canteens and camp kettles, though to go was almost certain death. The attempt succeeded, though in making it one man was killed and several wounded. The men were relieved and that night the animals were watered. The fight closed at dark, opening again next morning, and continuing until the afternoon of the 27th Meantime the men become more and more exhausted and all wondered what had become of Custer. A panic all at once was created among the Indians and they stampeded, from the hills and from the valleys, and the village was soon deserted except for the dead, Reno and his brave men felt that succor was nigh. Gen. Terry came in sight, and strong men wept upon each others necks, but no word was had from Custer. Hand shaking and congratulations were scarcely over when Lt. Bradley reported that he had found Custer dead, with one hundred and ninety cavalry men. Imagine the effect. Words cannot picture the feeling of these, his comrades and soldiers. Gen. Terry sought the spot and found it to be too true. Of those brave men who followed Custer, all perished; no one lives to tell the story of the battle. Those deployed as skirmshers, lay as they fell, shot down from every side, having been entirely surrounded in an open plain. The men in companies fell in platoons, and like those on the skirmish line, lay as they fell, with their officers behind them in their proper positions. Gen. Custer, who was shot through the head and body, seemed to have been among the last to fall, and around and near him lay the bodies of Col. Tom and Boston, his brothers, Col. Calhour, his brother-in-law, and his nephew young Reed, who insisted on accompaning the expedition for pleasure, Col. Cook and the members of the non-commissioned staff all dead—all stripped of clothing and many of them with bodies terribly mutilated. The squaws seem to have passed over the field and crushed the skulls of the wounded and dying with stones and clubs. The heads of some were severed from the body, the privates of some were cut off, while others bore traces of torture, arrows having been shot into their private parts while yet living or other means of torture adopted. The officers who fell are as follows: Gen. G. A. Custer, Cols. Geo. Yates, Miles Keough, James Calhoun, W. W. Cook, Capts. McIntosh, A. E. Smith, Lieutenants Riley, Critenden, Sturgis, Harrington, Hodgson, and Porter, Asst. Surgeon De Wolf. The only citizens killed were Boston Custer, Mr. Reed, Charles Reynolds, Isiah, the interperter from Ft. Rice and Mark Kellogg, the latter the Tribune correspondent. The body of Kellogg alone remained unstripped of clothing, and was not mutilated. Perhaps as they had learned to respect the Great Chief, Custer, and for that reason did not mutilate his remains, they had in like manner learned to respect this humble shover of the lead pencil and to that fact may be attributed this result. The wounded were sent to the rear some fourteen miles on horse litters striking the Far West sixty odd miles up the Big Horn which point they left on Monday at noon reaching Bismarck nine hundred miles distant at 10 p. m.

The burial of the dead was sad work but they were all decently interred. Many could not be reconized; among the latter class were some of the officers. This work being done the command wended its way back to the base where Gen. Terry, awaits supplies and approval of his plans for the future campaign.

The men are worn out with marching and fighting, and are almost wholly destitute of clothing.

The Indians numbered at least eighteen hundred lodges in their permanent camp, while those who fought Crook seems to have joined them, making their effective fighting force nearly four thousand. These were led by chiefs carrying flags of various colors, nine of whom were found in a burial tent on the field of battle, many other dead were found on the field, and near it ten squaws at one point in the ravine—evidently the work of Ree or Crow scouts.

The Indian dead were great in number, as they were constantly assaulting an inferior force The camp had the appearance of having abandoned in haste. The most georgeous ornaments were found on the bodies of the dead chiefs, and hundreds of finely dressed and painted robes and skins were thrown about the camp. The Indians were certainly severely punished.

We said of those who went into battle with Custer none are living —one Crow scout hid himself in the field, and witnessed and survived the battle. His story is plausable, and is accepted, but we have not the room for it now. The names of the wounded are as follows:

LIST OF WOUNDED

Private Davis Corey, Co. I, 7th Cav. right hip; Patrick McDonnall, D, left leg; Sergt. John Paul, H, back; Priv. Michael C. Madden, K, right leg; Wm. George, H, left side, died July 3d, at 4 a. m.; 1st Sergt. Wm. Heyn, A, left knee; Priv. John McVey, C, hips; Patrick Corcoran, K, right shoulder; Max Wilke, K, left foot; Alfred Whitaker, C, right elbow; Peter Thompson, C, right hand; Jacob Deal, A, face; J. H. Meyer, M, back; Roman Rutler, M, right shoulder; Daniel Newell, M, left thigh; J. Muller, H, right thigh; Elijah T. Shroude, A, right leg; Sergt. Patrick Carey, M, rigth hip; Privt. James E. Benett, C, body, died July 5th, at 3 o'clock; Francis Reeves, A, left side and body; James Wilbur, M, left leg; Jasper Marshall, L, left foot; Sergt. James T. Riley, E, back and left leg; Privt. John J. Phillips, H, face and both hands. Samuel Severn, H, both thighs; Frank Brunn, M, face and left thigh; Corp. Alex B. Bishop, H, right arm; Privt. Jas Foster, A, right arm; W. E. Harris, M, left breast; Chas. H. Bishop, H, right arm; Fred Homsted, A, left wrist; Sergt. Chas. White, M, right arm; Privt. Thos. P. Varner, M, right ear; Chas. Campbell, C, right shoulder; John Cooper, H, right elbow; John McGuire, C, right arm; Henry Black, H, right hand; Daniel McWilliams, H, right leg.

An Indian scout, name unknown, left off at Birthold; Sergt. M. Riley, Co. I, 7th Infantry, left off at Buford, Consumption; Privt. David Ackison, Co. E, 7th cav., left off, July 4th, at Buford, Constipation.

The total number of killed was two hundred and sixty one; wounded 52. Thirty-eight of the wounded were brought down on the Far West; three of them died en route. The remainder are cared for at the field hospital.

De Rudio had a narrow escape, and his escape is attributed to the noise of the beavers, jumping into the river during the engagement. De Rudio followed them, got out of sight, and after hiding for twelve hours or more, finally reached the command in safety.

The body of Lt. Hodgson did not fall into the hands of the Indians; that of Lt. McIntosh did, and was badly mutilated. McIntosh, though a half-breed, was a gentleman of culture and esteemed by all who knew him. He leaves a family at Lincoln, as does Gen. Custer, Cols. Calhoun, Yates, Cook Smith, and Lt. Porter. The unhappy Mrs. Calhoun, loses a husband, three brothers and a nephew. Lt. Harrington also had a family, but no trace of his remains was found. We are indebted to Col. Smith for the following list of the dead; to Dr. Porter for the list of wounded, which is also full:

KILLED

Field and staff, George A. Custer Brevt. Major General.

W. W. Cook, Brevt. Lt-Colonel.

Lord Asst. Surgeon, J. M. DeWolf, Acting Asst. Surgeon.

A.C. Staff, W. W. Sharrow Surg-Major.

Henry Voss, Chief Inspir.

A, Henry Dallans, ... Corp.
A, G. K. King, ... "
A, J. E. Armstrong, ... Privt.
A, James Drinaw, ... "
A, Wm. Moody, ... "
A, D. Rowlins, ... "
A, James McDonald, ... "
A, John Sullivan, ... "
A, Thos. P. Switzer, ... "
B, Benj. Hodgson, ... 2nd Lieut.
B, Richard Doran, ... Privt.
B, George Mask, ... "
C, T. W. Custer, ... Brevt. Lt.-Col.
C, H. M. Harrington, ... 2d Lt.

The body of Lt. Harrington was not found, but it is reasonably certan that he was killed.

C, Edwin Baba, ... 1st Sergt.
C, Finley, ... Sergt.
C, Finkle .... "
C, French, ... Corpl.
C Foley, ... "
C Ryan, ... "
C, Allen, ... Privt.
C, Criddle, ... "
C, King, ... "
C, Bucknell, ... "
C, Eisman, ... "
C, Engle, ... "
C, Brightfield, ... "
C, Fanand, ... "
C, Griffin, ... "
C, Hamel, ... "
C, Hattisoll, ... "
C, Kingsoutz, ... "
C, Lewis, ... "
C, Mayer, ... "
C, Mayer, ... "
C, Phillips, ... "
C, Russell, ... "
C, Rix, ... "
C, Ranter, ... "
C, Short, ... "
C, Shea, ... "
C, Shade, ... "
C, Stuart, ... "
C, St. John, ... "
C, Thadius, ... "
C, Van Allen, ... "
C, Warren, ... "
C, Windham, ... "
C, Wright, ... "
D, Vincent Charley Farrier
D, Patrick Golden, ... Privt.
D, Edward Hansen, ... "
E, A. E. Smith, ... Brevt. Capt.
E, E. Sturgis, ... 2d Lt.

The body of Lt. Sturgis was not found, but it is reasonably certain he was killed.

E, F. Hohmeyer, ... 1st Sergt.
E, Egnen, ... Sergt.
E, James, ... "
E, Hagan, ... Corp.
L, James Calhoun, ... 1st Lt.
L, Miller, ... Privt.
L, Tweed, ... "
L, Veller, ... "
L, Cashan, ... "
L, Kiefer, ... "
L, Andrews, ... "
L, Crisfield, ... "
L, Harrington .... "
L, Haugge, ... "
L, Kavaugh, ... "
L, Lobering, ... "
L, Mahoney, ... "
L, Schmidt, ... "
L, Lunon, ... "
L, Semenson, ... "
L, Riebold, ... "
L, O'Connell, ... "
L, J. J. Crittenden, ... 20th Inf.
L, Butler, ... 1st Sergt.
L, Warren, ... "
L, Harrison, ... Corpl.
L, Gilbert, ... "
L, Walsh, ... Teptr.
L, Adams, ... Privt.
L, Assdely, ... "
L, Burke, ... "
L, Cheever, ... "
L, McGue, ... "
L, McCarthy, ... "
L, Dugan, ... "
L, Maxwell, ... "
L, Scott, ... "
L, Babcock, ... "
L, Perkins, ... "
L, Tarbox, ... "
L, Dye, ... "
L, Tessler, ... "
L, Galvin, ... "
L, Graham, ... "
L, Hamilton, ... "
L, Rodgers, ... "
L, Snow, ... "
L, Hughes, ... "
K, D. Whitney, ... 1st Sergt
K, Hughes .... Sergt
K, J. J. Callahan .... Corpl
K, Julius Helmer .... Trptr
K, Eli U. T. Clair .... Privt
I, M. W. Keogh .... Col
I, J. E. Porter—the body of Lt. Porter was not found, but it is reasonably certain he was killed.
I, F. E. Varden .... 1st Sergt
I, J. Burtard .... "
I, John Wild .... Corpl
I, G. C. Morris .... "
I, S. T. Staplis .... "
I, J. M. Gucker .... "
I, J. Patton, ... Trptr
I, H. A. Baily .... Blacksmith
I, J. E. Broadhurst .... Privt
I, J. Barry .... "
I, J. Conners .... "
I, T. P. Downing .... "
I, Mason .... "
I, Blorm .... "
I, Meyer .... "
I, McElroy .... Trptr
I, Mooney .... "
I, Baker .... Privt
I, Boyle .... "
I, Bauth .... "
I, Conner .... "
I, Daring .... "
I, Davis .... "
I, Farrell .... "
I, Hiley .... "
I, Huber .... "
I, Hime .... "
I, Henderson .... "
I, Henderson .... "
I, Leddisson .... "
I, O'Conner .... "
I, Rood .... "
I, Reese .... "
I, Smith 1st .... "
I, Smith 2nd .... "
I, Smith 3rd .... "
I, Stella .... "
I, Stafford .... "
I, Schoole .... "
I, Smallwood .... "
I, Tarr .... "
I, Vaugant .... "
I, Walker .... "
I, Bragew .... "
I, [illegible] .... "
F, G. W. Yates .... Capt
F, W. Van Rieley .... 2d Lt
F, Kenney .... 1st Sergt
F, Nursey .... Sergt
F, Vickory .... "
F, Wilkinson .... "
F, Coleman .... Capt
F, Freeman .... "
F, Briody .... "
F, Brandon .... Farrier
F, Manning .... Blacksmith
F, Atchison .... Privt
F, Brown 1st .... "
F, Brown 2nd .... "
F, Bruce .... "
F, Brady .... "
F, Burnham .... "
F, Cather .... "
F, Carney .... "
F, Dohman .... "
F, Donnelly .... "
F, Gardiner .... "
F, Hammon .... "
F, Kline .... "
F, Krianth .... "
F, Luman .... "
F, Losse .... "
F, Milton Jas .... "
F, Madson .... "
F, Monroe .... "
F, Ruddew .... "
F, Omeling .... "
F, Sicfous .... "
F, Sanders .... "
F, Wanew .... "
F, Way .... "
F, Lerock .... "
F, Kidey .... "
F, E. C. Driscoll .... "
F, D. C. Gillette .... "
F, C. H. Gross .... "
F, F. P. Holcomb .... "
F, M. E. Horn .... "
F, Adam Hitismer .... "
F, P. Killey .... "
F, Fred Lehman .... "
F, Henry Lehman .... "
F, A. McIchargey .... "
F, J. Mitchell .... "
F, J. Noshaus .... "
F, J. O'Bryan .... "
F, J. Parker .... "
F, F. J. Pitter .... "
F, Geo. Post .... "
F, Jas. Quinn .... "
F, Wm. Reed .... "
F, J. W. Rossberg .... "
F, D. L. Lymons .... "
F, J. E. Troy .... "
F, Chas. Van Bramer .... "
F, W. B. Whaley .... "
G, Daniel McIntosh .... 1st Lt
G, Edward Botzer .... Sergt
G, M. Considine .... "
G, Jas Martin .... Capt
G, Otto Hageman .... "
G, Benj. Wells .... Farrier
G, Henry Dose .... Trptr
G, Crawford Selby .... Saddler
G, Benj. F. Rodgers .... Privt
G, Andrew J. Moore .... "
G, Jno. J. McGinniss .... "
G, Edward Stanley .... "
G, Henry Seafferman .... "
G, John Papp .... "
H, Geo Lee, ... Corpl
H, Julian D. Jones .... Privt
H, Thos. E. Meador .... "
M, Miles F. O'Hara .... Sergt.
M, Henry M. Scollier .... Corpl
M, Fred Stringer .... "
M, Henry Gordon .... Privt
M, H. Klotzbursher .... "
M, G. Lawrence .... "
M, W. D. Meyer .... "
M, G. E. Smith .... "
M, D. Somers .... "
M, J. Tanner .... "
M, H. Tenley .... "
M, H. C. Voyt .... "
Boston Custer .... Civilian
Arthur Reed .... "
Mark Kellogg .... "
Chas. Reynolds .... "
Frank C. Mann .... "

INDIAN SCOUTS

BloodyKnife
Bobtailed Bull,
Stab.

Total number of Commissioned officers killed 14
Actg asst Surg 1
Enlisted men 237
Civilians 5
Indian Scouts 3

An Indian memoir of Custer's defeat

"Five springs ago I, with many Sioux Indians, took down and packed up our tipis and moved from the Cheyenne River to the Rosebud River, where we camped a few days; then took down and packed up our lodges and moved to the Greasy Grass and pitched our lodges with the large camp of Sioux." With those words, conveyed in sign language to a U.S. Army surgeon who transcribed them into English, Chief Red Horse began a detailed narrative of the events surrounding George Custer's defeat on the Little Bighorn, which the Indians called the Greasy Grass River. Red Horse had played a prom-

inent role in the battle. Now five years later he offered his version of that momentous June day in 1876. The surgeon who took his testimony, Dr. Charles McChesney, also persuaded the Sioux chief to draw a series of pictographs of the battle. When completed this visual record covered 41 sheets of paper. The drawings, together with excerpts of Red Horse's narrative, give a vivid account of the action as it appeared to one of the victors.

Red Horse continued: "The day of the attack I and four women were a short distance from camp [below] digging wild turnips. Suddenly one of the

women attracted my attention to a cloud of dust rising a short distance from camp. I soon saw that soldiers were charging the Indian camp." This was the abortive cavalry charge led by Major Marcus Reno that opened the engagement (top, right) and ended with Reno and his cavalry fleeing for their lives (bottom, right). The pictures that follow, and Red Horse's narrative, carry the story through the annihilation of Custer's troops, concluding with the withdrawal of the Sioux from the valley of the Little Bighorn, where they had scored the greatest Indian victory during the decades of war on the plains.

"I was a Sioux chief in the council lodge," Red Horse recalled. "My lodge was pitched in the center of the camp." But a notation on this pictograph by Red Horse says the yellow lodge in the top row is neither the council lodge nor that of Red Horse, but a sacred Cheyenne lodge.

226

"The soldiers came on the trail made by the Sioux and attacked the lodges of the Unkpapas, farthest up the river." Red Horse's pictograph of Major Reno's force shows the cavalry advancing in orderly columns.

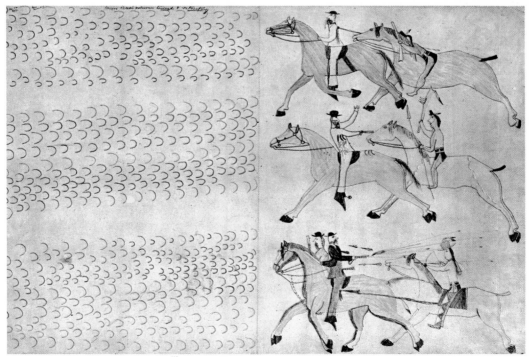

"All the Sioux now charged the soldiers and drove them in confusion across the river," up into the hills. Red Horse shows the cavalry riding back over its own hoofprints, indicating that they are in retreat.

Red Horse's pictograph shows the height of the battle. As he recalled it, "The Sioux charged the different soldiers [Custer's men] and drove them in confusion; these soldiers became foolish, many throwing away their guns and raising their hands, saying, 'Sioux, pity us; take us prisoners.'"

"The Sioux did not take a single soldier prisoner," Red Horse reported, "but killed all of them; none were left alive for even a few minutes. These soldiers discharged their guns but little. I took a gun and two belts off two dead soldiers." His drawing shows the dead cavalrymen.

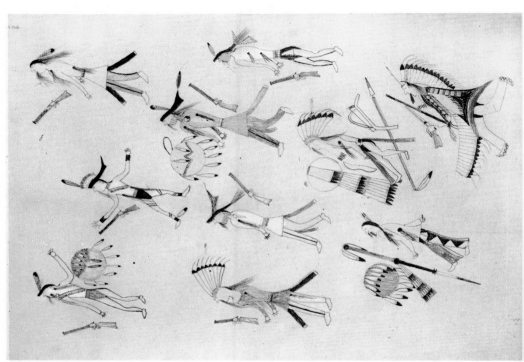

Although the Indians won the battle, they too suffered in the fighting. Red Horse drew this picture of Sioux casualties and said: "Now the Sioux had many killed. The soldiers killed 136 and wounded 160 Sioux."

Though Red Horse did not discuss the dead horses, he made this picture of their bodies around the fallen battalion colors. The flowing tails indicate these are cavalry horses; Indian horses' tails were tied up for war.

"The fight continued at long range," Red Horse recalled; Indians had surrounded Major Reno and his surviving cavalry when "a Sioux man saw the walking soldiers coming." This was an infantry column, under Colonel Gibbon, approaching from the north. The Sioux and their allies ended their attack and rode off to the Bighorn Mountains, as Red Horse's picture shows.

TEXT CREDITS

Chapter I: particularly useful source for information on the Indian peace council, *The Fighting Cheyennes* by George Bird Grinnell, University of Oklahoma Press, 1956; 20 — from "Picture Writing of the American Indians" by Garrick Mallery, 10th Ann. Rep. Bur. Amer. Ethnol. 1888-89, pp. 266-287. Chapter II: 55 — song, copyright © 1967 by Charles Hofmann, reprinted from *American Indians Sing* by Charles Hofmann by permission of The John Day Co., Inc., publisher; 62 — trading information from "The Assiniboin" by Edwin Thompson Denig, 46th Ann. Rep. Bur. Amer. Ethnol. 1928-29, p. 585, Smithsonian Institution, and *The Horse in Blackfoot Indian Culture* by John C. Ewers, Smithsonian Institution Press, 1969, pp. 217-219; 64 — quote and part of text based on *The Plains of the Great West* by Richard I. Dodge, G. P. Putnam's Sons, 1877, pp. 329-330; 74, 75 — list compiled from *The Horse in Blackfoot Indian Culture* by John C. Ewers, Smithsonian Institution Press, 1969, pp. 150-151. Chapter III: particularly useful sources for information on the Cheyennes, *The Cheyenne Indians* by George Bird Grinnell, Vols. I and II, Cooper Square Publishers, Inc., 1962, and *The Cheyennes* by Edward A. Hoebel, Holt, Rinehart & Winston, Inc., 1960; 85 — parts based on "Notes on Cheyenne Child Life" by Sister M. Inez Hilper, Amer. Anthrop., New Series, Jan.-March 1946, Vol. 48, No. 1, p. 60; 86 — quote from *The Journal of Jacob Fowler*, Elliott Coues, ed., University of Nebraska Press, 1970, p. 59; 88-91 — quotes from "The Narrative of a Southern Cheyenne Woman" by Truman Michelson, Smithsonian Misc. Col., Vol. 87, No. 5, March 21, 1932, Smithsonian Institution, pp. 4-8; 91 — tipi etiquette based on information from *The Indian Tipi* by Reginald and Gladys Laubin, University of Oklahoma Press, 1957, pp. 91-93; 101 — quote from *The Life and Adventures of a Quaker Among the Indians* by Thomas C. Battey, University of Oklahoma Press, 1968, pp. 240-241; 102 — songs from *The Indian Tipi* by Reginald and Gladys Laubin, University of Oklahoma Press, 1957, p. 2, "Notes on Some Cheyenne Songs" by George Bird Grinnell, Amer. Anthrop., Vol. 5, 1903, p. 316, "Societies and Ceremonial Associations in the Ogalala Division of the Teton-Dakota," by Clark Wissler, Amer. Mus. of Nat. Hist. Anthrop. Pap., Vol. XI, 1912; 104-105 — quotes and part of text from *Five Indian Tribes of the Upper Missouri* by Edwin Thompson Denig. Copyright 1961 by the University of Oklahoma Press, pp. 151-152, 196-200; 105 — quote from *The Cheyenne Indians* by George Bird Grinnell, Vol. I, Cooper Square Publishers, Inc., 1962, p. 336. Chapter IV: 123 — Pawnee sacrifice from *Pawnee Hero Stories and Folk-Tales* by George Bird Grinnell, reprinted by University of Nebraska Press, 1961, pp. 362-369; 132 — vision quest adapted from *Crazy Horse* by Mari Sandoz, University of Nebraska Press, 1961, pp. 29-43, 101-105, by permission of McIntosh and Otis, Inc.; 140 — sand painting information from "The Mountain Chant. A Navajo Ceremony," 5th Ann. Rep. Bur. Amer. Ethnol. 1883-84, pp. 444-450, Smithsonian Institution.

PICTURE CREDITS

The sources for the illustrations in this book are shown below. Credits from left to right are separated by semicolons and from top to bottom by dashes.

Cover — Herb Orth for LIFE, courtesy Western Americana Collection, Beinecke Library, Yale University. 2 — Alexander Gardner, courtesy Smithsonian Institution National Anthropological Archives. 6,7 — Courtesy History Division, Natural History Museum of Los Angeles County. 8 — Edward S. Curtis copied by Frank Lerner, courtesy Rare Book Division, The New York Public Library, Astor, Lenox and Tilden Foundations. 9,10 — Courtesy Smithsonian Institution National Anthropological Archives. 11 — Edward S. Curtis copied by Frank Lerner, courtesy Rare Book Division, The New York Public Library, Astor, Lenox and Tilden Foundations. 12 — Courtesy Smithsonian Institution National Anthropological Archives. 13 — L. A. Huffman, courtesy David R. Phillips. 14 — Henry B. Beville, courtesy Map Division, The National Archives. 16,17 — Courtesy History Division, Natural History Museum of Los Angeles County. 19 — Paulus Leeser, courtesy The Denver Art Museum — Drawing by Nicholas Fasciano based on drawing in "Games of the North American Indians" by Stewart Cullin, 24th Annual Report, Bureau of American Ethnology, 1902-1903, Smithsonian Institution. 20,21 — Benschneider, courtesy South Dakota State Historical Society. 26,27 — Paulus Leeser, courtesy The Denver Art Museum (2) — courtesy The Brooklyn Museum, Henry L. Batterman and Frank Sherman Benson Funds — Hillel Berger, courtesy Peabody Museum, Harvard University — courtesy The Brooklyn Museum, Henry L. Batterman and Frank Sherman Benson Funds — Lloyd Rule, courtesy The Denver Art Museum; Paulus Leeser, courtesy Smithsonian Institution. 28 — Paulus Leeser, courtesy The Denver Art Museum. 29 — Hillel Berger, courtesy Peabody Museum, Harvard University; Paulus Leeser, courtesy The Denver Art Museum; courtesy The Brooklyn Museum, Henry L. Batterman and Frank Sherman Benson Funds (2) — Paulus Leeser, courtesy Smithsonian Institution. 31 — Drawings by Nicholas Fasciano, based on material in *Indian Sign Language* by William Tompkins, copyright 1969 by Dover Publications. 33 — Map by Rafael Palacios. 34 — Courtesy History Division, Natural History Museum of Los Angeles County. 36 through 43 — Courtesy Thomas Gilcrease Institute of American History and Art. 44,45 — Edward S. Curtis copied by Paulus Leeser, courtesy Rare Book Division, The New York Public Library, Astor, Lenox and Tilden Foundations. 46,47 — Courtesy Library of Congress. 48 — Courtesy Thomas Gilcrease Institute of American History and Art. 51 — Map by Rafael Palacios, based on map found in *The Horse in Blackfoot Culture* by John Ewers, copyright 1969 by The Smithsonian Institution Press, p. 11. 52,53 — Courtesy Thomas Gilcrease Institute of American History and Art. 55 — Benschneider, courtesy South Dakota State Historical Society. 56 — Christian Barthelmess, courtesy Coffrin's Old West Gallery, Miles City, Montana. 57 — Paulus Leeser, courtesy The Denver Art Museum; drawings by Nicholas Fasciano based on drawings from *The Horse in Blackfoot Culture* by John Ewers, copyright 1969 by The Smithsonian Institution Press, pp. 104,132. 58 — Paulus Leeser, courtesy The Denver Art Museum. 59 — Drawings by Nicholas Fasciano. 61 — Paulus Leeser, courtesy The Denver Art Museum, except center, courtesy The Brooklyn Museum, Henry L. Batterman and Frank Sherman Benson Funds. 62,63 — Courtesy Thomas Gilcrease Institute of American History and Art. 65 — From *Sioux Indian Painting* by Hartley B. Alexander, Volume I, Editions d'Art, C. Szwedzicki, 1938. 66,67 — Frank Lerner, courtesy National Collection of Fine Arts, Smithsonian Institution. 68,69 — Courtesy National Collection of Fine Arts, Smithsonian Institution. 70,71 — Frank Lerner, courtesy National Collection of Fine Arts, Smithsonian Institution. 72,73 — Frank Lerner, courtesy National Collection of Fine Arts, Smithsonian Institution; courtesy National Collection of Fine Arts, Smithsonian Institution. 74,75 — Paulus Leeser, courtesy The Denver Art Museum. 76,77 — Courtesy History Division, Natural History Museum of Los Angeles County. 78,79 — Courtesy Smithsonian Institution National Anthropological Archives. 80,81 — Courtesy U.S. Army Field Artillery and Fort Sill Museum. 82,83,84 — Courtesy Smithsonian Institution National Anthropological Archives. 85 — Lloyd Rule, courtesy The Denver Art Museum. 86 — Courtesy Smithsonian Institution National Anthropological Archives. 87 — Lloyd Rule, courtesy The Denver Art Museum. 89 — Courtesy Smithsonian Institution National Anthropological Archives. 90 — Courtesy History Division, Natural History Museum of Los Angeles County. 92 — Drawings by Nicholas Fasciano, adapted from drawing of Arapaho tipi cover in the Vincent Colyer Collection, Smithsonian Institution, and drawings in *The Indian Tipi; Its History, Construction and Use* by Reginald and Gladys Laubin, copyright 1957 by the University of Oklahoma Press, pp. 34,86. 94 through 97 — Courtesy Rare Book Division, The New York Public Library, Astor, Lenox and Tilden Foundations. 99 — Paulus Leeser, courtesy The Denver Art Museum. 100 — Drawings by Nicholas Fasciano, based on drawings from *The Sioux* by Royal B. Hassrick, copyright 1967 by the University of Oklahoma Press, p. 287, and *The Indian Tipi* by Reginald and Gladys Laubin, copyright 1957 by the University of Oklahoma Press, p. 79. 102, 103 — Paulus Leeser, courtesy The Denver Art Museum. 106 through 109 — Edward S. Curtis copied by Frank Lerner, courtesy Rare Book Division, The New York Public Library, Astor, Lenox and Tilden Foundations. 110 — Courtesy The American Museum of Natural History — courtesy Southwest Museum, Los Angeles, California. 111 — Edward S. Curtis copied by Frank Lerner, courtesy Rare Book Division, The New York Public Library, Astor, Lenox and Tilden Foundations. 112 — Courtesy Smithsonian Institution National Anthropological Archives. 113 — Lloyd Rule, courtesy The Denver Art Museum. 114 — Courtesy Smithsonian Institution National Anthropological Archives. 115,116 — Paulus Leeser, courtesy The Denver Art Museum. 117 — Courtesy Library of Congress. 118,119 — Courtesy Smithsonian Institution National Anthropological Archives. 120,121 — Courtesy Minnesota Historical Society. 122 — Benschneider, courtesy The Denver Art Museum. 125 — Courtesy National Collection of Fine Arts, Smithsonian Institution. 126 — Edward S. Curtis copied by Paulus Leeser, courtesy Rare Book Division, The New York Public Library, Astor, Lenox and Tilden Foundations. 128 through 131 — Benschneider, courtesy The Denver Art Museum. 132 through 135 — Edward S. Curtis copied by Paulus Leeser, courtesy Rare Book Division, The New York Public Library, Astor, Lenox and Tilden Foundations. 136 — L. A. Huffman, courtesy David R. Phillips. 139 — Edward S. Curtis copied by Paulus Leeser, courtesy Rare Book Division, The New York Public Library, Astor, Lenox and Tilden Foundations — Paulus Leeser, courtesy The New York Public Library. 141 — Courtesy Fifth Annual Report of the Bureau of Ethnology, 1883-1884, Smithsonian Institution. 142,143 — Courtesy Collection of Fine Arts, Smithsonian Institution. 144,145 — Paulus Leeser, courtesy Western Americana Collection, Beinecke Library, Yale University. 146,147 — Courtesy The American Museum of Natural History. 148,149 — Courtesy National Collection of Fine Arts, Smithsonian Institution. 150,151 — L. A. Huffman, courtesy David R. Phillips. 152 — Courtesy Beinecke Rare Book and Manuscript Library, Yale University. 155 — Courtesy Thomas Gilcrease Institute of American History and Art. 156 — Courtesy Western History Collections, University of Oklahoma Library. 158 — Courtesy Montana Historical Society, Helena. 159 — Courtesy The National Archives. 160,161 — Courtesy U.S. Army Field Artillery and Fort Sill Museum. 162 — Courtesy Manitoba Archives. 164 — Courtesy Western History Collections, University of Oklahoma Library. 166 — L. A. Huffman, courtesy David R. Phillips. 167 — Courtesy Texas State Archives, Austin. 169 — Courtesy U.S. Army Field Artillery and Fort Sill Museum. 170,171 — Courtesy Minnesota Historical Society. 172,173 — Herb Orth for LIFE, courtesy Minnesota Historical Society. 174 through 179 — Courtesy Minnesota Historical Society. 180,181 — Courtesy Smithsonian Institution National Anthropological Archives. 182 — Courtesy Colorado College, Colorado Springs. 184,185 — Courtesy The State Historical Society of Colorado. 186 — Courtesy History Division, Natural History Museum of Los Angeles County. 189 — Courtesy Texas Collections, Baylor University. 190,191 — Courtesy Kansas State Historical Society, Topeka. 192 — Courtesy Montana Historical Society, Helena; courtesy Smithsonian Institution National Anthropological Archives (2) — courtesy Smithsonian Institution National Anthropological Archives; courtesy Kansas State Historical Society, Topeka; courtesy The State Historical Society of Colorado. 193 — Courtesy Smithsonian Institution National Anthropological Archives; courtesy Kansas State Historical Society, Topeka; courtesy The National Archives and Records Service — Bettmann Archive; courtesy Smithsonian Institution National Anthropological Archives; courtesy Bureau of Indian Affairs in the National Archives. 197 — Courtesy The American Numismatic Society, New York. 198,199 — Courtesy U.S. Signal Corps, Brady Collection in the National Archives. 201 through 204 — Courtesy National Collection of Fine Arts, Smithsonian Institution. 205 — Benschneider, courtesy National Park Service, Department of the Interior. 206 — Lloyd Rule, courtesy The Denver Art Museum. 207 — Courtesy Museum of the American Indian. 208,209 — Benschneider, courtesy National Park Service, Department of the Interior — Henry B. Beville, courtesy Smithsonian Institution (2); Paulus Leeser, courtesy The Denver Art Museum (2) — Lee Boltin, courtesy The American Museum of Natural History. 210,211 — Edward S. Curtis copied by Frank Lerner, courtesy Rare Book Division, The New York Public Library, Astor, Lenox and Tilden Foundations. 212 — Courtesy Denver Public Library, Western History Department. 215,216 — Courtesy National Park Service, Department of the Interior. 219 — Benschneider, courtesy National Park Service, Department of the Interior. 220,221 — Edward S. Curtis copied by Richard Henry, courtesy Rare Book Division, The New York Public Library, Astor, Lenox and Tilden Foundations. 223 — Map by Rafael Palacios. 224 — Courtesy West Point Museum Collections. 225 — Courtesy South Dakota State Historical Society. 226 through 233 — Henry B. Beville, courtesy Smithsonian Institution National Anthropological Archives.

Alexander, Hartley B., *Sioux Indian Painting,* Vols. I and II, Editions d'Art. C. Szwedzicki, 1938.

Amsden, Charles Avery, *Navajo Weaving.* The Rio Grande Press Inc., 1964.

Andrews, Ralph W., *Curtis' Western Indians.* Bonanza Books, 1962.

Andrist, Ralph K., *The Long Death: The Last Days of the Plains Indians.* Collier Books, 1964.

Bailey, L. R., *Indian Slave Trade in the Southwest.* Tower Publications, 1966.

Battey, Thomas C., *The Life and Adventures of a Quaker Among the Indians.* University of Oklahoma Press, 1968.

Belous, Russell E., and Robert Weinstein, *Will Soule, Indian Photographer at Fort Sill, Oklahoma 1869-74.* The Ward Ritchie Press, 1969.

Berthrong, Donald J., *The Southern Cheyennes.* University of Oklahoma Press, 1963.

Bourke, John G., *On the Border with Crook.* Rio Grande Press, 1969.

Brady, Cyrus Townsend, *Indian Fights and Fighters.* University of Nebraska Press, 1971.

Branch, E. Douglas, *The Hunting of the Buffalo.* University of Nebraska Press, 1962.

Brown, Dee, *Bury My Heart at Wounded Knee.* Holt, Rinehart & Winston, Inc., 1971.

Brown, Joseph Epes, ed., *The Sacred Pipe: Black Elk's Account of the Seven Rites of Oglala Sioux.* Penguin Books, Inc., 1971.

Carley, Kenneth, *The Sioux Uprising of 1862.* The Minnesota Historical Society, 1961.

Catlin, George, *North American Indians,* Vols. I and II. Ross and Haines, Inc., 1965.

Clark, William, *Indian Sign Language.* L. R. Hammersly & Co., 1885.

Coues, Elliott, ed., *The Journal of Jacob Fowler.* University of Nebraska Press, 1970.

Cremony, John C., *Life Among the Apaches, 1850-1868.* The Rio Grande Press, Inc., 1970.

Cullin, Stewart, "Games of North American Indians." 24th Ann. Rep. Bur. Amer. Ethnol. 1902-03. Smithsonian Institution.

Curtis, Edward S., *The North American Indian.* University Press, 1907-30.

Custer, George A., *My Life on the Plains,* Milo H. Quaife, ed. University of Nebraska Press, 1966.

Denig, Edwin Thompson, *Five Indian Tribes of the Upper Missouri.* John C. Ewers, ed. University of Oklahoma Press, 1961.

Dodge, Richard I., *The Plains of the Great West.* G. P. Putnam's Sons, 1877.

Eastman, Mary, *Dahcotah: Life and Legends of the Sioux.* Ross and Haines, Inc., 1962.

Ellis, Richard N., *General Pope and U.S. Indian Policy.* University of New Mexico Press, 1970.

Ewers, John C., *The Blackfeet.* University of Oklahoma Press, 1958.
The Horse in Blackfoot Indian Culture. Smithsonian Institution Press, 1969.
Indian Life on the Upper Missouri. University of Oklahoma Press, 1968.
Artists of the Old West. Doubleday and Company, Inc., 1965.

Feder, Norman, *Art of the American Indian.* Harry N. Abrams, Inc., 1971.

Foreman, Grant, *The Five Civilized Tribes.* University of Oklahoma Press, 1970.

Fritz, Henry L., *The Movement for Indian Assimilation 1860-90.* University of Pennsylvania Press, 1960.

Frost, Lawrence A., *The Custer Album.* Superior Publishing Company, 1964.

Geronimo, *Geronimo, His Own Story,* Dutton, 1970.

Graham, Colonel W. A., *The Custer Myth.* Bonanza Books, 1953.

Gregg, Josiah, *The Commerce of the Prairies.* University of Nebraska Press, 1967.

Grinnell, George Bird, *The Cheyenne Indians,* Vols. I and II. Cooper Square Publishers Inc., 1962.
The Fighting Cheyennes. University of Oklahoma Press, 1956.

Haines, Francis, *The Buffalo.* Thomas Y. Crowell Co., 1970.
Horses in America, Thomas Y. Crowell Co., 1971.

Hassrick, Royal B., *The Sioux — The Life and Customs of a Warrior Society.* University of Oklahoma Press, 1967.

Hilper, Sister M. Inez, "Notes on Cheyenne Child Life." American Anthropologist New Series, Jan.-March, 1946, Vol. 48, No. 1.

Hodge, Frederick W., ed., *Handbook of American Indians, North of Mexico,* Vols. I and II. Scholarly Press, 1968.

Hoebel, E. Adamson, *The Cheyennes.* Holt, Rinehart & Winston, Inc., 1960.

Hofmann, Charles, *American Indians Sing.* The John Day Company, 1967.

Hoig, Stan, *The Sand Creek Massacre.* University of Oklahoma Press, 1961.

Horan, James D., *Timothy O'Sullivan: America's Forgotten Photographer.* Doubleday and Company, Inc., 1966.

Hyde, George E., *Indians of the High Plains.* University of Oklahoma Press, 1970.
A Life of George Bent. University of Oklahoma Press, 1968.
Red Cloud's Folk. University of Oklahoma Press, 1957.

Jablow, Joseph, *The Cheyenne in Plains Indian Relations 1795-1840.* University of Washington Press, Seattle and London, 1966.

Jackson, Clarence, *Picture-Maker of the Old West, William Jackson.* Charles Scribner's Sons, 1947.

Jackson, Clyde L. and Grace, *Quanah Parker.* Exposition Press Inc., 1963.

Jones, Douglas C., *The Treaty of Medicine Lodge.* University of Oklahoma Press, 1966.

Kelly, Lawrence, *Navajo Roundup.* Pruett Publishing Co., 1970.

Laubin, Reginald and Gladys, *The Indian Tipi.* University of Oklahoma Press, 1957.

Lavender, David, *Bent's Fort.* Doubleday and Company, Inc., 1954.

Linton, Ralph, ed., *Acculturation in Seven American Indian Tribes.* Peter Smith, 1940.

Llewellyn, K. N., and E. Adamson Hoebel, *The Cheyenne Way.* University of Oklahoma Press, 1941.

Lowie, Robert H., *Indians of the Plains.* The Natural History Press, 1963.

Mallery, Garrick, "Picture Writing of the American Indians." 10th Ann. Rep. Bur. Amer. Ethnol. 1888-89. Smithsonian Institution.
"Sign Language among North American Indians." 2nd Ann. Rep. Bur. Amer. Ethnol. 1879-80. Smithsonian Institution.
"Pictographs of the North American Indian." 4th Ann. Rep. Bur. Amer. Ethnol. 1882-83. Smithsonian Institution.

Mardock, Robert Winston, *The Reformers and the American Indian.* University of Missouri Press, 1971.

Marquis, Thomas B., interpreter, *Wooden Leg, A Warrior Who Fought*

Custer. University of Nebraska Press, 1971.

Matthews, Dr. Washington, U.S.A. "The Mountain Chant. A Navajo Ceremony." 5th Ann. Rep. Bur. Amer. Ethnol. 1884. Smithsonian Institution.

Mayhall, Mildred P., *Indian Wars of Texas.* Texian Press, 1965.
The Kiowas. University of Oklahoma Press, 1962.

Michaelson, Truman, "The Narrative of a Southern Cheyenne Woman." Smithsonian Misc. Coll., Vol. 87, No. 5. 1932, Smithsonian Institution.

Mooney, James, *The Cheyenne Indians.* American Anthropological Association, Memoirs I.
"Calendar History of the Kiowa Indians." 17th Ann. Rep. Bur. Amer. Ethnol. Part I. 1895-96. Smithsonian Institution.
The Ghost-Dance Religion. University of Chicago Press, 1970.

Neihardt, John G., interpreter, *Black Elk Speaks.* University of Nebraska Press, 1961.

Nye, Wilbur Sturtevant, *Carbine and Lance: The Story of Old Fort Sill.* University of Oklahoma Press, 1969.

Olson, James C., *Red Cloud and the Sioux Problem.* University of Nebraska Press, 1965.

Priest, Loring B., *Uncle Sam's Stepchildren: The Reformation of United States Indian Policy 1865-87.* Octagon Books, 1969.

Roe, Frank Gilbert, *The Indian and the Horse.* University of Oklahoma Press, 1955.

Sandoz, Mari, *The Beaver Men.* Hastings House, Publishers, 1964.
Crazy Horse. University of Nebraska Press, 1961.

Sonnichsen, Charles L., *The Mescalero Apaches.* University of Oklahoma Press, 1966.

Stands In Timber, John, and Margot Liberty, *Cheyenne Memories.* Yale University Press, 1967.

Stone, Eric, *Medicine Among the American Indians.* Hafner Publishing · Company, 1962.

Thomas, Alfred Barnaby, *The Plains Indians and New Mexico, 1751-1778.* University of New Mexico Press, 1940.

Thompson, David, *David Thompson's Narrative of His Explorations in Western America 1784-1812.* The Champlain Society, 1962.

Thrapp, Dan L., *The Conquest of Apacheria.* University of Oklahoma Press, 1967.

Tomkins, William, *Indian Sign Language.* Dover Publications, Inc., 1969.

Turner, Katherine C., *Red Men Calling on the Great White Father.* University of Oklahoma Press, 1951.

Underhill, Ruth, *Red Man's Religion.* University of Chicago Press, 1965.

Utley, Robert M., *Custer Battlefield.* Historical Handbook Series No. I. National Park Service, U.S. Dept. of the Interior, 1969.

Villasenor, David, *Tapestries In Sand.* Naturegraph Company, 1966.

Vogel, Vergil J., *American Indian Medicine.* University of Oklahoma Press, 1970.

Wallace, Ernest, and E. Adamson Hoebel, *The Comanches: Lords of the South Plains.* University of Oklahoma Press, 1964.

Washburn, Wilcomb E., *Red Man's Land — White Man's Law.* Charles Scribner's Sons, 1971.

Webb, Walter Prescott, *The Great Plains.* Ginn and Company, 1959.

Weiner, Michael A., *Earth Medicine — Earth Foods.* The Macmillan Company, 1972.

Wied-Neuwied, Maximillian A. P., Prinz von, *Travels in the Interior of North America,* Reuben Gold Thwaites, ed. Cleveland, 1906.

Wissler, Clark, *Indians of the United States.* Doubleday and Company, Inc., 1966.
"Material Culture of the Blackfoot Indians." Amer. Mus. Nat. Hist. Anthrop. Pap. Vol. 5, Pt. I. 1910.

Wright, Muriel H., *A Guide to the Indian Tribes of Oklahoma.* University of Oklahoma Press, 1971.

ACKNOWLEDGMENTS

The editors of this book wish to thank the following persons and institutions for their assistance: Richard Conn, Curator of Native Art, Denver Art Museum, Colorado; John C. Ewers, Senior Ethnologist, Department of Anthropology, Smithsonian Institution, Washington, D.C.; Morris Opler, Department of Anthropology, University of Oklahoma, Norman; Robert M. Utley, Director, Office of Archeology and Historic Preservation, National Park Service, U.S. Department of the Interior, Washington, D.C., who read and commented on portions of the book.

Also, Casey Barthelmess, Miles City, Montana; Keith Basso, Department of Anthropology, University of Arizona, Tucson; Donald J. Berthrong, Purdue University, West Lafayette, Indiana; Lewis S. Brown, Helen Jones, The American Museum of Natural History, New York City; Jack Coffrin, Coffrin's Old West Gallery, Miles City, Montana; John Miller, Chief, and the staff of the American History Division, Maud D. Cole, Rare Books Division, The New York Public Library, New York City; James H. Davis, Picture Librarian, Western History Department, Denver Public Library, Colorado; Andrew Old Elk, Randall Kane, Elden Reyer, Custer Battlefield Museum, Crow Agency, Montana; Eugene D. Decker, Archivist, Kansas State Historical Society, Topeka, Kansas; Dr. Henry Fritz, St. Olaf College, Northfield, Minnesota; Dorothy Gimmestad, Assistant Head, Audio Visual Library, Minnesota Historical Society, St. Paul; Gillett Griswold, Director, U.S. Army Field Artillery and Fort Sill Museum, Oklahoma; Archibald Hanna, Curator, Yale University Western Americana Collection, New Haven, Connecticut; David B. Hartley, Museum Curator, Kenneth Stewart, South Dakota State Historical Society, Pierre; Abraham Hoffman, Curator, Jack Haley, Assistant Curator, Western History Collections, University of Oklahoma, Norman; Charles Hofmann, Toronto, Canada; Joan Hofmann, Beinecke Rare Book and Manuscript Library, Yale University, New Haven, Connecticut; Carol Johnson, Paula Richardson, Department of Anthropology, James F. Pinkney, Chief, Sales Section, Photographic Services, Smithsonian Institution, Washington, D.C.; Jerry L. Kearns, Head of Reference, Prints and Photographs Division, Library of Congress, Washington, D.C.; Nancy E. Malan, Archivist, National Archives and Records Service, Washington, D.C.; Terry W. Mangan, Alice L. Sharp, Mrs. Enid Thompson, State Historical Society of Colorado, Denver; Harriett C. Meloy, Librarian, Montana Historical Society Library, Helena; Arthur Olivas, Photo Archivist, Richard Rudisill, Museum of New Mexico, Santa Fe; Gary L. Roberts, Abraham Baldwin Agricultural College, Tifton, Georgia; Eleanor A. Snyder, National Collection of Fine Arts, Washington, D.C.; Oliver Willcox, Staff Photographer, Thomas Gilcrease Institute of American History and Art, Tulsa, Oklahoma.